THE WORLD IS ALWAYS
COMING TO AN END

CHICAGO VISIONS AND REVISIONS

Edited by Carlo Rotella, Bill Savage, Carl Smith, and Robert B. Stepto

THE WORLD IS ALWAYS COMING TO AN END

PULLING TOGETHER AND APART IN A CHICAGO NEIGHBORHOOD

CARLO ROTELLA

THE UNIVERSITY OF CHICAGO PRESS

Chicago and London

The University of Chicago Press, Chicago 60637
The University of Chicago Press, Ltd., London
© 2019 by Carlo Rotella

Published 2019
Printed in the United States of America

28 27 26 25 24 23 22 21 20 19   1 2 3 4 5

ISBN-13: 978-0-226-62403-7 (cloth)
ISBN-13: 978-0-226-62417-4 (e-book)
DOI: https://doi.org/10.7208/chicago/9780226624174.001.0001

Map of South Shore by Lauren Nassef.

Library of Congress Cataloging-in-Publication Data

Names: Rotella, Carlo, 1964– author.
Title: The world is always coming to an end: pulling together and apart in a
    Chicago neighborhood / Carlo Rotella.
Other titles: Chicago visions + revisions.
Description: Chicago; London: The University of Chicago Press, 2019. |
    Series: Chicago visions and revisions | Includes bibliographical references
    and index.
Identifiers: LCCN 2018050985 | ISBN 9780226624037 (cloth: alk. paper) |
    ISBN 9780226624174 (e-book)
Subjects: LCSH: South Shore (Chicago, Ill.) | Neighborhoods—Illinois—
    Chicago. | City and town life—Illinois—Chicago. | Rotella, Carlo, 1964–
Classification: LCC F548.68.S7 R67 2019 | DDC 977.3/11—dc23
LC record available at https://lccn.loc.gov/2018050985

♾ This paper meets the requirements of ANSI/NISO Z39.48-1992
(Permanence of Paper).

For the Earps, Trainers, Thigpens, and Passmans

Love your neighbour, yet pull not down your hedge.
GEORGE HERBERT, *Jacula Prudentum* (1640)

Tell the story of your village. If you tell it well, you will have told the story of the world.

ANDREA CAMILLERI

CONTENTS

JACKSON PARK

67TH STREET

S. CREGIER AVE.

JACKSON PARK HIGHLANDS

PARKSIDE

O'KEEFFE

SOUTH SHORE BANK

JEFFERY PLAZA

71ST STREET

S. EUCLID AVE.

ST. PHILIP NERI

BRYN MAWR WEST

S. STONY ISLAND AVE.

BOUCHET SCHOOL

BRYN MAWR EAST

75TH STREET

S. EAST END AVE.

S. JEFFERY BLVD.

AVALON REGAL THEATER

79TH STREET

INTRODUCTION

71ST AND OGLESBY TO 69TH AND EUCLID

While working on this book, I got in the daily habit, whenever I was in Chicago, of taking a walk between the two houses in South Shore in which I grew up. One is on the 7100 block of Oglesby, the other on the 6900 block of Euclid. They're not quite a mile apart, no more than a twenty-minute walk each way, but to go from one to the other is to pass through three distinct worlds. Those worlds, and the resonances and disjunctions between them, give shape to the place that shaped me.

Sometimes I start the walk at one house, sometimes at the other. Let's start this one, taken in the summer of 2016, on Oglesby. The compact brick house with a low-pitched overhanging roof and an offset front door in which I lived on that block between 1967 and 1973 is a bungalow—one of more than a thousand in South Shore, one of 80,000 in the great swath of neighborhoods that make up the city's bungalow belt. The bungalows on the 7100 block of Oglesby have the distinctive feel of city houses, ranked shoulder to shoulder on tight lots, each asserting its own defensible singularity but also taking its place among its peers, like an armored warrior in a shield wall. The block looks greener, more settled and maintained, than it did when I lived there, but it also feels more precarious to me, more vigilant and embattled. From early childhood I was attuned to the signature buzzing stillness of a block of houses in South Shore, an atmosphere of surface calm stretched over a banked, forted-up watchfulness. The buzz has heightened over the years, or I've become even more sensitive to it, or both.

There's a shooting just about every day somewhere in the neighborhood, and a great deal of robbery and theft. It doesn't approach the Wild

West highs of the early 1990s, when a nationwide spike in violent crime coincided with the maturing of the crack trade on the South Side, and by some measures street crime's not even up to the level of the lesser but still impressive early 1970s surge that gave South Shore a lasting reputation for danger; but it's a lot of action, especially for a neighborhood that has long prided itself on being one of the most desirable places to live on the South Side. A neighbor across the street from my old house on Oglesby parks at the curb end of his driveway with the car facing out and a cover on the windshield. Along with the scrupulously maintained house and lawn, the car seems to say, "Yeah, we work hard to have nice stuff and we take care of it, and we're home. Try us, and we'll take care of you, too."

There are larger forces at work on the neighborhood that can't be held at bay with locks, bars, dogs, or guns. The financial crisis of 2008 hit the area especially hard, leaving many householders upside down on their mortgages, and many properties still haven't regained their value. It got to be too much for the people living next door to my old house on Oglesby; they walked away from their mortgage and left their bungalow for the bank. The bungalow block was twentieth-century Chicago's quintessential landscape of middle-class solidity and working-class confidence in upward mobility, but today it's harder to enter or stay in the middle class. The middle strata of American society that grew so spectacularly in the postwar era are hollowing out, aging out, contracting, leaving a city of haves and have-nots separated by a deepening divide that makes it hard for them to see each other as neighbors. In South Shore, where the middle class has traditionally decided the community's priorities and how to pursue them, there has been a general retreat not just from public space but from public life, especially by those who can afford to insulate themselves with money, technology, educational credentials, and a willingness to get in the car and leave the neighborhood to do anything at all outside the home: send the kids to school, shop, go out to eat, see friends. The familiar form of the bungalow block endures, but as the social order housed in it changes, so do the ways that people who live there think and feel about themselves and their world.

*

We live in neighborhoods, and neighborhoods live in us.

Archaeologists and others who study cities around the world have found that neighborhoods are an urban universal, showing up wherever human beings settle in substantial numbers, including para-urban settlements like refugee camps, military bases, company towns, protest sites, and festival encampments. Distinctions between neighborhoods may be based on wealth, occupation, ethnicity, place of origin, religion, or some other principle, and they may be imposed from above or improvised from below, but people always end up in neighborhoods. It's apparently an aspect of being human, like opposable thumbs or vengeance.

This is important because the places in which we live, especially the places in which we grow up, lastingly mark and shape us: neighborhoods live in us. They aren't just neutral stages on which we act out our lives and feel the effect of global-scale economic and social forces. Rather, as the sociologist Robert Sampson puts it, neighborhoods are "important determinants of the quantity and quality of human behavior in their own right," affecting residents in distinctive ways that can be teased apart from overlapping influences like income and race. These are called neighborhood effects, and they're remarkably wide-ranging, long-lasting, and influential. You can see them show up across the life course—in birth weight and child mortality, school performance, economic attainment, rates of cancer and heart disease, life expectancy. So neighborhood effects can tell us important things about how to address public health problems, persistent economic inequality, violent crime, and other pressing social concerns. But the influence of neighborhood effects can also be traced in aspects of perception and mentality that we usually think of as personal character: altruism, sensitivity to disorder, attitude toward the rule of law, and other features of inner life.

Sampson, the leading scholar of neighborhood effects, has done much of his groundbreaking research in Chicago, and he has a rich trove of South Shore data. His findings help me generalize from the evidence I've been compiling using my own more qualitative, humanistic, journalistic, one-man, subjective, low-budget methods: interviewing people, going to meetings, monitoring the neighborhood's profile in the news media and popular culture, reading the literature of South Shore, going through old newspapers and letters and other papers collected in various archives around the city, walking around and hanging out, searching through my own memories and those of others for telling details that indicate—often in code—the receding and emergence of urban orders.

Social scientists like Sampson who analyze how neighborhood works deal mostly in evidence that can be quantified. I'm investigating what and how neighborhood *means*, tracing the mutually shaping fit between place and sensibility—cultural neighborhood effects, you might say. These don't have such obvious policy implications and can be a lot trickier to nail down than birth weight or income, but they play an essential part in understanding how people live in neighborhoods and vice versa. How people see their neighborhood and tell stories about it and otherwise infuse it with meaning affects not just how they feel and what they believe about the place but also their material decisions about whether to stay or go, whether to send their kids to the local schools, how to invest money and political leverage and other vital resources. As Sampson says, "When people act as if neighborhood matters, that helps to shape the concrete ways in which neighborhood really does matter."

The Sicilian crime writer Andrea Camilleri once said, "Tell the story of your village. If you tell it well, you will have told the story of the world." In this book I aim to say something about neighborhood in general by telling you something about one neighborhood in particular. Because neighborhood and the pervasiveness of its effects are universal, in going deep on the place I come from I'm also speaking to a more widely shared experience. Especially in our ultra-urbanized age, many of us carry around some version of this book in our heads, a book that goes: *This is the smaller-place-within-a-bigger-place that I come from, this is what that place means to me and to other people, and here's how that meaning shapes our works and days.*

*

As I walk up Oglesby to the corner, there's a palpable click of transition when I take the step that carries me beyond the hedge at the property line of the last house on the block. One moment I'm in one environment, between a neatly trimmed front lawn and parkway (what locals call the strip of grass between sidewalk and street) on a well-kept, tree-shaded bungalow block, and then there's an airlock sensation, one atmosphere draining out to make way for another flowing in, as I cross an alley, pass the blank cinder-block side wall of the building that houses the offices of the Fifth Ward's alderman, and turn the corner onto 71st Street.

Every neighborhood in the city has at least one traditional main street like this, and the airlock sensation of crossing between residential and commercial realms at the corners where it intersects with blocks of tight-packed housing is a fundamental experience of Chicago life. There are people out and about on 71st, running errands, hawking single cigarettes (called "loose squares") or DVDs, getting high or drunk, selling drugs, or just hanging out waiting for something to happen, but the street still feels desolate, stark and exposed. It's laid out extra-wide to accommodate the old Illinois Central tracks that run down its center at grade, the way trains passed through the city in the nineteenth century. Pedestrians coming in the distance seem like riders approaching in the desert. For much of the twentieth century, 71st was a busy old-fashioned main street. It had begun to thin out by the 1970s, but my Keds and birthday cakes were bought there, and I saw *Tarzan and the Great River* at the Hamilton Theater and *Car Wash* at the Jeffery Theater. Those businesses are long gone, eclipsed by faraway malls and big box stores, and they haven't been replaced. You can still buy a wig on 71st— South Shore has been over-endowed with cheap beauty supply stores for half a century—and there's a plucky bakery café, a new taco place, and a venerable no-frills pizza joint, but mostly there are empty storefronts and a scattering of convenience stores and dollar stores that sell junk and necessities to poor people. With a vacancy rate above 50%, the street feels too big for its remaining functions, like clothes that hang awkwardly off a once-robust old friend afflicted with a wasting disease.

*

Like *home* or *love*, *neighborhood* as a concept threatens to be too capacious to be practically useful. It describes both a place and a quality of feeling, a physical landscape and the flows of population, resources, and thought moving through it. The infrastructure of streets and parks and buildings may be there for the long haul, but any particular order—any particular way of life and the material basis for it—housed in this container is always taking form, in the process of disappearing, or both at once. And the term *neighborhood* can shrink or stretch in scale to fit a small cluster of buildings or an expansive quarter of the city composed of many sub-areas that qualify as neighborhoods in their own right. It's a several-faced and at times self-contradictory term, but neighborhood is my subject, so I should explain what I intend by it.

Is it even useful to call South Shore a neighborhood? It does have a clearly defined identity. South Shore is number 43 of the 77 "community areas" into which the city of Chicago is formally divided. Almost nine miles south of the Loop, South Shore is a lakefront residential district bounded by Lake Michigan, Jackson Park, Stony Island Avenue, and 79th Street—a rough rectangle of three square miles. Its population of about 50,000, down from a high of about 80,000, is over 95% African American, 34% of residents are below the poverty line, and it is above the average for Chicago in numbers of both high school dropouts and PhDs. South Shore ranks among the worst 25% of the community areas in measures of violent crime: there were 187 homicides—the sixth highest total citywide—between 2006 and mid-2015, and the rate went up in 2016 as part of a surge in gun violence. The schools are widely regarded as subpar, and rates of infant mortality, teen pregnancy, and low birth weight are disturbingly high. But South Shore has also long been known as one of the most physically attractive parts of the South Side, blessed with good housing stock, lovely parks and beaches, convenient public transportation, and a long-established reputation for respectability.

The community areas were originally mapped out a century ago by sociologists at the University of Chicago, known as the Chicago School. As part of their grand scheme to parse urban modernity, they broke up Chicago, their laboratory, into what they regarded as naturally occurring communities that had stable boundaries and displayed enduring characteristics, no matter who happened to live there. The community areas don't correspond to wards or police districts or other administrative maps, but decades of reference to them in policy, planning, data gathering, and business activity—as well as everyday conversation—

has given them a lasting authority and social purchase. Government officials and scholars and businesses and residents use the Chicago School's map of community areas in practical ways to organize the city.

Yet the official South Shore community area is too big and complicated to constitute a single organic social unit in which everyone regards everyone else as a neighbor. It's composed of several easily identified sub-areas that readily fit most people's notion of a neighborhood—the enclave of stately houses in the Jackson Park Highlands, the walkup apartment-building blocks of Parkside and O'Keeffe, the bungalow belt in Bryn Mawr East, the strip of lakefront high-rises along South Shore Drive, and so on. The residents of a sub-area often have less in common with those in the next one or even on the other side of their block than they might have with people in similar circumstances in Woodlawn, South Chicago, Hyde Park, and other nearby community areas. South Shore is just as much a composite mini-city of disparate parts as it is what the Chicago School sociologists thought of as a "natural" area, produced by "ecological" social processes.

But, before you give up on the official Chicago community area as a useful category for the study of neighborhood, remember that you can slice *any* neighborhood into ever-finer sections by making ever-subtler distinctions between social classes, housing types, and the like. The community area may be a fiction, but it's a convenient one that people treat as if it matters, and convenient fictions are essential features of how neighborhood works. The community area is what people on the street and in city hall mean when they say "South Shore," and what they say and think influences what they do.

Sampson argues that how you define neighborhood should depend on the question you're asking about it. For example, he says, "If you're looking at environmental toxins, service delivery, or reputation, then larger areas have more meaning, but if you're studying something more micro, like how parents supervise their kids, then you might look block by block." In daily life, we shift scales like this all the time without a second thought. If on your block you see someone who lives twenty blocks away, you'll wonder what she's doing so far from home, but if you run into that same person in the Loop or in Spokane, you'll greet her as a close neighbor. So, like Sampson, I take a flexible approach to neighborhood that places priority not on a seamless definition but on enabling moves that need to be made.

My rough working answer to "What is a neighborhood?" has four parts. First, and most important, a neighborhood is both community and container, the sum of a social arrangement plus the discrete chunk of geography that houses it, and the relationship between them. Second, the term *neighborhood* covers multiple and often nested scales, beginning at the level just above household and family (the level of the block, usually) and extending with waning force across progressively larger-scale but still plausibly walkable areas of the city until it stops being useful at some point short of the level of the city as a whole. The "plausibly walkable" part still matters, I think. Your mind is housed in a body, and your imaginative grasp and experience of neighborhood (a word that, after all, literally refers to physical proximity) are calibrated to the scale of that body, even if you drive everywhere and gain much of your knowledge about it online. Third, a neighborhood is part of a larger landscape composed of other neighborhoods, like and unlike it. Fourth, neighborhood is both fact and idea, each influencing the other, so that a full account of it must address both the material landscape inhabited by flesh-and-blood people and the imagined landscape inhabited by characters and mapped by words and images.

These four traits don't add up to a comprehensive definition, but they give me questions to ask, moves to make: describe the container, the lay of the land; take the quantitative and qualitative measure of the community or communities it contains; get a sense of the different scales of neighborhood nested in it and the points of contact and friction between them; see the whole neighborhood in relation to others around it; put it all in motion over time to see the play of persistence and succession as different phases of the city rise and fall; and consider the two-way traffic of influence between the material neighborhood and its double in the realm of imagination.

*

Walking west on 71st, I pass first Paxton Avenue and then Merrill, each of which has its own gang, known respectively as Pax Town and the

Merrill Boys. These corners used to be the territory of the Four Corner Hustlers, but in Chicago large formal gangs with expansive territorial ambitions have been breaking down into loose cliques that hang out on this block or that one, and the proportion of intra-gang shootings has gone up as social media slights replace battles over turf as reasons for a beef. Unlike the bungalow blocks south of 71st, the blocks north of 71st are thick with apartment buildings, many filled with tenants holding housing vouchers. The voucher program was supposed to allow poor people to exercise individual choice to escape the kind of warehousing exemplified by the Robert Taylor Homes, Cabrini-Green, and other high-rise housing projects that the city began tearing down in the 1990s. But they mostly ended up reconcentrated in places like South Shore, which has more voucher holders and evictions than any other community area in the city. There are often guys on the corner on this part of 71st, whistling and wigwagging signals up the block. Every so often one of the Chicago Police Department SUVs that ceaselessly prowl up and down 71st will roll in and break them up, and they'll gather on another corner. A recent study found that 47% of black men between the ages of twenty and twenty-four in Chicago were neither in school nor in the job market. On a board covering the display window of a failed convenience store at the corner of 71st and Merrill someone has written:

Men, _please_ respect yourself
Be a real man
And pull up your pants

*

Allan B. Hamilton, a real estate man whose family name used to grace one of those long-defunct movie theaters on 71st Street, once said, "The world is always coming to an end in South Shore." That was in 1969. South Shore, which had been over 90% white in 1960, would be 70% black by 1970, and over 95% black by 1980. Offering some historical perspective to those inclined to see this change as the end of the world, Hamilton noted that in the past South Shore's residents of English descent had feared imminent apocalypse when the Irish arrived, as did the Irish when Jews began moving in. Each time, the newcomers failed to destroy the neighborhood and South Shore had remained a pleasant place to live, retaining its respectable middle-class character. Black bungalow owners are just as house-proud as white ones, and their money spends the same, he was saying, so the neighborhood's merchants—many of whom were his tenants, and to whom his remarks were most pointedly directed—would do well to refrain from panic and carry on with business as usual. In a few more years, though, he would sell off his family's extensive holdings on 71st Street and join the exodus of white people and their money.

Hamilton's observation, with all its ironic overtones both intended and unintended, touches on a central South Shore paradox. On the one hand, South Shore is nowhere near as sensationally distressed as starkly depopulated zones of vacant houses and lots going back to prairie in Englewood or Garfield Park, and even at its worst it's nowhere near as iconically scary as were the high-rise towers of the Robert Taylor Homes that once marched for twenty blocks along the Dan Ryan Expressway. Those who don't live on the South Side tend to regard it all as a no-go zone uniformly rife with poverty and danger, with a provisional exception only for Hyde Park, home of the University of Chicago and many educated white people. Such simplistic thinking does poor justice to a varied and complex reality. Large stretches of South Shore, for instance, are quiet and green and no doubt disappointing for a naive visitor prepared by overheated news reporting and the self-promoting guns-in-the-camera bunkum of drill rappers to expect a cross between *The Wire* and *The Road*. South Shore can be staid—boring, in fact, as I sometimes remarked to myself in my teens—and nobody moves there for the excitement. Residents tend to prefer it that way, valuing solidity to the point of willingly accepting stolidity as its price, and they're suspicious of anyone who thinks otherwise.

One lesson of more general application that South Shore teaches is that neighborhood may feel solid and even stolid—mundane, knowable, boring—but it's also always in motion underfoot, with older orders rising and falling and piling up in layers of fragments and ruins through which succeeding newer orders are already emerging. Neighborhood is how we experience both order and flux, persistence and succession, the intensely familiar and the disorientingly unfamiliar, the daily round and the big picture at the same time. Major change can feel like a lot of little things of local and passing interest: the Joneses defaulting on their mortgage, the Johnsons moving back to Mississippi, the bank and supermarket going out of business, the usual worries about crime and alien newcomers. But when you look back later, you can see the outlines of tectonic shifts that show up in history textbooks: folk migrations, transformations of economic and social class structure, changes in the form and function of the city. Neighborhood, the first step beyond the household, is the most intimate public stage on which we live the consequences of history.

That's why, on the other hand, the world really is always coming to an end in South Shore. As Hamilton knew, the neighborhood has a history of successions, with waves of newcomers shouldering in and settling down only to feel shoved aside in turn by subsequent newcomers. Also, fear of violent crime has pervaded the neighborhood's public discourse and physical character for half a century. Houses and apartment buildings tend to be buttoned up tight; residents, accustomed to daily routines designed to minimize the chances of being victimized, are primed to choose between fight or flight. The neighborhood's variegated mix of housing stock, which brings different social classes into close proximity, is another source of tension. When the Chicago Housing Authority, implementing its Plan for Transformation, tore down high-rise projects all over the city in the late 1990s, their former residents were channeled to black neighborhoods on the South Side and West Side. South Shore, which had thousands of apartments and a shrinking population, received a disproportionate share of the displaced families—perhaps the largest share of any community area. Even though South Shore's worst era of violence actually predates the arrival of these displaced CHA residents, the stories of decline I frequently hear in the neighborhood attribute a great deal of disruption and degradation to this relatively small set of newcomers and the much larger group they are made to stand for—those who receive public assistance in the form of housing vouchers—all lumped together as "project people" or "Section Eight people" or "the element."

While there are resources in South Shore, especially among its sizable cohort of educated professionals, neither individual nor institutional wealth tends to run very deep, as is generally true of black neighborhoods compared to white ones. There's not much wealth or social capital held in reserve, not much slack built into the system, so even medium-sized problems tend to loom as major threats to the neighborhood's preferred way of life and self-image. That helps explain why South Shore's outward air of respectable calm seems to buzz with expectation of the next shock to the system, the next threat to order and stability.

I grew up in a middle-class world in South Shore, and this is fundamentally a middle-class book. It mostly explores the social realm occupied by those who are richer than poor and poorer than rich, like the bungalow dwellers and apartment owners who have traditionally dominated South Shore's public discourse. But that middle-class world is shrinking and changing, and not just in South Shore. America's social strata are realigning from a familiar and somewhat fluid tripartite arrangement—upper, middle, working—to a binary and more rigid one: haves and have-nots. Yes, being a have-not in America is not at all the same thing as being a have-not in Bangladesh or Ethiopia, and yes, even poor Americans live better than the vast majority of human beings on earth today or who have ever lived. But the experience of being a have-not is more relative and less absolute than we tend to assume. People measure their suffering or success against whoever is most available for comparison, and in South Shore people of widely divergent means often live no more than a block or two apart.

The numbers tell the story of a far-reaching transformation of American life. In the 1980 census, 52% of South Shore's population qualified as middle class, while 39% qualified as lower class and 9% as upper class. By 2014 the middle cohort had fallen out of the majority to 31% and the upper had slipped to 6%, while the lower had expanded to 63%, more than half of them under the poverty line. Over the same period, the income gap between the richest and poorest in the neighborhood grew drastically, outpacing both Cook County and the nation as a whole. The richest used to earn 11.8 times what the poorest did; now they earn more than 20 times as much.

Some of South Shore's middle-class residents have left for the suburbs or the South, but another important movement happens in the minds and habits of those who stay. Educated professionals who once thought of themselves as solidly in the middle become haves who seek to insulate themselves from the disorder and danger and bother of public life. It's not that they suddenly get richer, but rather that they become haves by default. Others who might lack the haves' educational or professional credentials but still would have once thought of themselves as middle class, or on the way there, now feel themselves slipping into the have-nots: upside down on a mortgage, perhaps, or insufficiently pensioned, and increasingly unable to preserve and hand on the gains that so many upwardly mobile South Side families made during the postwar boom.

The social order is changing around them at frog-boiling speed: slow enough to be imperceptible from day to day; yet fast enough, year to year, to be disorienting and dangerous. I see the speed bumps that residents have insisted on installing on residential blocks all over South Shore as expressing a wish to slow down and contain not just traffic, which isn't one of the neighborhood's significant problems, but also more abstract and intimidating processes beyond their control. There are poor people in this book, but no truly rich ones, and most fall somewhere in the middle—with the accent on the uncertain resonances of "somewhere," as we continue to revise our assumptions about who gets to be middle class in this country and what the label even means anymore.

That living on the South Side of Chicago is also about being middle class, and not just gangs and guns, shouldn't be news at this point. Other writers have abundantly demonstrated that it's also about respectability, cutting the grass, getting ahead, hanging on to gained ground, and doing right by both self and community in all the traditional ways. And it bears noting that what happens in black neighborhoods often happens in the rest of America a generation or so later. So the shallower wealth, greater proximity to the poor, and other distinctive traits of the black middle class that make its status especially precarious also tend to suit it for the role of canary in a coal mine. If you want to see what American cities are going to be like when we're done reversing the postwar expansion of the middle class, South Shore's a good place to look.

*

Continuing west, I arrive at 71st Street and Jeffery Boulevard, South Shore's central intersection, the kernel from which the neighborhood grew. German truck farmers settled here in the mid-nineteenth century. The Illinois Central built a station here in 1881, enabling a housing boom that picked up momentum when the World's Columbian Exposition was held in Jackson Park, just to the north of South Shore, in 1893. The South Shore Commission, once one of the most powerful neighborhood organizations in the country, had its offices at this intersection, as did the Afro-American Patrolmen's League. So did the South Shore Bank, an internationally renowned exponent of community development banking. The bank went out of business in 2010 and its building stands empty. Diagonally across from it is 65,000 square feet of vacant space in a shopping center financed by the bank. There was a Dominick's there, the neighborhood's only supermarket, but it closed in 2013 and has not been replaced.

There are more people out at 71st and Jeffery—changing buses, going to Walgreens, hanging out, selling loose squares and stronger smokables—but the scene still feels desultory, like the aftermath of a minor cataclysm. Passing through it, I have slipped without conscious effort into a middle-aged version of the persona I first adopted on 71st Street as a child: cordial but flat in affect; willing to engage but not eager for recognition; minding my own business in a way that projects purpose without challenge, self-effacement without diffidence. There and not-there, I'm in a slightly out-of-focus middle state between neighbor and ghost. Old moves come back to me instinctively. Without consciously deciding to, I slide a little to the left so that a light pole and a street tree screen until the last possible moment my approach to a corner where men are milling and shouting.

*

As the inmost ring of the world at large beyond the home, neighborhood typically provides the setting in which you begin to assemble and try out your equipment for living. By equipment for living I mean the tool kit of ideas, models, and techniques for understanding the world and making your way through it that you pick up from the people around you and from what you see and hear and read. Much of this useful stuff comes from sources either more intimate or more expansive than the neighborhood: from home and family, on the one hand, and from school lessons and the culture at large, on the other. In my case, I had immigrant parents who brought equipment with them from Spain and Sicily—a legacy of sardanas and opera, carpentry and dressmaking, classical mythology and a taste in art that ran to Renaissance Madonnas making gang-sign hand gestures and the arrow-feathered Saint Sebastian lolling in his bonds like a beautiful sleepy porcupine. Instead of neighborhood schools, I attended the University of Chicago's Laboratory Schools (known as Lab) in Hyde Park, where most of my classmates lived. I got to know—and got to know myself in—many places beyond South Shore, not just Hyde Park and downtown and my parents' hometowns but also Philip Marlowe's Los Angeles and Conan the Barbarian's Hyboria; Sherwood Forest and outer space; Funkytown and Kashmir and all the other faraway realms to which radios, TVs, and movie houses served as portals; and countless permutations of basketball court and baseball diamond and football field. Even so, even if my equipment for living came from all over, South Shore was my first proxy for the world at large, functioning as both filter and laboratory as I stepped from the shelter of home into the street and set about figuring out what to use and how to use it.

Take, for example, a minor childhood incident of which I happen to retain a vivid memory: a difference of opinion that arose when I informed my next-door neighbor Alfred Thigpen, who had just upended me with a hard slide during a game of running bases in front of our houses on Oglesby, that I had tagged him out. We were probably eight years old. I shed my glove and stepped hotly into a prefight face-off with him, but I was not optimistic about what would come next, given what Alfred's habit of executing rigorous hook slides on the sidewalk in tan corduroy flare pants suggested about his willingness to go all the way. (He went to Tuskegee and died young, murdered at the age of thirty-one while working as a bouncer.) I hurriedly reviewed my equipment for living in search of relevant models of manly self-assertion that might provide a way out of fighting without loss of face. Action heroes like Neal Adams's Batman, the red-fro'd Thor of *D'Aulaires' Norse Gods and Giants*, and the TV private eye Joe Mannix were useless here; they would just start swinging. But how would Don Kessinger, the Cubs' wading bird of a shortstop, respond if the rageball Pete Rose took him out with a flagrantly malign slide? And what would my father do? I had never seen him back down from anyone, but I had also never seen him drawn into a fistfight. How did he manage that? What about my sideburned, cigar-smoking Catalan hepcat-drummer uncle Ricard, who had a volatile temper but also a gift for joking around? Or, if Alfred and I had passed the point at which jokery could defuse the crisis, maybe I could somehow instantaneously learn to mimic the dire front of kids I saw on the blocks east of Yates Boulevard on my way to the public library, fearsome characters who managed to project menace without having to actually *do* anything to anybody. I never did come up with a viable alternative to fighting Alfred. As I wearily got up after each knockdown, resigned to taking my medicine, I was already telling myself that next time it would be wiser not to let things get so far so fast. Less Kirk, more Spock, with perhaps a dash of Uhura.

Facing off with Alfred was one of a series of neighborhood scenarios that obliged me to test my equipment for living. The scenarios advanced in complexity as I got older: navigating between the block on which I was well known and the train station on 71st Street where strangers converged, refining the art of getting next on a basketball court and trying to hold my own in the game, figuring out how to carry myself as a white guy in a predominantly black world set inside a world dominated by white people, and so on.

Born in 1964, I grew up in a time when neighborhood was more obviously important than it is now. The older you are, the more you remember a pre-internet, more pedestrian, less magnet- and charter-schooled city where childhood featured a lot of unsupervised free play in the street and the bounds of neighborhood had more authority in dictating who your friends would be, where you went to school and worked, who you might fall in love with, what you knew and liked. But the fundamental function of neighborhood hasn't changed all that much. In 2015 Michelle Obama, who was also born in 1964 and lived on Euclid five blocks down from me, told the graduating class of Chicago's King College Prep, "I was born and raised here on the South Side, in South Shore, and I am who I am today because of this community." It was as true of her audience as it was of her, even if during her speech some considerable proportion of them felt a potent urge to text, take selfies, or otherwise plunge through a handheld screen, removing themselves from the physical here and now into a disembodied realm of data. For them, as for her and for me, neighborhood is still a principal ground of first encounters with the world beyond the home, and it still plays an important part in the work of developing your equipment for living.

*

Continuing on 71st west of Jeffery I pass the blank empty hulks of the South Shore Bank building and the Jeffery Theater on my right, and the raised platform of Bryn Mawr station in the middle of the street on my left. Then, before I reach the antique neon sign of the defunct Red Pagoda (CHOP SUEY TO TAKE HOME) or the chained-shut grated storefront next door to it that used to be Wilson Brothers hardware, I turn right off 71st onto Euclid Avenue. A keyhole-shaped dead-end circle at the end of Euclid prevents access by car to or from 71st. Walking up Euclid, I pass a couple of fenced-off lots, a couple of small apartment buildings, and then, just as the sidewalk crosses the driveway of the first single-family house on Euclid, a near-mansion on a double lot where the Bourellys used to live, there's another click and another airlock moment. The low hum of 71st Street recedes and the wide tree-lined streets grow quiet except for birdcalls.

This is the Jackson Park Highlands, sixteen square blocks planned in the early twentieth century as a demonstration district featuring underground utilities, no internal alleys, and architecturally distinctive houses set well back from the street and each other on generous lots. Its quality of rarefied aloofness has been enhanced since I lived there by the creation of cul-de-sacs at almost every point on its periphery where its streets connect with the rest of South Shore, greatly increasing the feeling of being snugged in a well-defended genteel preserve. It feels as if there's more oxygen in the air here, more room to maneuver, more give in the lives being lived in the big houses on lush, landscaped grounds. Known for being the home of Jesse Jackson, Ramsey Lewis, Gale Sayers, and other notable figures in black Chicago, the Highlands is as nice as South Shore gets, as nice as the South Side gets, though these houses would cost more like $3 million or $4 million, not $400,000, on the North Side or in Boston, where I live now. So it's aloof gentility on a relative budget, fifteen minutes from the Loop by car or express bus but costing less than a typical McMansion in a far-flung commuter exurb of the sort that many Americans still consider the model of a good place to raise kids.

A block and a half into the Highlands, on the 6900 block of Euclid, I pass houses I still think of as the Parkers', Trainers', and Earps' and end up in front of a high-shouldered Tudor-style brick house with a brick driveway and no front door. I lived there from 1973 to the fall of 1982, when I went off to college on the East Coast, where I ended up staying. My parents lived in the house until 1989, when, with their three grown sons gone and mayoral politics making Chicago increasingly untenable for my father, who was chancellor of the city's community college system, they moved to New York City. When we lived in the Highlands, we were part of its substantial white minority, whose continuing presence makes this area unique in South Shore. Integrated and unified by upper-middle-class interest, the Highlands' residents have long regarded themselves as surrounded by slippery slopes. They treat as an existential threat any incursion from the larger neighborhood into their enclave, any attack on any of its fine houses or householders, any potential degradation of its physical beauty, or any unseemly business activity around its borders, and they respond promptly with mutual aid and by insisting on attention from the police and other authorities.

Like the more modest bungalows on Oglesby, the elegant houses and grounds of the Highlands have become harder targets in the years since I left home. There are more burglar bars on windows, and watchdogs barking furiously behind high fences. There are a lot more high fences. There are security cameras, too, and electric gates sealing driveways, neither of which anybody had when I was a kid. There's almost nobody out at night, which was true before, but there are also fewer people out during the day—and some significant proportion of them are landscapers, a type I didn't see around much in the 1970s. Many fewer children play on the streets and sidewalks, and they are much less likely to go down to 71st Street in search of amusement or to run an errand for a parent, both because parents let kids do less free-range wandering than in the past and because there's less for them to do out there. I always found the Highlands beautiful but eerie, and it seems more beautiful and eerier than ever these days.

*

No matter how carefully I have done my job of research and writing, no matter how scrupulously I have tried to get things right, people who know something about South Shore or places like it will feel I got at least some of it wrong. That's to be expected, given the sense of ownership people tend to feel for a neighborhood. *It wasn't that way*, they will say, or *It used to be that way but things have changed recently, and now you're behind the times* (which is why in the chapters that follow I write mostly in the past tense, to reflect the fact that the neighborhood and its people remained in motion when I stopped doing principal research in mid 2016, right about when I took this walk from Oglesby to Euclid). People who feel in the know will say that class difference, or racism, or crime, or community spirit, or something else was more or less important than I make it out to be.

I know this will happen because I have some of the same reactions to what I read about South Shore. People from South Shore don't get blasé about their unassuming, unfamous neighborhood entering public discourse in the way that people from Hyde Park, Greenwich Village, Beverly Hills, or the Lower Ninth Ward do. It's always a thrill to see South Shore turn up in the culture at large, as it does in the *Barbershop* movies, the closing moments of the film version of *Glengarry Glen Ross*, a video in which Kanye West shows Jay-Z around his old neighborhood, and discussion of the Obama Presidential Center in Jackson Park, which went from speculative possibility to imminent fact during the final months of my research. However, that thrill is typically paired with irritation at errors of fact, misinterpretations, or failure to catch the tone and texture of the place with sufficient nuance. I have yet to read anything about Michelle Obama's early years that doesn't inspire me to say, "No, no, *no*," in my head or even out loud, appalled at some mistake or false note that only someone from the neighborhood would notice or care about. Even her own accounts of growing up in South Shore vary considerably in emphasis. At times she has dwelt on how close and safe the community and her extended family felt, and how South Shore has changed since then; at other times she has stressed the structural denial of opportunity against which she had to contend to make her way in the world. The different versions aren't incompatible, but they're a reminder that neighborhood is a many-faceted subject that provides plenty of material for multiple accounts.

I try to bear in mind what the sociologist Harvey Molotch wrote in the introduction to *Managed Integration*, his excellent, ironically titled study of South Shore's transformation in the 1960s: "Life is too complicated for me to have been anything more than a little bit right." It's not just that any neighborhood is capacious enough to contain contradictory truths and competing versions of reality. It's that neighborhood is an amalgam of fact and experience, sensibility and data. Sharing space in the container of any neighborhood are very different slices of generational perspective, class outlook, personal style, ways of knowing the world—all of which leads to differing points of view that are not easily reconciled.

That doesn't mean, though, that neighborhood is all things to all people. For example, South Shore tends to have relatively low levels of collective efficacy, sociologists' term for a community's ability to accomplish needful things by taking advantage of the mutual trust and confidence in shared values that grow from social ties. But tell that to residents active in South Shore's public life and they'll say, "What are you talking about? I'm neighborly as all hell, and I know a dozen people in South Shore who are just as involved as I am." And they'll have a point. They are indeed passionately committed to the neighborhood, and they know others who are as well, and it could be that the situation is improving in this respect, as some people in South Shore have told me—though at least as many said it wasn't. But in the aggregate, South Shore's relatively weak collective efficacy is not a matter of opinion, as is clear not just from my interviews with residents and community leaders, and not just from the evidence of the eyes, but also from Robert Sampson's copious data.

Still, I recognize that what I'm trying to get right is *my* South Shore, which exists in part in the verifiable material world and in part in my head and in part in the words, pictures, music, and imaginations of others. My South Shore centers on Bryn Mawr East, the Jackson Park Highlands, and the stretch of 71st Street connecting them—a dumbbell shape about a mile long, with the two houses in which I grew up providing the cores of the lumps at each end and 71st forming the bar between them—and my South Shore is firmly founded in the past, especially the 1970s, the era when a neighborhood order began to cohere there that's now mature and perhaps even threatened with eclipse and succession. Part of what makes neighborhood so powerful and evocative a subject is that it shapes sensibility, your instrument for encountering and knowing the world.

In exploring this dynamic, I will alternate between two kinds of chapters. There are shorter, more first-person chapters that give you a feel for South Shore in the 1970s and the equipment for living I assembled and began to put to use there in understanding the neighborhood and my place in it. They frame longer, more journalistic chapters that return to South Shore in recent years to examine how current residents are living the consequences of what's happened to the neighborhood since then. I have grouped these chapters into two parts: Part I on the neighborhood-as-community, focusing on how residents engage with one another and how that affects their experience of South Shore; Part II on the neighborhood-as-container, diving deeper into the landscape and history of place to identify forces that shape those engagements and experiences.

*

Walking from the house on Oglesby to the house on Euclid through the abutting worlds of a single neighborhood, I'm tracing a pattern deeply imprinted on me—my first and truest atlas of what's out there beyond family and home, my first and most formative guide to how to carry yourself when abroad in it. I'm also navigating through flows of people, money, materials, power, and ideas that shape the neighborhood and the lives of everyone in it—not just surveying the effects of those flows with my eyes and ears and feeling them on my skin, but registering them as well in my impulses to linger here and cross there and say "How you doin'?" to one stranger but tacitly agree with another to mutually unsee each other. Nothing really happens on this walk, and yet it's replete with the consequences of a great deal that has happened to a great many people, and of powerful forces affecting not only South Shore but neighborhoods across the city and the country.

This book isn't a lament for my old neighborhood, lost community, or lost youth. I can appreciate those kinds of stories, but I distrust them as a narrative and analytical path of least resistance that can turn into a sentimental rut. I came back to South Shore to see how the neighborhood has developed and matured, examine how the lives of current residents fit the contours of the neighborhood's landscape and history, and try to draw lessons of more general application from intense attention to one small place and its effect on the people who live in it. I've come back equipped with ways of seeing that bear the marks not only of growing up there but also of working as an academic and a journalist, of all the places I've lived since I left home and of all the places I've written about—usually because I was drawn to them by questions first raised for me by growing up in South Shore: How do cities change, and how do we live the consequences and the meanings of those changes?

In H. P. Lovecraft's *The Dream-Quest of Unknown Kadath*, one of the pulp fantasy stories from which I drew equipment for living after discovering them in the stacks of the South Shore branch of the Chicago Public Library, the intrepid Randolph Carter searches all over dreamland for a tantalizing city he has glimpsed in the remote distances of the night. He travels on yak- and zebra-back, climbs forbidding mountains, braves soul-destroying voids, and still the city eludes him. Finally, the pschent-crowned Nyarlathotep reveals to Carter that he has been looking in the wrong places: "Behold! It is not over unknown seas but back over well-known years that your quest must go; back to the bright strange things of infancy and the quick sun-drenched glimpses of magic that old scenes brought to wide young eyes. For know you, that your gold and marble city of wonder is only the sum of what you have seen and loved in youth." Carter's alluring mystery city, it turns out, is an amalgam of Providence, Newport, and other such homely New England places that he—like Lovecraft—has known intimately from childhood.

That's what South Shore has been to me. So: forward, backward, onward.

PART I

COMMUNITY

A STRANGE SENSE OF COMMUNITY

"I want to get you past Lamentations and into a new book of the Bible, Implementations," said Carol Adams from the stage of the auditorium at the Bouchet Elementary Math & Science Academy, at 73rd and Jeffery. Adams, seventy-two, was one of South Shore's most accomplished and connected citizens, with a long history of activism in the neighborhood that went all the way back to the 1970s, an era of community-organizing successes when residents got together to stop the South Shore Bank from leaving, force the city to turn the old South Shore Country Club into a "palace for the people" called the South Shore Cultural Center, and shut down a troublemaking tavern strip. Adams had studied with the Chicago School sociologist Horace R. Cayton Jr., coauthor of the classic South Side study *Black Metropolis*, and gone on to a distinguished career in academia and public service, managing thirteen departments and a $500 million budget at the Chicago Housing Authority, heading the Illinois Department of Human Services, and directing the DuSable Museum of African American History. If "money talks to money and power talks to power," as she liked to say, Adams could get both of them on the phone. On this Saturday morning in February 2016, though, community was talking to community. She was speaking at the opening session of a daylong event, South Shore Rising, billed as the debut of South Shore Works, a new "transformative community network and planning initiative" that would bring together local leaders and their organizations to pursue "revitalization through community re-investment."

Facing her in rows of hard wooden seats worn smooth by generations of restless grade-school pupils (including Michelle Obama, who was salutatorian in 1977, when the school was still called Bryn Mawr) were perhaps two hundred local activists and social entrepreneurs. They were pillars of the community who attend meetings and say yes, who start neighborhood groups or join one and end up running it, neighbors to whom others turn when something needs doing. Most were women, most over fifty, and, except for a dozen or so whites, Hispanics, and Asians scattered among them, they were all black. Val Free, the main organizer of the event, was the principal force in the Planning Coalition and the Southeast Side Block Club Alliance, which sought to create and strengthen block clubs to form the backbone of a neighborhood network that could act on the whole community's behalf. Introducing Adams, with whom she had cofounded South Shore Works, Free described her as "my friend, my mentor, my roll dog." Also present were Yvette Moyo, who in 2014 had founded the booster magazine the *South Shore Current*; Teyonda Wertz, president of the neighborhood's chamber of commerce; Michelle Boone, commissioner of the city's Department of Cultural Affairs and Special Events; Suzanne Armstrong, proprietor of the Quarry, a venue on 75th Street for jazz and spoken word performances, a weekly farmers market, and other events, and also home to the *South Shore Current*; and Henry English, the long-serving president and CEO of the Black United Fund of Illinois. English—a big man with a limp who had long ago served as treasurer for the Black Panther Party and had taken part in the struggle to save the old South Shore Country Club— had influential connections to the city's black political elite. Charles Kyle, a young activist who had lost patience with English and the rest of South Shore's community-organizing old guard, had described their feuds and jockeying for position to me as "Game of Thrones." Kyle and others among the younger generation of neighborhood activists were not present at South Shore Rising, and the Jackson Park Highlands Association, aloof in its cul-de-sac'ed enclave, was not prominently represented, but otherwise many of South Shore's major players were there, with aldermen and other city officials scheduled to appear at a culminative afternoon session.

Adams was exhorting these concerned, engaged neighbors to come together and lead the community in standing up against encroaching forces that threatened their way of life. In her remarks she drew freely on a recent column in the *South Shore Current* in which she'd written, "Longtime residents of South Shore are known to reminisce about how the community was when they moved into it—the businesses along the commercial strip, the great schools, the lovely homes, the cultural amenities and the safety and security. We lament the current conditions where gunfire rings out at night, vacant lots and debris litter our business corridors and we can't even lure a major grocery [store] into our community." Her list of woes—in a booster magazine expressly intended *not* to reproduce the usual crime stories—also included break-ins and robberies, corner stores engaged in criminal activity, aggressive beggars, "vagrants" who "sleep (and worse) in the Metra station," and the ubiquitous hawkers of "loose squares" who pathetically amounted to "our new economic development plan."

In Adams's telling, the present emerging crisis was troubling in a different way than decades-old concerns about disorder and class tensions. South Shore, like other black neighborhoods, had been hit extra-hard by the financial panic of 2008. As property values foundered in the resulting extended trough, institutional investors and other outsiders had bought at bargain prices. Some building owners were renting their apartments to holders of housing vouchers, making what they could while waiting for South Shore to change. When the moment seemed right, they would get rid of the voucher holders and convert the apartments to upscale condos. Longtime neighbors, especially senior citizens on fixed incomes, were already losing their homes and being turned out on the street. Landlords were also warehousing commercial property, asking absurdly high prices that kept it vacant, waiting for that notional wave of enriching gentrification to roll over the neighborhood. The whole process, Adams asserted, had the look of "planned destabilization," not just the disinterested action of market forces. "You reside on some of the most valuable property in the city of Chicago," she explained, meaning its potential rather than its current depressed valuation, "moments from the beach and minutes from downtown." She broadly implied that powerful forces in both the private and public sectors were intent on clearing black people off this prime real estate so that white people could occupy—or, as those with a sense of South Shore's history saw it, *re*occupy—the neighborhood. If her neighbors failed to fully and shrewdly invest their collective resources in the defense of their own neighborhood, they would suffer the consequences. As she had put it in her column, "if you aren't at the table, you're on the menu."

A formidable woman with a rising shock of tight curls, Adams forcefully advanced a logical argument but also took pains to convey its emotional truth. She mixed registers, dropping Don Kingisms such as "trickeration" and "politricks" into her diction to pull a corner of the mantle of street authority around her analysis. She played Cassandra, monitory and dire: "If you let it go, shame on you," she said. "Our children will wonder, *you* will wonder, when you live somewhere the bus doesn't run and there's no Metra service and it takes two hours to get to work downtown, why we gave up on this neighborhood and lost it." And like a stern but loving parent, she reminded her audience that the people of South Shore would need to do better about organizing themselves, as they are not known for their gung-ho community spirit. "We charge conspiracy and we fear gentrification," Adams had written in her column, "but WE DO NOT ORGANIZE!" The significant proportion of Chicago's black professionals and managers who live in South Shore "run the rest of the city . . . work in government and the corporate world and in cultural arts and human services," and they "run national civil rights organizations and world-famous religious institutions" and "decide how philanthropic dollars are invested in neighborhoods just like ours." But when those capable professionals get home from work, she said, "We're tired and we want to go to sleep. We run the world, but we don't do it in South Shore."

The portrait of South Shore's black middle class drawn by Adams and other speakers at South Shore Rising presented it as squeezed from below and above: by poor black people, abandoned to their fate by government, who sowed disorder and eroded respectability; and by private capital and state power acting in the interest of well-connected rich white people who coveted lakeside real estate. Enumerating the resources this embattled middle class could draw on in self-defense,

Adams had to go beyond the traditional list of the attractions of the container, the physical amenities and locational advantages that made South Shore so appealing. After all, these attractions, in combination with depressed real estate prices, were precisely what had caught the notice of predatory real estate buyers. Instead, she emphasized South Shore's untapped reserves of "human capital." Just as its residents had grown used to spending their money elsewhere, they also exercised too much of their expertise and influence elsewhere—habits they had to change before they let the neighborhood be degraded to the point that it could be bought out from under them.

Mobilizing that human capital and investing it effectively in the neighborhood entailed defining an "us" to wield it. It also seemed to require defining a "them"—actually, two "thems"—to oppose. Anton Seals, a younger ally who spoke before Adams, said, "We have to sell a new narrative, not 'they that are coming' but 'us that are here.'" When I'd spoken with Seals a couple of days before, he'd said to an imaginary audience of potential white gentrifiers, "Hey, you *left*; now you want to come *back*?" When people in South Shore talked about "gentrification," even those who qualified by income and education as gentry in their own right, they meant white people displacing black people. But it wasn't clear that such a process was meaningfully under way. South Shore had lost a net of 12,790 black residents, about a fifth of its population, between 2000 and 2014, but white newcomers were not flooding in to replace them. Between 2000 and 2010, the net gain in white residents of South Shore was 30, and by 2014 it had risen only to 194 (out of a total of 897 white residents of South Shore). And yet many people I talked to in South Shore confidently reported that more and more white buyers were snapping up houses and apartments in the area.

But at South Shore Rising, "them" also meant a second foil, a group less self-consciously purposeful than white gentry on the march but just as threatening: the black poor, consistently characterized as a transient underclass, unengaged in neighborhood organizations and unlikely to vote, both vulnerable and prone to criminality, unwittingly partnered with the very perps who had sold them down the river—white capital and the state—in the sense that the black poor prepared the battlefield for the coming invasion of white gentry by unraveling and degrading the neighborhood from within.

One besetting wrinkle of the situation of South Shore's black middle class was that success in dealing with one "them" could weaken barriers against the other. Many improvements they desired—reductions in crime and visible disorder, fewer shady convenience stores and more sit-down restaurants and other such respectable businesses on the commercial strips—would be attractive as well to white "pioneers" looking for signs that South Shore had crossed the threshold from high-risk trouble spot into affordable neighborhood in transition. A juice bar or yoga place on 71st Street could serve as a tipping point. On the other hand, successfully keeping white gentrifiers at bay would also tend to keep away the higher-end businesses that came with them, which would in turn help keep housing prices depressed and ensure the continuing dominion on the half-empty commercial strips of low-end "ghetto" businesses and the unemployed people who hung out around them.

If there was an uncomfortably close consonance of interest at South Shore Rising between black haves and one "them," white haves, there was little serious attempt at bridge-building across the equally uncomfortable divide that separated black haves from the other "them," black have-nots. I was there all day, and I did not hear voices purporting to speak to or for the slightly over one-third of the neighborhood's population, including half its children, who fell below the poverty line. This is typical of public meetings in South Shore, where homeowners' voices and concerns tend to be heard to the exclusion of those of everyone else—not just poor people but also another almost one-third of the population whose household incomes place them above the poverty line but below the middle class, and renters at almost any income level. Just a few weeks before, the news had been full of the study showing that in 2014, 47% of black men between the ages of twenty and twenty-four in Chicago had been unemployed and not in school. The prevailing tone at South Shore Rising held that of course providing better education and job opportunities to these have-nots—rather than, say, moving them out en masse or urging the police to hammer them into quiescence—would be the most desirable way to address the problem they represented. But by whatever means it could be reached, the objective was to get them to pull up their pants and stop shooting each other. As a developer named Ghian Foreman put it, "We shouldn't be afraid to teach them the rules of engagement" that govern life in a middle-class neighborhood.

Some neighborhood veterans I had been talking to in South Shore declared themselves happy to welcome white people and their money, but even those who preached black solidarity and black community, who were in the majority at South Shore Rising, might admit under duress to being willing to replace the poor with white hipsters. The young activist Ava St. Claire, who didn't attend South Shore Rising, told me, "Nobody wants to say they want it, but they do want gentrification." The catch was that, even if such a trade could somehow be engineered, there would be no way to stop the flow. If South Shore reached the point that every third resident was white, and new places to eat, drink, and exercise were opening to cater to them, less adventurous white urbanites would then consider the neighborhood fit for habitation. They would be likely to come and keep coming, each wave indicating that the coast was clear for less adventurous ones to follow, and pretty soon South Shore's remaining black residents would find that they were vanishing Indians à la *Dances with Wolves*, guarantors of a waning authenticity for a wave of Kevin Costners crossing the frontiers of 67th Street and Stony Island Avenue into a hot new lakefront housing market.

Adams and other speakers at South Shore Rising, offering a litany of "us" and "ours," paraphrased Barack Obama's campaign rhetoric: "We are the people we've been waiting for." But it was going to be a challenge to bring together and effectively mobilize that "we" to act in their own interests. The difficulty arose not just from the multiple and often contradictory nature of those interests but also because the whole endeavor went against the deep-set privatist grain of the neighborhood's culture. As it confronted the prospect of a transformation potentially as drastic as the turnover from white to black in the 1960s and 1970s, contemporary South Shore's leadership could ponder historical parallels to the story of the South Shore Commission, the community organization that back in the day had first tried to stop the flow of black newcomers into the neighborhood and then tried with equal lack of success to "manage" it. Now another middle-class constituency, this time a black one, was trying to organize to defend its purchase on the neighborhood in the face of racial and class succession. There was a new round of warnings that current residents will regret having allowed themselves to be pushed out of an urban Eden, and there were efforts to mobilize South Shore's human capital. Such a group would have to prevail, again, against social and market forces bearing down from the outside as well as a tendency to pull apart operating from within. "They" were coming, again, and "we" were once again scrambling to form ranks to receive them.

*

Over the years I've collected images that speak to me of South Shore. A photograph taken in 1900 of young duck hunters posing with their long guns in a spindle-treed expanse of swamp at what is now the intersection of 79th and Euclid reminds me that a century is forever in an American city—although, as my brother Sal pointed out when I sent him the picture along with a Google Maps street view of the same intersection a century later that featured the Tough Times thrift shop and a graffitist's plea to "STOP THE VIOLENCE" scrawled across the blank sign of a defunct chain auto-service shop, a consistent theme of "people packing heat" joins the inner-city present to the prairie past. A series of booking photos available online from the state of Florida traces the descent into alcoholic drifter-dom of a once-proud troublemaker who in my childhood was my block's shirtless-and-denim-vested street-fighting Achilles. I find myself drawn as well to a picture Marc PoKempner took of a kid in a parka crossing 71st Street as snow falls. The marquee of the Jeffery Theater in the background, advertising a double bill of Ernest Borgnine in *Shoot* and James Earl Jones in *Deadly Hero*, pegs the scene to early 1976. I had a parka just like that kid's when I was little, and I can feel the chill on the skin of my face within the hood's fuzzy fringe, the sense of imminence resolved as the flakes come down at last out of a sky that's been threatening snow all day. The flood of recognition and recall cued by these pictures makes something turn over in my chest like a whale surfacing and then sounding again with a stately roll of its tail. But when it comes to images that capture an essential quality

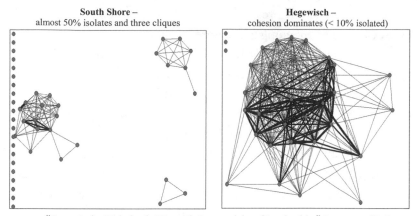

FIG. 1. "Community Variation in Network Connectivity of Leadership." Courtesy of Robert Sampson.

of South Shore, especially a quality that doesn't easily lend itself to a visual rendering, a figure on page 17 of Robert Sampson's book *Great American City: Chicago and the Enduring Neighborhood Effect*, published in 2012, may take the prize.

At first glance it seems far less evocative than the photographs. Dryly labeled "Community variation in network connectivity of leadership," it contrasts South Shore to Hegewisch, a formerly industrial neighborhood on the far South Side named for a rolling-stock baron. Each neighborhood's key leaders—the aldermen, ward committeemen, state representatives and senators, school principals, local school council members, bankers, realtors, ministers, priests, police commanders, neighborhood relations officers, tenant association presidents, health agency directors, community social service managers, and others to whom residents go to get things done—are represented by individual dots. A line between a pair of dots indicates a direct or indirect connection between leaders. The Hegewisch side of the figure looks like a schematic drawing of the Death Star's plumbing system, a deeply three-dimensional network that encompasses almost every dot. The South Shore side has three small networks, each composed of a few dots and floating in white space apart from the others, and a row of dots along the left margin, none of them connected by even a single line to any other. That's a picture of leaders who, while they may work with other influential people downtown or in other neighborhoods, either don't know each other or belong to separate, even hostile networks.

South Shore and Hegewisch are comparable in terms of income, but they have very different structures and cultures of leadership, which helps explain why South Shore has considerably weaker collective efficacy—the sociological term for how well a community gets together to do things for the public good. Hegewisch ranks near the top of the city's community areas in collective efficacy, South Shore in the bottom third. Sampson's research, now more than a decade old but still very pertinent, shows that while South Shore's key leaders are fairly busy and residents do participate at an average rate in civic organizations within and beyond the neighborhood, the yield of their efforts in South Shore itself is low. Leaders don't trust each other very much, they're not very effective in getting things done in South Shore, and residents accurately perceive both those leaders and themselves as not very effective.

More broadly, Sampson found that residents of South Shore were fairly disconnected from their leaders and each other. His data showed exceptionally low rates of reciprocal exchange (cooperation among neighbors—for example, in attending to children) as well as below-average levels of adult-child connections and perception of shared values with neighbors. South Shore also came in just about dead last among Chicago's community areas in anonymous altruism, which Sampson measured by leaving stamped letters around a neighborhood and seeing how many were picked up and mailed by helpful strangers. Sampson found that in South Shore high levels of sensitivity to disorder, perception of violence, and fear of crime led not to getting together to address shared concerns but to the opposite. Violence and crime seem all the more outrageous and indicative of weak community when they happen in South Shore precisely because residents believe that it's supposed to be in better shape—that is, more middle-class—than more notoriously "ghetto" neighborhoods farther inland like Grand Crossing or Englewood. So every shooting, every robbery or theft or gang incident, drives residents further in upon themselves by seeming to confirm that the community has fallen apart. If it hasn't, how could these things be happening in South Shore?

Sampson's figure grows more profound the more I look at it. He found a way to render an ethos, a mentality, a social and political fact of life that's abstract yet crucial to understanding South Shore's leaders, its residents, and the lessons they teach about neighborhood. Compared to people in other community areas in Chicago, including poorer and more crime-ridden ones, the people of South Shore tend to invest less of their money, time, feeling, and selfhood in their neighbors or the larger community. They do invest these resources in what they consider their own turf—in their own business enterprises, in their homes, and to a limited extent in their blocks or their apartment buildings—and they may invest these resources beyond the boundaries of South Shore, but as a group they commit relatively little to the social entity or polity of the neighborhood.

This is not to deny that there's strong feeling for South Shore among its residents. I shared in such feeling when I lived there and, even though I moved away long ago, I still feel its pull. But even among the most committed and long-term residents, that strong feeling is more the cool pride of respectability than the hot passion of street solidarity you'll find in more visibly distressed and rambunctious districts. There's a quiet conviction that at least some of South Shore—this end of the block, this side of Yates—remains a nice place to live and that it's still supposed to mean something if you live there. This conviction, however, comes paired with complementary horror at high rates of violent crime, depressed shopping strips, and other conditions that might be taken for signs of the ghetto emerging from an ostensibly middle-class district like the monster bursting from the chest of an unsuspecting astronaut in *Alien*. Residents' distancing from each other and the neighborhood-as-community is mirrored among their leaders, and low connectivity among leaders correlates with low collective efficacy. There are significant exceptions, of course, and those exceptions will understandably object to the foregoing generalizations, but the larger pattern is unmistakable.

Don't just take my word for it, or Sampson's. Listen to the voices of players represented by Sampson's dots, activists whose passion, calling, and livelihood it is to organize their neighbors to get things done for the public good in South Shore. They paint a consistent picture of a place where the distance between leaders mirrors the distance between neighbors.

"We are the low man on the totem pole when it comes to community unity," Val Free of the Planning Coalition, an organization dedicated to fostering more of that unity and deploying it as leverage on the neighborhood's behalf, told me in 2014. "It's haves versus have-nots, owners versus renters, owners versus Section Eight," she went on. "We still have failing schools, a weak economic corridor, the grocery store [closing]. These are common concerns that might bring people together, but there are people who won't put their guard down."

"It's a bedroom community with a strange sense of community," Henry English of the Black United Fund of Illinois, South Shore's most influential nongovernmental organization, told me. "They live here because it's accessible, they go to work and come home, and very few go out to experience their neighborhood," he explained. "They're like, 'I don't want to let you know I'm here.' People hide out here. Look at Jesse"—Jackson, that is, a longtime resident of the Jackson Park Highlands. "He saves the world but not the community he lives in."

"Even among forward-looking people, there's distrust between youth and elders," said Ava St. Claire, marketing director for the Far South Community Development Corporation and one of the neighborhood's tech-savviest activists. "I was a suburban kid who watched *Sesame Street* and thought I was going to come to the city and save it, and I was like, 'I'm gonna get me some of that black-elders-guiding-you-through-life thing!' But it wasn't like that." In her view, generational tension played an important role in preventing lines from developing between Sampson's dots.

"The new people didn't ruin the neighborhood," said Teyonda Wertz, executive director of the South Shore Chamber of Commerce, referring to incoming holders of housing vouchers, especially those relocated from Chicago Housing Authority projects. "The people who live here didn't invest in it," she told me. It's rare to hear such a candidly critical assessment of a community from a professional booster.

The tendency to withhold from investing oneself in the

neighborhood-as-community goes back a long way and connects to a larger standoffish ethos. In 1968, at the height of South Shore's racial turnover, in a newspaper essay defending the ethical integrity of white residents who chose to move out as black neighbors moved in and crime went up, Pat Somers Cronin wrote that if incoming black neighbors "were looking for an official welcome in South Shore, they chose the wrong community"—not because it was filled with grand mal racists but because its culture didn't favor such displays. Addressing herself as a proxy for other departing residents, she went on: "You have lived here for 40 years, and you know the area well. It is not social. Newcomers— white or Negro—are not, and never were, feted in any way. For years, the lake has attracted a certain kind of person who, more than anything, wants passionately to be left alone; an indication not of selfishness but of intense personal concern with family and career." This is all the more striking because Cronin's essay otherwise fits comfortably with the period's many other laments for the immigrant-ethnic urban village in decline, a genre that usually tends to emphasize how cozily tight-knit the old neighborhood was.

South Shore wasn't, and isn't, tight-knit. All kinds of observers offer all kinds of explanations, making for a long list of contributing factors: residents' tendency to place greater value on physical amenities like the lakefront than on a feeling of community, a mix of building stock that exacerbates class tensions and makes it harder for businesses to succeed, a bedroom-community culture of inturned individualism and privatism, weak institutions, fractious and misguided leadership, political fragmentation proceeding from the parceling out of the community area into three different wards, a worn-out middle class that fought its big battles in the 1970s and has turned away from public life as it ages out, class divisions widened by growing income inequality, the accrued effects of racial and class discrimination by both government and the private sector, the influx of former residents of public housing and other voucher holders without sufficient services to smooth their entry into the community, and a pattern of strategic disinvestment and selective profiteering by outside interests matched by the insular withdrawal of the neighborhood's most powerful and connected elites. Some of these factors arise from structural conditions of long standing, others from more recent or transient developments; overlapping with and amplifying one another, they all make it harder for residents to see each other as neighbors.

Whatever the exact combination of causes of the problem of South Shore's low collective efficacy, the efforts of local organizers who are trying to do something about it can tell us something important about the way the neighborhood works—and therefore, I hope, something important about the way neighborhood in general works. One basic lesson that South Shore teaches is that behind even the most heartfelt love for a neighborhood lies an especially contingent, partial, flexible, and ultimately optional kind of belonging. So collective efficacy works best when leaders operate with the grain and within the limits of residents' willingness to invest themselves in the community of the neighborhood. When going against that grain, even the most motivated, well-connected leaders fighting for sympathetic causes find themselves unable to meet the challenges raised by market forces, social processes, and the deep-rooted privatism that causes residents to shy from risking a sortie out of their urban fortresses of solitude.

And maybe South Shore's sense of community really isn't all that strange after all. In some ways it seems pretty typical of our urban moment and national mood. A deep divide between haves and have-nots, loss of faith in the state, an out-of-control gun culture, and a technology-assisted retreat from public space all sound resonantly familiar far beyond the boundaries of the neighborhood.

*

The South Shore Rising event moved through the day from speeches of welcome to breakout sessions on economic development, housing, the arts, and health, then on to a working lunch and an intermittently contentious plenary talk-back session with elected officials, and ended with a parting call to further action. It was par for the course for a community meeting in South Shore, as was the gradual waning of energy as the shared feeling of coming together to make a fresh start gave way to a growing sense of business as usual, culminating in the ritual of aldermen talking circles around the usual difficult questions posed by the usual concerned citizens representing the usual interests. There were exhortations to work together in a time of crisis, passionate interjections and digressions, revisiting of old injuries, and issuing of warnings against looming threats. The breaking news went around that McCaffery Interests—the main player in the titanic Lakeside development planned for the site of U.S. Steel's old South Works just southeast of South Shore—had pulled out and sold its stake back to U.S. Steel, sending the project back to the drawing board. What did it mean for South Shore? A setback for the forces of gentrification? Another blow to economic development plans and property values? A lot of people in attendance paid close attention throughout, some taking notes, and raised their hand and spoke with considered care when they had something to say. A tiny, bent old woman talked out of turn almost nonstop, echoing speakers' phrases and finishing sentences for them, sometimes clapping or making exaggerated conducting motions while others talked, every once in a while calling out comments like "Racism! Racist white people taking our things!" A thick-armed man in late middle age wearing a black leather kepi got up late in the day to say, "I want to talk about South Shore not as an economic place but as a place with real people in it, and not about exercising our First Amendment rights but about our Second Amendment rights—concealed carry, the right to defend our homes." He went on at some length, the Voice of the Gun casting a pall over the room as it reminded all present that any effort to exercise collective will was always threatening to break down into the war of each against all.

As I often do at meetings, I found myself wondering what this one might be accomplishing. At least a portion of the community was trying to pull together to look out for itself, and some of the speakers referred back to the victories of the 1970s to remind their neighbors that South Shore had once been capable of remarkable feats of collective efficacy. Recent events indicated a crying need for a revival on that front, and the ongoing grocery store disaster was Exhibit A.

The Dominick's in Jeffery Plaza, the strip-mall development on 71st Street financed by the South Shore Bank, had closed in late 2013 en the whole chain collapsed. That left South Shore, a community of almost 50,000, without a full-service supermarket other than an iffy Jewel at 75th and Stony Island, on the neighborhood's western edge. South Shore was a textbook food desert, except that it was inhabited by a lot of people who weren't poor. The vacancy also left the highly visible 65,000-square-foot corpse of the dead supermarket at the neighborhood's main intersection, kitty-corner from the dead bank building vacated first by what remained of the South Shore Bank (at that point called ShoreBank) in 2010 and then by its successor, Urban Partnership Bank, in 2014. Convincing a profit-seeking corporation to locate a supermarket at that intersection wasn't a purely civic matter, of course, but it seemed reasonable for citizens to expect themselves and their elected representatives to help make it happen. After all, there were plenty of potential consumers in South Shore, and not much nearby competition. Swiftly getting a new supermarket into the space seemed a fair test of the neighborhood's ability to organize—to show off its attractions to a potential tenant, and to put pressure on elected representatives to accelerate and smooth the process. Compared to past successes like stopping the bank from leaving or forcing the city to turn the old country club into a public cultural center, it seemed like a manageable task. Bringing in a new supermarket also seemed at first blush like the perfect cause for assembling a coalition that extended beyond the usual middle-class homeowners. Organizers at the forefront of the supermarket campaign stressed the simple unifying fact that everybody needs to eat.

But that fact is neither so simple nor so unifying as it was a generation or two ago. Class difference divides American foodways more sharply than ever these days, and middle-class shoppers with choices have grown ever more used to getting in the car to find their particular market niche for food, as they have for finding schools for their kids and other necessities. Our increasingly segmented consumer culture, rising inequality, and the habit of reliance on cars—all in addition to the empty storefronts on 71st Street and South Shore's reputation for crime—have made it harder for a supermarket chain to believe that a store in South Shore would earn a suitable return. A Whole Foods might be too upscale for a neighborhood with high poverty levels and a school dropout rate above the city's average, a Sav-A-Lot too downscale for a neighborhood with an above-average number of PhDs and a sizable cohort of households with incomes over $90,000—and South Shore, confoundingly, was both. Dominick's, like Jewel, had occupied the middle ground, but that middle ground has been shrinking and fragmenting along with the middle class for decades in South Shore, as it has in the rest of the nation. When South Shore Rising convened, well over two years after the Dominick's closed, there was still no supermarket and no realistic prospect of having one. Even if a store was eventually recruited, the long vacancy said much about the neighborhood.

When I went to see Henry English in the offices of the Black United Fund on 71st Street a few blocks west of Jeffery in May 2014, almost two years before South Shore Rising, he and others were already trying to get the grocery store campaign into full swing. The fund had supported local arts organizations, workplace programs, and schools for almost thirty years, but he and other leaders were finding it difficult to work together and get neighbors together to solve the problem, despite shared strong sentiments. He said, "When I first got here"—in 1976, when he joined the fight to save the country club—"people seemed pretty engaged." He credited the vigor of the neighborhood's area councils, which united block clubs into larger constituencies; the connective effect of the South Shore Commission's community newspaper, the *South Shore Scene*; and the schools for providing structure. "When people who lived in South Shore shopped on Seventy-First and went to school in South Shore," he said, "they were more connected." Of course, people who lived in South Shore were doing these things in 2014, but they were poor people, with 98% of students in the three schools nearest to 71st Street qualifying as "economically disadvantaged." English wasn't talking about them. After the South Shore Commission and its newspaper went out of business in the 1980s, he said, the old networks "went into disarray, and when the old residents began retiring, their activism never got replaced." Now, he said, only the Jackson Park Highlands Association was still active among the old area councils, "but they're just about people not breaking into their crib"—insular self-defense, not community-wide engagement. Nor did he put much faith in South Shore's elected officials, especially the Fifth Ward's alderman, Leslie Hairston, with whom he had a long-running feud. Without mentioning her by name, he and his allies told me on several occasions that they wished for "better political leadership" and "more effective representation." Teyonda Wertz, head of the chamber of commerce, once told me that nobody wanted to openly cross Hairston, because "you kill a snake by cutting off the head, and nobody wants to volunteer to be the head."

But English's reservations did not shake his long-run optimism. He expected eventual gentrification, integration, sidewalk cafés on 71st Street, a more soulful and more residential version of Hyde Park. "Educated professionals from elsewhere will come in," he said. "There's nothing left in Hyde Park they can afford, nothing downtown. They have to come here, but the schools have to come up some first." He sat back in his chair and smiled, finding a less uncomfortable position for his legs. "If I survive to eighty," he went on, "I'll see a lot of change." He didn't make it. In early March 2016, one week after the South Shore Rising event, he died at the age of seventy-three in a crash on Lake Shore Drive on his way to a get-out-the-vote event for Hillary Clinton, initiating a crisis of succession in the neighborhood's non-elected leadership.

When I talked about the grocery store campaign with Alderman Hairston in June 2015, a year after I discussed it with English and almost a year before South Shore Rising, it had been dragging on long enough that residents had begun to give up hope and complain about her leadership. Hairston, a woman not inclined to do much backing down, had a wide-eyed, mobile expression that readily reflected her feelings. She had been a few grades ahead of me at Lab; I used to ride the bus with her and her younger brother, who back then had an unsettling habit of turning his eyelids inside out. When I visited her in 2015, she had been alderman of the Fifth Ward for fifteen years and had been easily reelected yet again that February. Residents of South Shore might criticize her—"They don't want to pay taxes," she said, "but they still want us to stop the shooting"—but she commanded plenty of clout and a reliable corps of voters. She had tried various well-publicized means, including talk of exercising eminent domain, to pressure supermarket chains, the absentee landlord, and the mayor to take action on the grocery store, but so far there had been no results. She blamed racism for that: media that stereotyped South Shore as gang-infested and crime-ridden, chains that cooked their own market research to justify avoiding black neighborhoods, mayors who dumped voucher holders in South Shore and wouldn't lift a finger to help out a black neighborhood on the South Side. "It took *five years* to do the Starbucks deal," she said acidly, referring to the Starbucks on the western edge of South Shore at 71st and Stony Island. "They sell *coffee!*"—meaning that everybody drinks coffee, regardless of race. "That's the racism of corporate America." When I suggested that making common cause with Henry English and his Black United Fund might help in the fight against the effects of such prejudice, she responded, "He has property on Seventy-First Street, so he has a vested interest in peddling his vision of recovery and gentrification. He's about getting grants. He doesn't do shit."

Hairston's and English's offices were a dozen blocks apart on 71st Street. Both had Africana on the walls, worn carpeting, the feel of cut-rate institutionality. They were the kind of places that don't look like much but serve as conduits for the flow of power and money—in the form of government funds, foundation grants, jobs programs, and the like—into the neighborhood from outside it. Players like Hairston and English derive their leverage and influence from managing that flow. It wasn't the fault of South Shore's leaders that Dominick's had gone out of business and other supermarket chains had not rushed to fill the space, but if (recalling Sampson's graphic) the two cliques centered on the dots housed in those two offices had more lines between them, the crisis might already have been over.

The grocery store situation came up, inevitably, during the talk-back session with elected officials toward the end of South Shore Rising. Hairston assured the crowd, as she had over the previous two-plus years, that "we have the landlord at the table with a grocer," this time "an African American–owned grocer." But, she added, "racism is not dead; it's part of corporate America's mind-set. Poorer communities have grocery stores, so the only problem here must be our skin color." This didn't necessarily follow—some of those poorer communities with supermarkets were black—and some people I interviewed dismissed Hairston's racism argument as mere ass-covering by an alderman who couldn't get the job done, or only cared about the part of her ward that was in Hyde Park, or couldn't get along with the mayor. But nobody called her on it at South Shore Rising, and the questioning moved on to the topic of whether South Shore had indeed received the largest number of refugees from dismantled projects as a result of the CHA's Plan for Transformation.

*

The cohort of younger activists who did not attend South Shore Rising had plausible reasons to be elsewhere that day, but they did feel shut out by its organizers. As they saw it, South Shore's established leaders held their power too close, handed it only in grudging little doses to their anointed successors, sometimes actually tried to stop the next generation from doing anything new on the community's behalf, and weren't trying to do anything meaningful about the class divide that constituted the neighborhood's worst problem. In particular, younger activists felt that their attempts to bridge that class divide had set their elders against them.

Casting about for a way to describe the generational dynamics, Jedidiah Brown, pastor of the Chosen Generation Church at 75th and Phillips, cited an Old Testament passage, Numbers 32:13: "And the Lord's anger was kindled against Israel, and he made them wander in the wilderness forty years, until all the generation, that had done evil in the sight of the Lord, was consumed." The parallel to South Shore, Brown explained, was that "there's an entire generation who sees the potential where they're going, yet they're intentionally dysfunctional, so a whole generation has to die before they can get anywhere." We were talking in a Burger King on Stony Island in May 2016, three months after South Shore Rising. Henry English had died in March, and Talmadge Betts, the veteran program officer in charge of the Black United Fund's anti-violence and prisoner reentry programs, had died in April. "That generation is dying off," Brown continued. "On the one hand, it makes my heart ache, but, on the other, it makes me feel free, too." He believed that English and other civil rights–era veterans had protected their turf and their control of resources—which Brown felt they had hoarded and misused—by hamstringing and sidelining ambitious young activists. In his youthful hubris, he sometimes found himself thinking, "Damn, the old guard is not gonna let me fix this"—whether "this" was South Shore's class divide or some other daunting problem.

Brown, on break from his day job at a private security company that subcontracted for the Chicago Housing Authority, was wearing a blue tac squad jumpsuit with a slim flashlight and a tube of hand sanitizer neatly tucked under the epaulets. It was a new job. He had held it for two weeks and had already had two guns pointed at him, he said. He'd been fired from his previous job when he became a viral video celebrity and the target of death threats after he rushed the podium at an abortive Donald Trump campaign rally at the University of Illinois at Chicago, leading to a melee in which he clocked a Trump partisan and tussled with security guards. Shaven-headed, fit, bespectacled, an intense charismatic figure well supplied with self-esteem and a sense of dramatic timing, Brown once persuaded a young man who had tried to shoot him the day before to accompany him to an anti-violence event.

Brown's church concentrated its services for the poor in South Shore, which he described as "kind of a mini Chicago" because of its social divisions and unrealized potential. He said, "You take the Fifth Ward part"—the northern end of South Shore centering on 71st Street. "It's an area not invested into, a lot of dysfunctional siloed work. You have the Highlands and—how should I say it?—they don't give a damn about everybody else. Residents don't shop local. Police response is very different in different parts of the neighborhood." The most difficult part of trying to unify this divided community, he said, was "to get two separate worlds, separate realities, to converse." Trying to find areas of common interest had proven frustratingly futile, and it was a challenge to find a rhetorical style that brought different constituencies together. "You have to tap into what interests them to get them into the same room," he said, "and you have to find the fluff words, get away from haves and have-nots—'cause that's what South Shore is, in isolated form, haves and have-nots." Nobody wanted to confront this truth, he felt. "It's a delusional neighborhood, 'cause they think they're progressive. People don't want to hear the hard truth. You have to tell them something they can hear."

So far, Brown had not found the right fluff words. He candidly admitted that he had not been successful in bridging the divide to create greater community in South Shore. When he came to the neighborhood from Englewood five years earlier, he had seen great potential—"a beautiful neighborhood, affluent African Americans, major arteries to the Loop"—but also a weak sense of community. "Nobody was speaking to say hi, hello, and South Shore is the first place where I saw dead people in the street and other people just going about their business around them. Not even Englewood was like that." He had tried all kinds of approaches to the problem, from confrontational to cooperative, spectacular to low profile, and he had even run unsuccessfully for alderman against Leslie Hairston, and he had found himself stymied at every turn by established leaders who regarded him as a threat to their share of power and influence. He felt that his efforts—and those of other young activists, like Ava St. Claire and Charles Kyle—to reach the law-abiding poor and involve them in the life of the community had inspired especially concerted opposition. "They are victims of the element *and* the government," he said. "You got to give them a voice and make them visible, but they need to feel they have a champion. You had Charles, Ava, me, working together to try to reach them. But the agendas and perspectives came up." When I asked for specifics, he would go no further than to refer darkly to "a COINTELPRO-like thing from the board of BUFI" (COINTELPRO was the covert FBI program that targeted Martin Luther King Jr. and the Black Panthers, among others; BUFI was Henry English's Black United Fund of Illinois) and to "aldermen who are threatened by anyone who wants to do something new."

Brown was beginning to grow discouraged. He was assembling resources for one more big push to make a difference in South Shore, and if it didn't work, he would try a less intractable neighborhood. Like other young activists who felt themselves on the outside in South Shore, he was constantly performing a cost-benefit analysis: Do I dig in and make a stand here to try to develop the neighborhood's unrealized possibilities, or am I throwing away my youthful energy on a futile crusade? (On February 12, 2017, Brown appeared live on Facebook sitting in his car downtown with gospel music playing and gun in hand, obviously distraught and speaking disjointedly to the camera about his own death, the recent death of a young cousin, and his own continuing inability to improve conditions in his community. Police peacefully disarmed him after a standoff that shut down Lake Shore Drive for ninety minutes.)

Trying to explain why some activists her age "have completely cut ourselves off from people over fifty," Ava St. Claire cited Shakespeare rather than the Bible. She had in mind the image in *Macbeth* of "a mother pulling the baby from her teat and smashing it against the wall." As she saw it, "A lot of the older folks don't have the energy to do the footwork. So we bust our asses to do it, and then they mow you over, throw you under the bus. They give you this masterful title, you're signing off on Excel sheets, think you're doing something, and then it turns out you find out they're fooling around with the money, and they hide things from you. They're eating the young like Jabba the Hutt." Svelte and stylish, St. Claire was the picture of youthful energy and competence. We were sitting in easy chairs in the lobby of the South Shore Cultural Center, enjoying the ongoing benefit of one of the older generation's greatest successes in the exercise of collective efficacy.

With her background in planning, St. Claire had wanted to work with established organizations to teach people in South Shore about the process of development. She believed that poor people in particular would never stand a chance against the powerful forces bearing down on them unless they understood the logic guiding those forces. "You have to understand how development works, just like Black Lives Matter needs to understand policing, which they don't," she said. But she felt that the leaders who ran those organizations, deep in the habit of focusing on their middle-class constituency's concerns, didn't seem very interested in having her spread such knowledge around. "You keep getting slapped down," she said, "and you give up."

St. Claire put a larger historical frame around the tensions between old heads and young turks. "The symptoms show up in different ways," she said, "but the Rubicon is that since the eighties the skills required to be middle class have gone way up." Once upon a time, during the era of the New Deal order, a career often meant working for decades for a single employer, a career that led to an adequately pensioned retirement, with security guaranteed by a tacit Fordist compact among corporations, unions, and government. She was typical of the succeeding order in that she cobbled together a living from multiple contingent sources—community development work, a graphic design business—a tenuous arrangement that forced her to reinvent herself every few years. Her husband, a sheriff's deputy, also ran a business on the side and had a small nonprofit that worked with young men in danger of falling out of the school-and-work track and into the street life. "We're widgeting everything out in little pieces," she said. "I understand how someone who's sixty-two is not up for that. It's frustrating for us, and it's scary for them." A lot of people can't keep up, and some don't even try. "Black guys shooting each other and white guys overdosing on drugs is the same kind of despair," she said. "They don't have the tools to do what's being asked of them," whether they're members of an older generation not up to hustling to hang on to their place or of a younger one under-equipped by the educational system and cut off in the contingent lower end of the labor market from career trajectories that would allow them to gradually build expertise and credentials.

Not only is it getting harder to be middle class in a society increasingly divided between haves and have-nots, but there's not much faith in the ability and will of the state, the traditional counterbalance to market forces, to do anything about it. She said, "Younger people are saying, 'Nobody's going to come save us!'" And South Shore's aging middle class is jealously, if understandably, hanging on to what's left of the advancement it achieved in the past. "The eighties was a land of milk and honey," she said with conviction, though she wasn't old enough to remember the era firsthand. "All these people were rolling in dough from a thimbleful of work. Now you need to do a double handful of work to get a thimbleful of money. Everybody I know with a job has two jobs. *Every*body. We have no dependence on government or anything else." Instead, they share, barter, widget it out in little pieces. "But government funds? Wait for grants? I'd sell corn dogs on the corner first."

South Shore's middle-class activists, both the old guard and the rising generation, have been scrambling for resources, often in competition with each other. "A lot of the elders want the things that come with middle-class life, but they don't want to give things up, and the deal has changed," St. Claire said. "It's people protecting their interest. I hate to say it, but we totally have to wait for them to die." When I mentioned that Jedidiah Brown had said something similar, she said, "He's a good example, teat to the wall." When Brown opposed Leslie Hairston in the election of 2015, it wasn't just her allies who attacked him. Some of her rivals who initially encouraged Brown to run turned on him. "It starts with whispers, rumors," St. Claire said. "Then they start not supporting you. Then they reach out to *your* elders and mentors to say, 'I don't know about this guy,' working to undermine your reputation. Teat to the wall."

In Charles Kyle's view, this is fairly typical of neighborhood politics in black Chicago. "You see political figures and community heads on the South Side and West Side, you see them flanked by people their age, people they know," he said when I talked to him in his windowless cinder-block office at Hyde Park Career Academy, where he was a counselor in a program called Becoming a Man. "They're not transformative about bringing on people with new opinions who will make a change in the neighborhood." Kyle, who had previously worked for state representative Monique Davis, was familiar with political business as usual, Chicago-style. Because the generation of leaders rooted in the civil rights era—the generation of Jesse Jackson, Cook County Board President Toni Preckwinkle, and Congressman Bobby Rush—had not done a good job of nurturing their successors, black Chicago had failed to produce viable candidates to challenge the eminently beatable mayor, Rahm Emanuel. Furthermore, the death of a figure from that old guard like Henry English, who had sustained his influence by doling out the Black United Fund's resources according to a pattern long favored by the city's patronage kingpins, was guaranteed to leave a classic power vacuum. "There are no lines of succession in our community," he said. "The people who go to Carol Adams are as old as she is. When you look at a Pilsen"—a Hispanic neighborhood with a strong tradition of inclusive grassroots organizing—"I see all the community organizations working together, people from seventy to eighteen, working together.

We"—meaning black neighborhoods in general and South Shore in particular—"don't empower people in our communities like that. Not everybody gets invited to the table."

The one prominent community activist I encountered in South Shore who made a point of having nothing bad to say about anyone else was Julia Hunter. A full-time social worker who supervised foster care, a single mother of an adult son, she was younger than Adams and English but older than Kyle, St. Claire, and Brown. She sympathized with the younger generation's frustration, but within the limits of her studied neutrality. "I love them, and the older people need to learn how to transform and release the stick, and Ava is the keeper of my website, but there's always two sides to a story," she said. When she first became involved in community activism, she had naively expected solidarity. "I thought there was all this unity, and I found all these divisions," she said. "There are some big heads, and you can't always fix it." Hunter, an easygoing and organized woman with deep reserves of patience and goodwill, realized that if she couldn't heal the breaches between antagonists like Alderman Hairston and Henry English, it would be useful to "at least get the *resources* to cross over and help each other." So she decided to collect and disseminate, via her website, information about available services and programs, everything from after-school programs to theater in the park to training in various trades. She tried to create cohesion by encouraging different groups in South Shore and across the greater South Side to concentrate on projects on which they could work together: a summer arts program, say, or a positive loitering event, in which law-abiding citizens temporarily reclaimed a trouble-prone spot by gathering there to clean it up or otherwise make themselves visibly present. Her objective was to direct the resources to the people who needed them most. These were often the people who had the least money and power, knew the least about what was going on in the neighborhood, and would be pushed out first if it showed signs of improvement. "Nobody's got a problem about that," she said, meaning that South Shore's elites would be happy to see the poor go. "Everybody's in their lane. I don't want to say selfish, but in their lane."

Hunter described herself as a typically closed-off middle-class homeowner who, after many years of living in her own lane in South Shore, woke up to the need for more community. "I lived here, I went to work, and I came home to be to myself. God has blessed me pretty well, and I had a good life—vacations, nice house, nice things." But when her son got to be fifteen or so, he got pulled into the street life, suffering a couple of beatings and eventually joining a gang for protection at school. He survived his gang phase and moved on, but she began to consider the constant action on nearby corners, the problem buildings, the empty storefronts and shady businesses, the vacant houses, not as reasons to stay shut off from the neighborhood but as reasons to become more involved. "I saw all these blue lights going up and down Seventy-Ninth Street, and I felt this feeling of isolation," she said. "Our community can't just be blue lights and guys hanging on the corner. It's hard to live in a community and be happy if the community is not happy." She admitted that her perspective "can be fairy-tale-ish"—she once told me, "I believe every place should be a Mayberry"—but in 2016 she thought she saw a few more lines forming between the dots representing the neighborhood's leaders on Sampson's chart. "I think it might be getting better in the last few years," she said. "The leaders know each other, even if they're fighting each other."

One morning I was talking with Hunter in front of her house on the 7800 block of Saginaw, not far from the corner of 79th Street. A typical South Shore vista confronted us: her two-flat, owned by her family for two generations; a similarly well-kept house across the street, with immaculately trimmed lawn; then two small apartment buildings; then a parking lot on the corner where young men were hanging out. We looked down the block at them, and Hunter started talking about the lack of job opportunities, the failings of the public schools, the lack of sufficient training in the trades. We watched one guy in a white muscle shirt and ball cap walk aimlessly in circles for a while in the morning sun and then hunker down to gaze at his phone. "That guy doesn't know about South Shore Works," she said. The human costs of South Shore's unaddressed class divide made the squabbling of its leaders seem especially wasteful. "You get jealous of Englewood because they are so together," she said. "You get tired of always fighting."

*

You could see South Shore Rising as a lot of talk leading to nothing more than a not-much-visited South Shore Works Facebook page, and therefore a waste of time, but it was also a genuine attempt to do on a larger scale what Julia Hunter (who didn't attend) was trying to do: connect the dots to make common cause against forces operating at a scale that dwarfed any one individual. All the talk might lead to something, and it might not, but it did at least succeed in drawing a self-portrait of the neighborhood. Watching South Shore's black middle-class activists try to define themselves in relation to those who were black but not middle class and those who were middle class but not black, I was reminded how such seemingly uneventful meetings can play out the tension between pulling together and coming apart that charges a neighborhood with much of its inner life. Just as powerful forces of change are at work behind the stillness of a drowsing bungalow block on which nothing much seems to be happening, those forces and the passions and ideas they inspire move beneath the surface of the most rote-seeming community meeting.

During a session on arts and culture at South Shore Rising, a white priest named Wolf Werling with a cascading Old Testament beard, noting that his family had been in the neighborhood for four generations, talked about previous eras: Jews' struggles against anti-Semitism, conflict between high- and low-caste Irish parishes, and the like. His point seemed to be that the history of division, difference, and succession in South Shore went well beyond the question of whether it would be black or white in 2036. "I'm still not sure what identity we're offering here," he said, implicitly bundling the current agitation to keep South Shore black with the 1960s-era agitation to keep it white. A woman sitting nearby suggested that the neighborhood's identity could be inclusively "multiple," but Michelle Boone, the city's arts commissioner, who lived with her mother in a high-rise apartment on South Shore Drive, shook her head and responded, "But if we don't define that identity, somebody else will." Boone was wearing sweats, signaling her presence as a neighbor rather than a city official, but she navigated the city's ethnic, racial, and cultural politics for a living, and she was, as usual, thinking strategically.

Another woman, who had previously been silent, spoke up: "I don't think so much of Irish or Jewish or African American. I think of South Shore as a place where people want to live who want to have a viable life. The people who live here now feel threatened that we'll be pushed away from the table. This is an African American community. We are open to other people living here, but we don't want to disappear. Everybody else is gonna come, 'cause that's what they're gonna do, and we need to put ourselves out there with confidence."

Margaret Murphy-Webb, a jazz singer and veteran police officer, said, "I want to know how on board our politicians really are for revitalizing this community. How on board are the politicians, the Park District, the people that we need?" She and her husband, the first-call jazz and funk bassist Chuck Webb, were trying to revive the tradition of jazz festivals that had helped bring together support for the South Shore Cultural Center in the early 1980s, and she said she was getting no help from "the alderman," meaning Leslie Hairston. "Are we getting lip service?" Murphy-Webb asked. Boone said, "Yes, you are. We haven't done a good job of telling our story; it's just crime, and South Shore disappears into 'the South Side'" pathologized, along with the West Side, as a vast inner-city forbidden zone of violence and decline. Boone concluded, "You get a good story, some momentum, and the politicians will come to you."

A good story, confidence, some momentum: generating these was the objective of South Shore Rising and ultimately of South Shore Works. But, as a sentiment to organize around, "This is an African American community; we don't want to disappear" was not likely to produce those results. It proposed a broad moral claim to community solidarity rather than a specific appeal to the individual self-interest of homeowners whose depressed property values would rise if white gentrification ever happened in earnest. As a motivating ideology it didn't exactly resemble "This is a white community; we don't want to disappear," the implicit appeal that had failed to work for the South Shore Commission a half century before, but the two messages had a certain complementary similarity. If the residents of Irish and Jewish South Shore in the 1960s, feeling large forces converging on them, had been like late-imperial Romans feeling themselves menaced by advancing Goths, twenty-first-century South Shore's black middle class were like the inhabitants of Roman Italy in late antiquity—descended from Goths but now Romans themselves, even though they had once been regarded as barbarous outsiders—warily eyeing encroaching hosts of Lombards and Byzantines and other new-order invaders.

*

I go back and forth on the best way to understand South Shore, or any neighborhood. Geography, folk migration, the flow of capital—they all seem from some angles to be determinative, to be the force that explains the distribution and effect of other forces, the cause among causes. Then there's the class-and-race conundrum. A career in academia and a half century of exposure to American public life has made me skeptical of race as the default explanation of choice for everything. You'll hear all sorts of commentators say that we avoid the subject of race, but I think the opposite is true. Americans love to talk about race, can't get enough of it, especially if it allows them to avoid talking about class. And for that reason, every instinct in me wants class to come out on top in a competition with race to explain South Shore. That's a false opposition, of course, because the two subjects are folded together, especially in the sense that racial difference in this country matters mostly because it translates into class difference, which means that the color of your skin helps dictate your access to resources and power. But still, you can tease apart class and race to some degree, at least enough to get a better look at the relationship between them.

So I keep going back and forth. Sometimes I look at South Shore and I think that class, not race, is indeed the deeper influence, the more potent explanation for the shapes that social order has taken there. The middle class and those aspiring to it have consistently tried to fashion a suitable habitat for themselves, which means not only maintaining amenities like the South Shore Cultural Center but also controlling the black poor and separating themselves from them, a pattern that goes back a long way. Black middle-class activists have comfortably made common cause with white middle-class neighbors in those efforts. Like the claim of shared whiteness in the late 1960s, the claim of shared blackness has consistently proven a weak ideology in South Shore. Black tavern owners on 75th Street failed when they tried to invoke it against black neighbors organizing to shut them down in the 1970s. Young activists like Charles Kyle, Ava St. Claire, Jedidiah Brown, and Val Free discovered the claim's weakness all over again in recent years when they tried to bridge the divide between black haves and have-nots that their elders seemed to accept as a feature of the social landscape. As Julia Hunter put it, "The color that matters is green." The Jackson Park Highlands serves as strong evidence for putting class first in understanding South Shore. It has been a racially integrated, stable enclave for decades, set apart from the rest of South Shore by class difference pure and simple. The packs of boys who came into the Highlands looking to mess with some rich kids when I was young never made much distinction between white and black targets of opportunity. There are times when I think theirs was the most sophisticated analysis of the neighborhood.

But at other times I find myself grudgingly conceding that, whether I like it or not, maybe the story of South Shore really is all about race. After all, racial segregation explains the close proximity of the black middle class and the black poor in the first place—and, indeed, if that proximity was not a given in American life, if it wasn't a rule of segregation that the black poor will follow where the black middle class goes, then much of the resistance to the initial black migration into South Shore would never have materialized. If being black makes you less likely to have access to resources, financial or educational or otherwise, and if being black makes you more likely to find yourself jammed together with black people of other classes, then maybe race does come before class in the chain of causation—which means that much of the evidence I just cited of class being a powerful determinant of the shape of history and life in South Shore becomes evidence of race being an even more powerful determinant. I consider how much more strenuous the official response would have been if the couple of hundred people shot to death in South Shore over the past decade had been white.

Probably the National Guard would have been sent in long ago. Yes, but wouldn't the response also have been more vigorous—if not quite *that* vigorous—if the victims had been mostly black homeowners rather than black and poor and in the street life? A career community activist and veteran of the South Shore Bank named Steve Perkins told me in 2014 that, given the neighborhood's advantages in location and housing stock, "South Shore should be thriving, but no black neighborhoods are. The black community of Chicago is in deep, deep trouble, and the mayor has written them off." In the end, is being a black neighborhood South Shore's determinative problem these days? I can't settle on one way to see it, probably because there isn't one way to see it.

*

When South Shore Rising was over, I left the school and took a walk down 71st Street. It was an extremely mild Saturday afternoon in late winter, pushing 60 degrees, too warm for the anonymous camouflage-armor of hood and gloves. People were out—a few shoppers, more hangers-out, especially on the sunny north side of the street. Loose squares were indeed for sale, as were bootleg DVDs and drugs. A guy in a gray hoodie, no more than twenty years old, fell silently into step with me for a while as I walked. He was drinking off the dregs of a bottle of Rémy Martin, killing the day, like Fetty Wap or a winehead three times his age. Guys like him in the street life formed a minority of the nearly half of the city's young black men who weren't in school and didn't have jobs, but they were generally taken for the public face of that group. They weren't included in the community collectively imagined by the concerned, engaged citizens who had gathered earlier that day in the Bouchet school.

"What is social responsibility?" Charles Kyle had asked himself when we talked at Hyde Park High. "What is *my* social responsibility?" He imagined what kind of an answer the head of the Mariano's supermarket chain, who considered and rejected the possibility of opening a store to replace the Dominick's on 71st Street, might give. "If I'm Bob Mariano and people in South Shore are saying we want a store, and he comes to visit and he can see people selling loose cigarettes, and he comes back and sees it at night, and he says, 'I don't think we can make money here,' why should he?" Kyle flatly rejected Leslie Hairston's charge of corporate racism; as he saw it, Mariano was just doing the money math. But what was the proper answer for a neighbor? "What about people who own a house, and cut their grass, and go to Leslie's meetings?" he said. "What's your responsibility?" If you forted-up and just looked out for your property and yourself and the amenities that made the neighborhood feel like home to you, you might look up one day and find yourself isolated among strangers, or even living among newcomers who regard you as a freakish holdover. Kyle cited Harlem and Brooklyn as places where recent real estate booms had increasingly put longtime black residents in such a position.

Maybe taking care of your own business wasn't enough. Maybe South Shore's middle-class activists should be trying to make common cause with poorer neighbors, encouraging them to show up to meetings and above all to vote, so that politicians would take them seriously. Carol Adams and Val Free had begun to talk about the strategic wisdom of concentrating on housing issues as a way to start forming a united front, but it wasn't having much effect yet. For the moment, class appeared to trump race, and division appeared to be exerting a stronger pull than cohesion. "Compare South Shore to Englewood," Kyle said. "There's a lot more organizing of poor people in Englewood, and you can hear the difference in the rhetoric of a twenty-year veteran of Englewood versus a twenty-year veteran in South Shore"—where the crypto-bootstrappy "pull up your pants" and pejorative terms like "the element" are still commonly heard in polite public conversation, even among otherwise sensitive community organizers. "You're looking at this one-third in poverty and then this top group well over $100,000 in income," Kyle went on, "and the top group is pushing on the Val Frees and Anton Seals," who were in line to succeed the cohort of Adams and English, and whose desire to reach across class divides could be blunted by senior allies and board members with more exclusively middle-class agendas. "And then you get me, Ava, Jedidiah, the younger ones," he said, "and we're saying, 'Fuck this, we want a juice bar or we're taking our talent to South Beach.'" It was a telling moment to invoke LeBron James, raising the prospect of black people with choices leaving the urban North. Chicago's growing Hispanic population was just about to pass its declining black population, pushing African Americans into demographic third place behind Hispanics and whites and raising a fresh threat of political marginality. Noting that his undergraduate degree was in biology, Kyle said, "I know how energy works. We're all trying to push the community forward, but we're all fighting each other."

A police SUV was working 71st Street on that sunny Saturday afternoon after South Shore Rising. It would pull to the curb to scatter a clot of idlers, and they'd flow to another spot a block or so down and after a while get excited about something and start yelling and posturing, then the SUV would roll in and break them up again. Some residents of South Shore referred to this stretch of 71st as a "blue-light district" because the cops were busy there at all hours. One of the guys out on the street, easy to pick out by the distinctive skeleton-like pattern emblazoned in white on his black sweats, circulated almost nonstop, hanging with one crew on one corner and then another crew on another, wandering out into the street to block traffic, whistling up the block and making outsize hand signals. I watched him for a while. He was busy, but just marking time: not selling drugs, not running with an intimidatingly obvious gang; just hanging out with other hangers-out, empty-handed, going nowhere. Most everybody on 71st Street that day was black; most everybody was a have-not by the neighborhood's standards. Which mattered more, black or have-not? I think the latter, but couldn't tell you for sure. Either way, that difficult question is at the heart of the story of South Shore since the 1960s.

EQUIPMENT FOR LIVING

—

HISTORY

In their childhoods, my parents ducked the kind of glancing blows that the twentieth century doled out in passing while it was working up to other, more comprehensive horrors. Neither of them had to dig out from the ruins of a Dresden or Nagasaki, but they both had ample opportunity to grow familiar with big trouble in its classical midcentury form: wet-combed zealots in epaulets and peaked officers' caps, mounted on the spacious running boards of long-snouted cars, giving orders that could only lead to sorrow for everyone; the men going off to fight and die; the women and children huddling under cover while bombers stooped in the sky over their cities and explosions bloomed. Franco's air force and their German mentors did their best to kill my mother in Barcelona in the course of developing the art of destroying cities from above. The British air force had a go at my father in Asmara during the Second World War. Both of my parents remember vividly the uncomprehending pleasure they took as young children in the spectacle of the first raid—for my father it was a shot-down plane trailing smoke as it corkscrewed earthward, for my mother the unfolding petals of flares falling softly in the night sky in advance of a bombing run—until their mothers hauled them off to a shelter as bombs began to fall on the neighborhood.

Like millions of children of the 1930s all around the world, my parents were taught the gospel of the master wall: the one best-sheltering wall of a building, stronger than the others for reasons that transcended architectonics and verged into mysticism, against which to stand when the bombs began to fall. My father—who was born in the Sicilian town of Barcellona but grew up in Eritrea, where there was work for his parents, a carpenter and a seamstress—knew it as *la parete maestra*, or simply *il Muro* (the Wall). His mother, wearying of repeatedly rushing to the curved tunnel her husband and the other men had dug into a nearby hill, took to remaining in her own house during air raids and taking cover against *il Muro*—until one day a red-hot hunk of metal plowed through the roof and narrowly missed her, instantly reconciling her to the sweaty inconvenience and crowding of the hillside shelter.

When the sirens sounded in Barcelona, Spain, where my mother grew up, the women would shout, *"Nens, a la paret mestre"* (Children, to the master wall). At first, my mother and her cousins would be herded down to the *refugio* in the basement of their building, but later, after repeated raids had bred fatalism among the adults, the children stayed upstairs and were lined up against the magical wall, stiff and shivering, as the racket of guns and the deeper detonations of exploding bombs rolled closer. All the while she would imagine the wall suspended in midair, herself and the other children attached to it like a row of pinned butterflies, floating away through the roaring mayhem of planes, flares, antiaircraft fire, and bomb blasts toward a serene destination that in later years she learned, from watching *Star Trek* with her own children, to call a parallel universe.

The war gave my mother a lifetime's worth of memories to conjure with, and to return to in her dreams. In one of her earliest memories, she is waiting with her mother, grandmother, and great-grandmother in a barn-like, dilapidated train station with high ceilings crisscrossed by long wooden beams on which dozens of little birds are perched, silent and immobile. The women, too, are uncharacteristically mute. A pall of disquiet hangs over the scene, and an asphyxiating heat that their cheap paper fans barely stir. It is July 1936, and urgent word has come from Barcelona, interrupting their visit to the great-grandmother's village in Aragon: the war is beginning; come home right away while it's still possible to travel. A small, fluffy thing drops from above and lands at my mother's feet with a dull thud. Then another, and another, the thuds multiplying as one by one the birds fall, unable to breathe what she remembers as "the incandescent midafternoon air." She recoils from the limp, yielding deadness of the little bodies.

The men of the family, Catalan Loyalists, went away to war. Her father, a gentle musician who discovered that he was even more afraid of killing than of being killed, became a stretcher bearer. At some point he fell in with a crew of anarchist hard cases who commandeered a train that had a piano on it. Family lore maintains that it was on this train, on this piano, playing for the anarchists, that he composed one of his finest pieces, a haunting ballad entitled "Inquietud."

Despite having much better musicians, poets, and theorists, his side lost. And so, another memory: my mother, five years old, holding her mother's hand as they make a long, terrifying walk across Barcelona, trying to get home to their apartment, which they have temporarily vacated to avoid the worst of the bombing. Their objective is to reoccupy the apartment and somehow prevent Franco's forces from confiscating it when the city falls. Retreating Loyalists and foreign volunteers stream through the streets, heading for the French frontier. The little girl and her mother wait for a break in traffic on Gran Vía, a broad boulevard on which military trucks, private cars, ambulances, and armored vehicles hurry out of town. A flatbed truck comes by, overloaded with men in uniform chanting their battle cry, *"No pasarán, no pasarán"* (They shall not pass), which sounds forlorn now that the enemy have broken their line and routed them. The truck stalls with a jerk that throws one of its occupants onto the pavement right in front of my mother. The soldier, so young that he's almost a child himself, tries to get up and crawl back onto the truck bed, but his leg is broken and he can't make it. He lies there, desperately calling, *"No em deixeu! Espereu-me! No em deixeu!"* (Don't leave me! Wait for me!) The driver restarts the truck's engine and it moves off. All these years later, she can still see the young man on the pavement, his eyes dark with pain, his arms raised in supplication, and she can also see her mother, sobbing, looking down at him for a long moment before she and her daughter, like his comrades, leave him in the street to fend for himself.

And there he remained, in my mother's dreams. So did her cousin Ramonet, who as a baby was once somehow left behind in his crib on the glass-enclosed back porch when everyone rushed to the basement during an air raid. He was recovered intact by my mother's mother, my Yaya, a matronly violinist given to imposing bouffants and impassioned vibrato, who displayed unlikely vertical speed in dashing up a dozen flights of stairs from the *refugio* to save him. In my mother's dreams, though, Yaya didn't get there in time: the baby Ramonet she sees in her sleep is forever soaked in his own blood, pierced like Saint Sebastian by a thousand glass shards.

My mother remembers three things her mother did once they made it across Gran Vía to their apartment on Carrer de Bailén. With tears streaming down her face, she hammered to pieces a bust of the Catalan patriot Francesc Macià. She burned their Catalan flag. And, as instructed by the victorious enemy's radio broadcasts, she hung a large white sheet from the balcony to indicate surrender.

Which is all to say that when my parents went house-hunting on the South Side of Chicago in 1967, impelled by the news that the walk-up apartment building in Hyde Park in which they lived was to be torn down to make room for a high-rise, what was happening in South Shore did not qualify, to them, as big trouble. Black people moving in, white people getting out, excitable talk about a spike in crime, urban crisis, and decline—but not a Stuka or a peaked cap in sight. And the rest of the calculus came out just fine. South Shore was within easy commuting distance of the University of Chicago, the most potent local incarnation of their chosen *paret mestre*: a good school, from which to proceed to good work. They were both pursuing doctorates there while holding down full-time academic jobs at other colleges, and the university also had a lab school to which they intended to send their three young sons. Also, the eagerness of white people to move out kept prices down, at least for other white people, so that in South Shore my parents could get what felt to them like a lot of house—that is, a standard Chicago bungalow—for the money.

Yes, there would be rioting on the South Side in 1968 after Martin Luther King Jr. was killed, a good deal of it just a few blocks away on the other side of Stony Island Avenue in Woodlawn, and troops would be deployed in response, bringing back childhood memories of defeated and conquering armies marching through the streets of their hometowns. But it was over in a few days, with nothing more to show for all the excitement than a couple of hundred burned-out buildings, fewer than a dozen fresh corpses, and the usual hard feelings—a very minor affair, in other words, by the century's high standards. The same goes for the riots downtown four months later at the Democratic Convention. Mayor Daley and Abbie Hoffman thought it was a big deal, and so did Dan Rather and Norman Mailer, but there was no indiscriminate machine-gunning by either side, there were no hanged bodies twisting from streetlights. You call those revolutionaries? You call that a draconian response?

And yes, there were atomic warheads on Nike missiles stationed at the base a few blocks north of us in Jackson Park, part of a defensive ring around Chicago designed on the principle that detonating those warheads up to 150,000 feet above the city would wipe out incoming waves of bombers and missiles. Cold War logic deemed a regrettable but necessary cascade of friendly fallout preferable to utter annihilation by multiple nuclear direct hits. Among other assets to protect, there was the strategically vital concentration of steel mills and other heavy industry that began just south and east of South Shore. But city people like my parents couldn't imagine an ideal spot, a *paret mestre* of a neighborhood on the South Side or the North Side or anywhere else in their adopted country, that would offer even a little safety from an all-out nuclear war. Any place under the dubious protection of the Nike umbrella was as bad or as good as any other. Better the abstract risk of an unlikely obliteration, in any case, than what they'd left behind in the Old Country: short rations, bad prospects, too many fascists and communists and other true believers unequipped to respect the first and only commandment.

Affari suoi, Sicilians say: leave other people to their business. How many more rules of life do you need? Unless and until bombers appear over the city's rooflines to put an end to life as you know it, you find a mate and pull in harness like a sled dog, you raise your family, you attend to the business of making it, and you leave others to their own affairs. As long as the neighbors "say hello and cutta da grass," as my Sicilian grandmother used to put it—my Nonna, the seamstress, who lived to make it to America because that hunk of red-hot metal missed her while she stood pressed against *il Muro* in Asmara—and as long as those neighbors don't turn out to have peaked caps in their closets (or, if they do have them, as long as the peaked caps *stay* in their closets), it doesn't much matter who they are.

You pick your ground and make your stand, but always with the knowledge that any chosen ground is in motion under your feet, under the foundations of whatever shelter you have managed to fashion or appropriate for you and yours, be it thatched hut or stone-built, rake-flanked Vauban fortress. Great flows of people, money, power, and ideas constantly undo and remake the neighborhood, the city, the world. Barcelona was founded by either Hercules or Hamilcar Barca, and ruled at one time or another by, among others, the Carthaginians, Romans, Visigoths, Arabs, Carolingian Franks, the Arabs again under Almanzor, and all manner of Catalan and Spanish factions, all the way up through Franco and then the separatists who waited until he was dead and it was time to make new busts of Macià and get back to the business of being stridently Catalan. And Barcellona—well, just about every warrior crew that ever sailed the Mediterranean has been through that part of Sicily with swords in hand, including the Greeks, Romans, Arabs, Normans, Catalans (who renamed the Sicilian village for their own city across the sea), Germans, British, and Americans—and the Italians, of course, northerners who passionately if unconvincingly professed belief in the rule of law and the nation-state and other outlandish ideas that the people of Barcellona put up with only to the extent that they have to.

The stories and layered cityscapes of my parents' hometowns, old settled places that nevertheless have always been in the process of coming apart and being thrown together at the same time, suggest that a stable lasting order is an illusion. It took me a while to figure that out. I grew up thinking of the Catalans and Sicilians who formed my extended family as representative of ancient peoples immemorially grounded on their respective turf, Barcelona and Barcellona, and it's true that these families handed down historical inheritances that my parents carried with them to the South Side of Chicago and relied on as equipment for living. But I came around to understanding that succession and flux, a ceaseless play of flows unpredictably throwing off fragments of the past that persist in unlikely places, are the truer norm. That goes double, triple, in America, where change is so piously welcomed and obsolescent orders so eagerly scrapped that a hundred years, or really any period longer than the span of a single observant and memorious life, might as well be forever.

SOMETHING FOR EVERYBODY

WFMT, the insufferable Cultured Person's Radio Station to which my parents listened when I was a kid, used to play a recording made in 1972 in which Yuri Rasovsky gets laughs from a live audience by pronouncing the names of streets and other locations around town. It's the essence of local humor, a map made of inside jokes that are funny to the extent they give continuing life to neighborhood stereotypes while simultaneously mocking them. A derelict souse says, "West Mad—*hic*—ison"; a gravitas-rich black voice, enunciating every syllable of a hard-won name change, says "Doc-tor Martin Luther King Jun-ior Mem-o-rial Drive"; "Meigs Field," drawn out and Dopplered, becomes the sound of a small plane missing the runway and hitting the lake with a glass-of-water-sized splash. There's a South Shore joke, too: a terrified white voice, out of breath from running or hysteria, gasps, "Seventy-First and Jeffery!" The perception of South Shore as white people's worst nightmare achieved citywide circulation and acquired seemingly eternal life when almost all of the neighborhood's white residents were leaving it in the 1960s and early 1970s. Even then, when street crime did rise dramatically, and even now, when South Shore has been a black neighborhood for two generations, if you were to hang out at 71st Street and Jeffery Boulevard on any given day, you would see the occasional white person waiting for a bus or going to Walgreens, unmolested among the black majority. But the joke—which is not so much a joke as simply a way of saying the name of South Shore's principal intersection—hangs primarily on what people *say* about South Shore, the social and cultural history and enduring reputation of which are at once brutally compressed and remarkably well expressed by how Rasovsky says those three words.

Crime did rise sharply in South Shore during its era of racial turnover, well above and beyond the general nationwide increase in crime in those years as the baby boom generation reached prime wrongdoing age. Crime had previously been low in South Shore, so it came as a shock when the neighborhood's rate of FBI-designated index crimes—murder, assault, rape, robbery, burglary, larceny, car theft (arson was added later)—soared from well under the citywide average to double and almost triple that average, among the city's highest. You can catch a taste of that shock in a mid-1970s letter pleading for "extra special" protection sent by a librarian at South Shore's public library to the commander of the police department's Fourth District. "We are having a book sale on Friday and Saturday and are fairly certain they will break-in to try to get the money from the sale," she wrote, noting that this had happened after the previous book sale, one of twenty break-ins over the past twenty months. In that climate, lesser quality-of-life offenses like vandalism, public drinking, loitering, and aggressive panhandling were also taken as signs of pervasive and growing disorder. It was all made scarier by the general assumption, which persists to this day, that South Shore was supposed to be more civil and peaceable than other neighborhoods on the South Side.

The fear of crime that became lastingly associated with South Shore in that era may have been inspired by more than a reasoned assessment of the chances of being victimized, but it wasn't unfounded, nor was it simply reducible to white people reacting to the arrival of black people. By the mid-1970s, with the turnover from white to black largely completed, vacancy rates on South Shore's main shopping streets had reached 20%, property values had stalled, tax delinquency rates were climbing, and the black middle class had begun to reckon with the realization that moving to South Shore had not separated them from the poor, who arrived right behind them as usual. Also as usual, crime made itself available as the most accessible part of this larger complex of problems, so talking about muggings, murders, and burglaries became established as a way for just about everyone—black, white, or otherwise—to talk about what was wrong with South Shore. Various neighbors moved away for all kinds of reasons when I lived in South Shore, but the way the story of their departure got told often took the form of "enough is enough" after a gunpoint robbery, home invasion, or similar last-straw outrage. Donda West, for instance, decided to move out of South Shore when some older boys with a knife tried to take her son Kanye's bike. "Call it black flight," she wrote in a memoir.

Residents of South Shore today are still saying, "Seventy-First and Jeffery!" Crime, followed by bad schools and terrible retail, heads the standard list of the neighborhood's drawbacks, and crime is always ready to hand as a subject of conversation, like the weather. A shooting is almost the only reason South Shore ever makes it into the local news, and even those who object to this tendency of the media often use crime to organize their own chronologies: "This was back before they broke in the second time," or "The Jacksons moved in after the Johnsons got held up." Talking about almost any neighborhood-related subject can take the form of talking about crime. When in 1997, coming off the peak in homicides that accompanied the arrival in full effect of the crack business across the South Side, I asked a priest at St. Philip Neri how the parish had changed during his time there, the first thing he said was, "We do a lot of gangbanger funerals."

People express a preoccupation with crime not just in the stories they tell but in the landscape they inhabit and make, in the stories told by the neighborhood's fences, burglar bars, security cameras, dogs, and other defensive adaptations of physical space. They make the eerie stillness of South Shore's residential blocks seem even more tautly pronounced than the buzzing false calm that I remember so well from childhood. Other than a cat picking its way through the fallen leaves on a lawn, nothing seems to move, and yet I have the sense that people are peering out from the safety of their homes. I know that's what they're doing in the Highlands, because while I was on the Jackson Park Highlands Association's email list (from 2013 to 2016) one of the most common kinds of messages I saw was a real-time report of potential threats moving through the neighborhood, spotted from a window: a pack of teenagers looking into parked cars or backyards, a stray pit bull, a suspicious car.

There's a block club sign in Terror Town, an area in the opposite corner of South Shore from the Highlands known for concentrated gun violence and drug dealing, that includes, among its itemized injunctions against this and that, one that reads: "No socialization or vandalism," as if the two forms of activity in public space are equally suspect. These days, they kind of are.

This all speaks of changes not just in the neighborhood but in the world, and the import of those changes can't be fully grasped or expressed by reducing them to crime stories. For example, kids not playing outside as much as they used to and being under much tighter adult supervision than in the past has less to do with crime than with shifts in what it means to be a good parent, and with technological changes that have fused children to their screens and keep them indoors more than ever. Children in the neighborhood I live in now, far from Chicago, don't play on the street much anymore, either, and it has a violent crime rate as close to zero as you can find in an American city, while as a child I played all day in the street and wandered South Shore at will in a period when its crime rate really was rising precipitously. Many parents in twenty-first-century South Shore told me that they didn't let their kids play on the block because they were worried about rising crime, but for the past two decades the neighborhood's crime rate has been mostly falling. The causal arrow may well point more significantly in the other direction: fewer kids and adults in public space means fewer eyes on the street, which contributes to more crime, and the retreat from public space also means that more people get more of their neighborhood news from TV, online news feeds, social media, and other such sources, which tend to play up fear-inducing crime reports.

South Shore's boosters blame the media—lazy or racist or both—for perpetuating the neighborhood's "Seventy-First and Jeffery!" image, which scares off investment and encourages the retreat from public space and civic life. Some of those boosters counter-circulate other sorts of stories that play up South Shore's traditional bedroom-community virtues or portray it as an emergent cultural hot spot, rebranded as the affordable and hip Soul Coast. Their attempt to partially decouple fear of crime from crime itself fits with what social scientists have found:

fear of crime is only indirectly linked to actual crimes and, given their realistic chances of victimization, many more people are afraid than should be, the least likely to be victimized report the most fear, and the most likely to be victimized report the least. As Robert J. Bursik and Harold G. Grasmick put it, "The fear of crime is the outcome of more subtle processes than a simple response to perceived risk." They point in particular to research, some of it conducted in South Shore, showing that residents will tolerate relatively high crime if a neighborhood is satisfying in other ways, but when "the economic future of an area is uncertain" or "there are visible signs of incivilities and disorder," then "high reported levels of fear of crime may actually serve as an indicator of a more general concern that the area is out of control." This "urban unease" goes far beyond rational calculation of the chances of becoming the victim of an index crime and becomes a way to respond to a neighborhood's other qualities and problems.

Adding in all the other factors that may influence fear of crime— everything from how you get your news to your degree of exposure to reruns of *Criminal Minds* to the degree to which you equate blackness or poverty or sagging pants with disorder—takes us well into the realm of symbolic responses that are tangled up with general attitudes toward one's neighborhood and the greater social order. And, as Robert Sampson's research has demonstrated, a neighborhood's reputation is "sticky"—it's contagious and it lasts. One of the most important factors in predicting current residents' fear of crime is the level of fear felt by other residents in the past.

It's more accurate to say that the people of South Shore talk and think a lot about crime, and think a great deal *with* crime, rather than simply fear it. While they do, in fact, demonstrate a fairly high degree of fear of crime, they tend to dismiss such fear as a craven response more typical of outsiders who lack their local street knowledge. For them, "crime" is an everyday problem to be addressed with good urban technique, and it's also the immediate, recognizable face of more diffusely threatening conditions. These conditions can be very local, like the mix of housing stock that together with the dynamics of racial residential segregation puts haves and have-nots in intimate contact. Residents who complain that neighbors relocated from CHA housing projects to apartment buildings in South Shore have been responsible for a crime wave are seizing on a convenient way to understand the latest episode in a long, vexed history of class tension and status anxiety in neighborhoods awkwardly assigned the one-size-fits-all label "the black community." The conditions compressed into South Shore's crime stories can also be metropolitan, national, or global in scale, far-reaching economic and social changes that can be hard to articulate when we rely on stories about shootings, stick-ups, or break-ins in the neighborhood to address them. But we live even the grandest-scale transformations at the intimate level of home, block, and neighborhood, and we handle complexity with the equipment at our disposal. Responding to the imminent threat of street crime is a way to both engage and not engage a larger set of potentially threatening conditions that shape life in the neighborhood, a way to simultaneously try to make sense of those conditions' consequences and avoid confronting their full import.

If you can't do anything about deindustrialization or the decline of the middle class, if you can't safeguard yourself from the big-time white-collar gangsters on Wall Street and in Washington who somehow undid your job security and left you upside down on your mortgage, you can at least try to be ready when predators from around the way stick a gun in your face on the street or come in through an unbarred window to despoil you. You can choose to take the collective approach to security—getting together with neighbors and local civic institutions to work with the police, other government agencies, and nongovernmental organizations to address your neighborhood's problems. But even some of those who participate in such communitarian efforts to build herd immunity to crime, in addition to many who don't, also pursue a more individualistic response, seeking personal rather than collective efficacy in response to a threat. This being America, there's something you can do on your own that feels like taking steps to protect yourself and your loved ones—whether you're a have or a have-not, a homeowner or a kid on the corner—and you can do it without attending a single meeting or relying on anyone else to ante up for the common good. You can arm yourself against a difficult world. You can get a gun.

*

David Lemieux—former Black Panther, retired Chicago Police detective, son of a Haitian father and a white mother, who described himself as "a free spirit raised by a free spirit"—was a man with an analysis. "What we see is by design," he told me, "and I'm not talking about divine design." We were sitting in a Starbucks in Hyde Park, next door to Jimmy's, a tavern I frequented in high school, at least when Mr. Wilson, who taught fifth grade and coached my brother on the basketball team, wasn't moonlighting behind the bar. Across the street was St. Thomas the Apostle, where Lemieux attended elementary school in the 1960s. Sixty-one years old, an imposing figure with extensive dreads and a quietly commanding manner, he fingered his scruff of beard and mustache as he broke down the situation for me: "It's part of the methodology of control to criminalize a segment of society. They rewrite the true cultural narrative to make it out for the benefit of the system." He recommended that I read Michelle Alexander's *The New Jim Crow*. "It's slavery by another name," he said. "You can control behavior in absentia. Crack and gangster rap culture, shit, it's *bull*shit. It's not art imitating life; that's a lot of hype. Criminal behavior in your own neighborhood isn't rebelliousness—It's just psychopathic criminal behavior."

His train of thought covered a lot of ground, ranging out from the South Side across the city and the culture, with connections to revolutionary Angola at one point, the work of the Nazi film propagandist Leni Riefenstahl at another. "If you're German in 1935," he said, "you're like, '*Whoa! That's incredible!*' If they'd had computer graphics . . ."—well, they'd have come up with something like what we've got now: "Facebook culture, electronic stimulation, self-debasing terrifying scenarios," all pressing black people to eagerly accept and enact a script that makes them vulnerable to being sucked into the legal system at an early age, fixing them in the criminal underclass. When as a homicide detective he went way out west on 95th Street to suburban Oak Lawn to interview gunshot victims at Christ Hospital (where they were taken because the South Side lacked a Level I trauma center), it had galled him to see white kids congregate at a Starbucks or Potbelly without attracting the attention of police. "They're not rich, but their social construct is not written the same way as ours," he said. "We are the face of criminality. That didn't start with Willie Horton," the felon who became a centerpiece of George H. W. Bush's presidential campaign in 1988. Nor did it happen by accident or as a result of less-than-purposeful cultural process, he believed. If he sounded like a crackpot conspiracy theorist, so be it. "I don't think it's an evil genius in a fortress doing this," he said. "I think it's Halliburton and Monsanto, Cheney, the oligarchs, the one-percenters."

Lemieux was also a man with a gun. He put in twenty-six years on the police force, most of them in plainclothes, and like other retired cops he carried himself as if he were still on the job and just happened to be off duty, and he still carried a gun. He was a proponent of allowing citizens to carry concealed firearms not just because it would equip them to fight back against criminals but also because he plainly liked the idea of an armed populace able to resist official oppressors. He joined the Black Panther Party's Chicago chapter at the age of sixteen, in 1969, and he may well be the only Chicago cop who ever joined the force with the express purpose of becoming a Black Panther with a badge. He also played a character named Pretty Willie, a street-gang member turned revolutionary brother who's touchy about his fair skin and straight hair, in *The Spook Who Sat by the Door*, a 1973 insurrection fantasy in which a renegade black CIA agent sticks it to the man by arming Chicago street gangs with advanced weapons and training them to rob banks and shoot up cops and National Guardsmen—by turning them, in other words, into the right kind of young men with guns to serve as instruments of his critique of white power. The young David (pronounced "Daveed") Lemieux was an interesting chin-bearded face off the street, picked for the part by a filmmaker obviously influenced by Gillo Pontecorvo's use of charismatic non-actors in *The Battle of Algiers*. Lemieux displayed a good deal of natural screen presence as he delivered lines on the order of "I was born black, I live black, and I'm'a die probably *because* I'm black, because some cracker that knows I'm black better than you, nig-gah, is probably gonna put a bullet in the back of my *head*."

Lemieux first moved to South Shore in 1973, and when he joined the police in 1982, he could walk to work at Third District headquarters, west on 71st Street all the way to Cottage Grove. Back then, when he lived at 79th and Oglesby, he used to take long walks up the lakefront to 71st Street, over to Jeffery, and then back east to Yates and home. "I wasn't worrying about crime," he said, "and there weren't kids mean-mugging, trying to intimidate." Now, though he lived steps away from 71st, he didn't walk there much. "I'm not afraid of being harmed . . . ," he said, and when I interrupted to ask if that was because he was armed, he nodded deeply and said, "Every *second* of every *day*." He went on: ". . . But I am pained by what I see. Teenage boys with their ass hanging out, that pains me. It's buffoonish." In his view, the head buffoon was Chief Keef, most prominent of Chicago's gun-crazy drill rappers—some of them, like the rising stars Lil Herb (aka G Herbo) and Lil Bibby, from South Shore. Capo, a member of Chief Keef's Glo Gang crew, would later be gunned down in South Shore—last time I checked, you could still watch him bleed out and die on the 7700 block of South Kingston in a cellphone video on YouTube—and the shooter's getaway car would kill a baby in a stroller during the ensuing police chase.

The bleakness of contemporary South Shore's commercial strips also deterred Lemieux from taking a stroll. "There's nowhere to go," he said. "Why isn't Seventy-First, Seventy-Fifth, a booming business district? Why is the Dominick's gone?" Why the loose cigarettes for sale, the vacant storefronts? "The curse of the indigenous peoples, maybe," he said, smiling bleakly at his own joke. He knew the real cause to be purposeful, systematic disinvestment from the black inner city, abetted by official neglect. "The potential is there, the clientele is there. The Starbucks at Seventy-First and Stony Island does a lot of business. Yeah, there are people camped out in front"—panhandling and cadging from patrons—"but that's just poor policing. Real police grounded in the community know the wheat from the chaff."

There was a strong historical dimension to his analysis—a story of decline, stage-managed by the powerful, that framed and suffused every resonant detail. Back in the day, he said, "the criminal element was not dominant; you could find them, they were there, but it wasn't everywhere," and there were authoritative alternatives to the stone gangster pose. "One thing about the sixties, the social narrative was Dr. King, the Black Panthers," he said. "Not everybody was serious, but that was the narrative. There was still sensationalism, but it was positive sensationalism, to a degree." He even allowed the Blackstone Rangers and other gangs of the pre-crack era, the kind of gangs wishfully lionized by *The Spook Who Sat by the Door*, a touch of virtue in retrospect, earned by their commitment to the neighborhood. There was an element of trust, he said, between old and young, and when he moved to South Shore in the 1970s there were still businesses on 71st Street—Don D Fashion, the Coffee Cup—that attracted people of all ages to the commercial main drag. Even the violent electronic stimulation was less toxic to black viewers, in his view. "When I was a kid, TV was either World War Two, cops and robbers, or cowboys and Indians," he said. "Nobody on screen looked like you—it was a fantasy from jump street, and you wanted to be the good guys. But now it's to where when you see violence on the screen, it's the bad guys against the worse guys, and now *everybody* looks like you. You've got boys and girls following some bullshit crippled behavior."

He remembered police work in South Shore as more relaxed, too, once upon a time. Compared to what he calls "the godforsaken West Side," and to Woodlawn and other high-action South Side neighborhoods, South Shore was a relatively quiet beat in 1982. The big rises in street crime during the 1960s and early 1970s had leveled off, and the neighborhood had settled into new routines and developed new community networks after its sudden turnover from white to black. White cops in the Third District got South Shore duty because it was seen as easier, he said, while black cops were assigned to more violent neighborhoods west of Stony Island. White officers had keys to the defunct South Shore Country Club, "and they didn't do anything."

The arrival of crack cocaine on the South Side later in the 1980s blew up that cozy arrangement. "That also put the nail in the coffin on relations between youth and elders," he said. "The internal compass you had, moral or social, no matter what your particular ism or schism is, what crack cocaine did is it changed that completely. You started having teenagers, children, selling an addictive drug to adults, telling them what to do. Even a kid not involved in that kind of enterprise, if you live in the community you witness that subordination of adults to youth. I never, ever observed that as an adolescent." Crack, an accelerant and multiplier of the effects of many other kinds of change, turned South Shore into a high-action neighborhood. "There were a lot of people buying the cultural narrative," he said. "Things really changed. Wasn't so much shooting at first . . . ," but soon there was, as the local gangs got down to violent business. In a grim parody of the postindustrial labor market, they broke down into ever more ad hoc and contingent drug-dealing factions even as they claimed allegiance with corporation-like citywide and national combines. Crack helped push gun violence and other street crime to new highs in South Shore in the 1990s.

Lemieux was telling me a crime story about how the world had changed, a story not just about crack and guns and policing but also about Facebook, hip-hop, obsolescent main streets, how kids today don't respect their elders, and the larger system of woes visited upon the black inner city. This is one principal thing we use crime stories for: compressing complexity into a lode of deep crime that we manage to simultaneously expose and bury even deeper when we dwell on the spectacular surface crimes that compel our attention. When I asked what he thought could be done to address the world historical-scale problem outlined by his Gramscian-Foucauldian analysis, he said, "The wrong people are the police." That made a kind of sense. Surgeons usually want to cut, and police tend to think that better police work will help fix almost anything. If the Weimar Republic had had a better tac squad, it might have nipped Hitler in the bud when he was still a punk-ass gangster.

"I think very globally," said Lemieux, "but I try to act locally." As he saw it, the police were too often just like the gangbangers. "It wouldn't matter if you had Nelson Mandela as superintendent of the Chicago Police," he said, "because you have a bunch of twenty-five- to thirty-five-year-old shitheads don't give a fuck what's happening at Seventieth and Paxton, and you see all these people of my own tribe who want to be a gangster whatever." Mixing these two wrong kinds of men with guns produces a nightmarish spiral of confrontation and violence, with the police adding to the problem by actively channeling young black men into the legal system. "But if you're grounded in something, you're able to resist it a little," he said. "If you live in the neighborhood, you have to comport yourself differently" when policing it. He and his partner, Gerald Hamilton, who also lived in South Shore, would haul kids back to their families if they could, rather than arresting them. "We'd take them home—curfew enforcement, meet the parents." That, he was sure, was how things had worked in Irish South Shore before his time. "If Tommy O'Leary is a cop and he sees Sean O'Sullivan is fucking up, he doesn't put him in the system. He uses his police discretion. He slaps the taste out of his mouth and takes him home to his mother. That's grounded in the community." But that was all long ago, at least in places like South Shore. He said, "You think white police will confiscate some white kid's car because a kid in the backseat had a bag of weed? That's how the police destroy families, and they don't do it to white families." Under the auspices of the nonprofit Black Star Project, in retirement he ran a seminar program that taught young people of color what to do if stopped by the police. It was called "Keeping OUR Children Out of the Just-Us System."

When he was done breaking it down for me and drinking coffee, Lemieux headed out into the deepening night, his stride rolling a little, dreads falling over the collar of his fatigue jacket and down his back. Physical confidence came off him like a bow wave, and his eyes, scanning the street in the perpetual routine of threat assessment that becomes second nature to a police officer, were alight with conviction. The world had gone bad around him in big complicated ways he couldn't fix, and shadowy figures were directing great flows of capital and culture with the intent of further subjugating and perhaps destroying his tribe, but he had an analysis and he had a gun. Nobody with even a little sense, no matter how hopelessly in thrall to the wrong cultural narrative, could take a look at this man and decide that it would be a good idea to mess with him.

*

Sampson's community area surveys measured fear of crime in South Shore in the 1990s and 2000s, and it ran fairly high—around the 59th percentile, above average among Chicago's community areas. The perception of violence and disorder in South Shore by its residents ran even higher, around the 75th percentile, roughly commensurate with the neighborhood's rank in actual levels of violent crime. Given the obsession with talking about crime in South Shore, you might well expect the opposite, that residents would fear crime out of proportion to actual levels of it. Why didn't the surveys show them to be as fearful of crime in South Shore as are people elsewhere in the metro area—Hyde Park, downtown, the North Side, the suburbs—who regard South Shore as dangerous and shun it?

First, the proximity of higher-crime and visibly poorer community areas offers constant perspective. No matter how bad it gets in South Shore—and 187 homicides between 2006 and mid-2015 is a lot, especially for a neighborhood that looks as good as parts of South Shore do—and no matter how appalled or outraged they are by shootings or theft, residents of South Shore are always aware that it's worse in Englewood and on the West Side.

Second, South Shore's residents have a strong ethos of forting-up. They tend to have confidence in their own individual enterprise and personal efficacy, even if their faith in community is weak and they regard the neighborhood as in some ways a disappointment. They may be concerned about crime and its effect on property values and the neighborhood's reputation, but they tend to believe that they'll take care of their own business in ways that will forestall their becoming a victim, even if others around them become victims. Sampson told me he was surprised when a fellow sociologist at the University of Chicago who lived in the Highlands responded to being robbed at gunpoint with anger rather than fear—*I can't believe I left the drawbridge down and let them punk me on my own property* rather than *Oh, God, they're coming for me and there's nothing I can do*—but I've been seeing the same reaction for decades. My neighbors often viewed being victimized as a failure of their own technique, the revealing of a mendable gap in their life-fortress's defenses.

And third, the people of South Shore constantly do the crime math, substituting calculation for panic. Yes, it can seem crazy to get used to checking your flanks and scanning for trouble at all times; staying inside when the sun goes down, like a character in a vampire movie; and minimizing exposure in public space, scuttling from home to car and back again, as if on a planet with hostile wildlife and unbreathable air. As Steve Perkins, who waged a long struggle in partnership with the South Shore Bank for the improvement of 71st Street before finally moving away, put it, "Who wants to get used to living like that?" But other residents do get used to living like that. Calvin Holmes—also a banker active in community development lending, who lived in a midrise condo on 67th Street with a glorious view of Jackson Park and the lake and the Loop beyond—told me, "Am I street-defensive and street-smart? Yes, but I don't feel like I'm going to meet my maker every day. I don't feel under siege. At this price point, it's worth the gamble." When my empty-nester parents moved from Chicago to Manhattan in 1989, they were pleased to be able to walk around their neighborhood at night in streets filled with all kinds of people doing the same. It reminded them of Barcelona or Rome, they said—a comparison that made sense if you contrasted the minimal violent-crime math they had to do in those places to the advanced calculus they had been used to doing in South Shore.

*

"The idea with interlocking fields of fire is you should know what you can cover from every window," Maurice was saying. We were in the backyard of his mother's big brick house in the Jackson Park Highlands, just across the street from Maurice's own house, which was even bigger—five bedrooms, six baths, 8,600 square feet. These were substantial century-old houses on double lots, built to last.

Birds were calling in the summer afternoon heat, but it was lush and cool in the overgrown yard of Maurice's mother's house, at the end of a long driveway guarded by a reinforced electronic gate and a No Trespassing sign. There had been distress in the Highlands the previous winter when a polar vortex had brought on extreme low temperatures that disabled the remote controls of such gates, forcing residents to leave them open or to dart from the shelter of their cars to operate them by hand. Maurice, a public defender who speculated in real estate and led classes for citizens who wanted to secure a license to carry a concealed firearm, had directed my attention to the sightlines from the windows on the second-story rear of his mother's house in the course of explaining that his own house was harder to defend because it was bigger and on a corner. His father, who put in thirty-four years on the police force, had always warned him against living in a corner house, what with all the extra frontage to cover, but the opportunity to acquire a distressed mansion at a rock-bottom price had been too good to pass up. Still, because his mother's place offered the less-exposed defensive position, in a last-stand situation Maurice would take his daughters, wife, and guns over there.

We had been talking about life in the Highlands. When my family moved there in 1973 from its bungalow on Oglesby, it had felt like a major step up for us. As one resident of several decades' tenure described the Highlands, "It's a peninsula with a sense of forces around it, surrounded by South Shore" on three sides, fronting Jackson Park on the other. Its residents make common cause like minor gentry occupying a string of hilltop castles in a borderland thick with bandits. "The neighbors, we talk, we see each other, but we're not as tight as on some other blocks," said Maurice. "Now, Sixty-Seventh and Euclid, they're tight. They see *anything*, they call the police." He served in the army in Iraq and Afghanistan, and his military training—preparing sector sketches of foxholes and interlocking fire zones—had given him a vocabulary for the kind of cooperation he had in mind. "There shouldn't be a place on our block where someone can walk without being caught by a camera," he said, and they could certainly do more with phone trees, group email lists, and other mutual support systems. "The world, in my opinion, is going to hell," he said, "and this neighborhood is gonna be one of the last places left standing"—if its residents made the effort to be suitably prepared. "I joke about it," he said, "but it's not necessarily a joke."

Nor was his talk of zones of fire merely metaphorical. Maurice usually carried a gun, and he kept copious firepower in reserve: a dozen or so handguns, and several automatic shotguns and rifles. I associate this kind of arsenal with a distinctively American strain of madness. Guns are like cats in that while owning one merely identifies one as a gun or cat person, and owning a second can be chalked up to enthusiasm or the result of plausible circumstances following upon possession of the first, owning three begins to demand a fuller explanation, and the assumption of nuttiness that can't be explained away scales up rapidly from there. But I don't regard Maurice as crazy. I grew up with him. We lived in the same neighborhood and he was a grade behind me at Lab, where he played in the violin section of the middle school orchestra with me and on the high school basketball team with my brother Sal. His family, like mine, made the move up from South Shore's bungalow belt to a big house in the Highlands, and his family's trajectory was more heroic. While my parents had PhDs from the University of Chicago, Maurice's father was a police officer who astutely acquired apartment buildings in Washington Park, an area he patrolled, and made the financial and imaginative stretch to send his son to Lab. Maurice, who became a lawyer, embodies the kind of social mobility that South Shore has traditionally offered. But there aren't as many people making such moves these days in South Shore, and those who did, like his parents, are aging out. Good union jobs—the kind traditionally held by the skilled industrial workers whose unions had their glory days in the 1950s and 1960s and by members of the public-sector unions that expanded in the 1970s—gave stability to the bungalow blocks that served as launching pads for upward mobility, and such jobs have grown rarer on the South Side and in general. And unions, of course, have taken a fall—in membership (as a percentage of the labor force), in influence, and in the value our culture places on them.

What's left, increasingly, are stagnant wages, income inequality, reduced upward mobility, haves and have-nots. Maurice—who had owned Section 8 apartment buildings, defended indigent felons, spent time in the projects, and served in the military with a variety of Americans from unfancy backgrounds—had had plenty of opportunity to grow familiar with this new order. He was acutely aware that he had ended up on the side that has secured the lion's share of the wealth, valuable stuff, and desirable life chances, and that the other side feels it has been screwed. When I consider the obsession with self-defense against crime that guided his response to that structural state of affairs, I find that while I believe that on balance all he was accomplishing by owning all those guns was to make the world a slightly more awful place without even making his family any safer, I can't dismiss it out of hand.

Maurice grew up in a bungalow on the 7200 block of East End, in South Shore on the other side of the Illinois Central tracks from the Highlands. He remembered it fondly as a solid old-school block. His friends there came from two-parent home-owning families who had moved in during the 1960s. Those friends mostly went to Catholic high schools like Hales Franciscan and Mendel, affordable options outside the neighborhood that their parents perceived as better than the local public schools, and they went on to college and careers. "I would say they're middle class," he said, "and doing all right." His parents left the block for the Highlands in 1985, when he was in college, and he moved to his own place in the Highlands in 2010. By then his old block on East End, not to mention childhood in America and the ability of the bungalow belt to produce another generation of upward mobility, had changed, and there was nothing much to hold him there. "When I grew up on that block, there were a lot of kids, and we went house to house, and our parents interacted," he told me. "That was gone. Most of the people on the block, we didn't know them. No one came out. I didn't feel comfortable when my kids went out to play."

Back when he was a kid, shuttling between East End and school at Lab gave Maurice whiplash. His father had taught him to make a way in the neighborhood—how not to look like a victim, how to stand up for himself. Maurice, who grew up to be six foot five with a condor-like wingspan and a deep voice, was always the biggest kid. "I don't want you starting fights or being a bully, but I want you to end fights," his father had always told him, and they practiced scenarios in which Maurice had to take a gun away from an assailant. In elementary school, navigating among Lab's ironists, eccentrics, and budding stoners, he frequently got his signals crossed. "Living in two worlds caused me some confusion," he said. "My dad had to come to school because I'd gotten in three fights in one day, depending who got in my way, who stepped on my feet—literally, a guy who stepped on my foot in line. I didn't use my words. I thought it was a code: if it was an accident, you say I'm sorry;

if it wasn't an accident, it was the start of war. I gave them a chance to apologize, and if not . . ."—then Maurice stood up for himself, 72nd and East End style. I asked him who he fought with, expecting to hear the names of boys I remember as pugilists. "I used to get into it with Anne Kitagawa," he said, smiling. Oh, right: this was Lab, after all, where if you got in a beef, it would not be with an aspiring Vice Lord but instead with a child of professors, in this case a girl who would grow up to be a museum curator specializing in Asian art. Her mother, Evelyn Kitagawa, was a Chicago School sociologist who took a leading role in preparing the neighborhood fact books I have consulted for historical statistics on South Shore. "I started to calm down around sixth grade," Maurice said. Maybe playing the violin helped.

The worldview principally shaped by his father and South Shore was tempered by Lab, but not fundamentally altered. Maurice reminded me that in drivers' ed we had been taught the IPDE method of defensive driving: identify, predict, decide, execute. He took it as a model for life. Even walking down the sidewalk, he would be actively scanning his lanes, predicting approaching threats and escape routes. This outlook was further refined by military service. During his year away from home, his reserve unit hit all the high spots: Kuwait, Iraq, Afghanistan. He inspected post offices in combat zones, traveling constantly and overseeing the transport of large sums of cash. "I actually felt safer and more comfortable walking the streets of Iraq in 2004 than I do here," he said. "I had an M16 with a grenade launcher, I carried a nine-millimeter sidearm, wore a Kevlar vest. I felt that if I could see them coming, I could shoot them first." The rules of engagement were supposed to constrain him, but he paid them little mind. "It didn't make sense to have the magazine in my cargo pants," he said. "I was locked and loaded."

Similarly, at home he began carrying a gun even before he found a loophole in the law—which has been made less restrictive since then—that allowed citizens to secure a concealed carry permit. "There are times when you have to make decisions about your safety," he said. Carrying a gun is an article of faith, an efficacious personal response to the condition of the world, and that faith is righteous enough to transcend the letter of the law. "It's about having it more than using it,"

Maurice said. "The laws haven't changed that much, and you're still a leper if you have a gun. You're still committing a crime if somebody sees you with a gun. So you only pull it out in a life-threatening situation. I don't think you should do anything differently because you have a gun. If you wouldn't do it without a gun, then don't do it because you have a gun. But it gives you confidence."

His clients, people of limited means in trouble with the law, crave that same confidence, and he didn't begrudge it to them. "What a lot of people don't realize is that gangbangers join gangs for protection," he said. "When I'm in court, all I see are Aggravated Unlawful Use of a Weapon cases, but I do believe that even convicted criminals should be able to protect themselves. I have a lot of clients who picked up a felony down the path of life, and they've cleaned themselves up, but they can't carry because they're a felon, and they live in a neighborhood where they have to protect themselves." No matter where he might find himself, be it Kabul or South Shore, Maurice understood himself to live in one of those neighborhoods, too.

We strolled across the street from his mother's house to Maurice's, an imposing mass of pale brick with a stone balustrade running along the third-story terrace, and a cupola on high. It had been a foreclosure, vacant for four years, when he snapped it up with a lowball offer in the aftermath of the real estate crash of 2008. We went around back. The huge yard was untended, the pool long dry, its concrete cracked and strewn with leaves. His dogs, pit bull–lab mixes, raged and leaped behind a fence, trying to get at me. "Oh, yeah, everybody's got dogs," he said. "There are feral cats living back here, too. A fox was coming around here, but they ran him off." Standing amid the ruinous beauty of the yard, he said that he would like his daughters to settle in the Highlands, where they could live among successful and civic-minded neighbors, but he soon got back to talking about crime. "I would say it's getting worse," he said. "A lot of shit around us is trickling over to us. We've witnessed people coming down the street trying car doors, our cars have been broken into four times, robberies, things like that, and we've had quite a few shootings. Whatever they say 'the numbers are down,' I don't trust the numbers." We checked out the garage, in which he no longer parked his enormous SUV. "I identified this as a danger zone," he said. "If you walk in the front gate of the yard, you can get around into the garage, and then if I park in there and get out, I'm locked in with you." Something like this had happened to neighbors who were robbed at gunpoint. It wasn't going to happen to him. He and his wife parked at the curb in a spot covered by one of the house's surveillance cameras.

There was less violent crime in the Highlands than in other parts of South Shore, but its residents felt besieged, especially by thieves. It was not just paranoia. Young men, alone or in duos or crews, did come through the neighborhood looking to take whatever wasn't nailed down, and even things that were. The Highlands email group tracked their progress and detailed their depredations after they had passed through. One summer weekend in 2015 produced a half-dozen reports of smash-and-grab burglaries in which heavy objects had been used to break windows or doors. A neighbor recommended that all residents remove paving stones from their yards and front lawns to deprive the invaders of makeshift battering rams. Grainy security-camera videos of guys in hoodies breaking into cars in driveways circulated on the email group, as well as requests for footage from neighbors' cameras after some fresh outrage, debates about hiring a private security service, fantasies about gating off their enclave from the rest of South Shore, expressions of concern that crime was an epidemic or tidal wave that was getting worse and worse, and stoic reminders that things had always been this way in the Highlands and if residents pulled together they could weather the latest storm.

My stroll with Maurice reached the sidewalk in front of his house. The talk turned to South Shore's depressed commercial strips and its schools with poor reputations. Like most other people with choices who live in South Shore, Maurice and his family didn't do much in the neighborhood other than live in their well-fortified house. His daughters had attended selective-enrollment public schools in other parts of the city, and the family also left the neighborhood to spend money. "I don't shop here," he said. "I get upset whenever I do. I feel you get overcharged and treated like a piece of crap. I don't even go to the Home Depot on Eighty-Seventh Street. I refuse to be around those people, who have been mistreated and don't know how to treat others." He went to the suburbs to buy groceries and home-improvement supplies, or to Indiana, just a few minutes away, where it was also cheaper to fill up his gas tank. "I'm a Sav-A-Lot-type person," he said. "I guess I'm part of the problem, because the people in this area don't want to go to the stores here." The desolation of 71st Street looked like the embodiment of fear of crime and helped perpetuate that fear, but it was also the desolation of an obsolete main street in an age when those who had choices would get in the car or go online to shop.

Even if the rest of South Shore held little appeal for him, Maurice believed that it was in the self-interest of the residents of the Highlands to establish partnerships with surrounding areas, especially Parkside, one of South Shore's poorest and most crime-plagued sections, which is separated from the Highlands by only an alley. "I'm for making Parkside a better place," he said. "I think our neighborhood needs to expand, and we need to sort of demonstrate the social expectations." This was a regular theme for him, squarely in a long tradition of the respectable black middle class volunteering to demonstrate bourgeois virtues to those in need of cultivating them. "It can be simple things, correcting the way you live—like loud talking, drinking on your front porch, not putting things in the garbage can," Maurice said. "Many people don't have a positive outlook on life. They're not expecting to be twenty-five, so they're not planning on it. They haven't been exposed to better." As a landlord he had rented to Section 8 tenants, some of whom proved difficult, including one family who inexplicably smashed in all the brand-new doors in their apartment. "Section Eight is reliable in that the government pays well and on time, but you have to decide whether it's worth it," he said. "It's a different group of people and it can be a mess." Managing such buildings was part of the reason he started carrying a gun in the first place. Still, he said, "I want to go to Parkside, give kids some hope about what they can do, as opposed to what they can't do."

As we were talking, a half-dozen boys, no more than ten or twelve years old, came along the street toward us, one of those crews from other areas of South Shore who will make a swing through the Highlands, taking a look at the big houses and their grounds, checking out what there might be to see and do. Maurice ostentatiously ignored them as they approached in a loose skirmish line; the boys, looking at nothing in particular and everything at once, were intensely aware of the blue-suited giant in their path. As they drew near, he leaned in a little to say to me, "You know, I'm naked right now," meaning that this was a rare moment when he didn't have a gun on him, and mentioned that he had yet to give me a tour of his collection. "Let's just say," he confided, nodding toward the forbidding bulk of his house, "I've got something for *everybody*." The boys abruptly changed direction like a flock of starlings and went off west on 68th Street, toward Parkside.

I went back to see Maurice sixteen months later, on an evening in late October 2015. This was my first look at the interior of his house, which was somber and grand, half-empty, the curtains drawn. The living room was almost devoid of furniture, a vast expanse of dark wood floor under an elaborately detailed ceiling, the fireplace densely carved with figures of cherubs and vines. It was hard to believe that a public defender could own such a palace, but stretching to buy the place had not left copious funds for renovating and decorating it, and it looked more like an investment than a home. Maurice had been watching *Monday Night Football* on a large-screen TV in an alcove off the kitchen. There was a holstered revolver on the coffee table in front of his seat.

Maurice and his wife were getting divorced, and she had moved out, taking the dogs. The house had the feel of a remote keep ruled by a suzerain whose retainers have decamped, but Maurice described himself as more optimistic than before about the neighborhood. "It was a good summer," he said. "Not many incidents." He saw the situation improving on the South Side. The University of Chicago had continued expanding into Woodlawn, pushing well south of 60th Street, and had also bought up land in Washington Park, his father's old patrol area. There was a lot of renovation going on to the west, on the other side of Stony Island, and there were some signs of gentrification in South Shore itself. He praised Leslie Hairston, fellow Lab alum and alderman, for encouraging it. "I think it's happening," he said, meaning that at long last investment capital was beginning to arrive. Good houses in

South Shore were beginning to attract the attention of bargain-hunters like the investor who had recently bought the bungalow on East End in which Maurice grew up. And, most gratifyingly, vigilance in the Highlands seemed to be having an effect. "It really is deterring crime," said Maurice. "I haven't heard so many reports of cars being broken into."

We fell to talking about Glenn Evans, the former commander of the police department's Third District, which includes the Highlands. Evans had been removed from command and charged with aggravated battery and official misconduct for allegedly putting his gun in the mouth of a suspect while holding a Taser to the suspect's crotch and threatening to kill him. The commander said he had seen the man at a bus stop on 71st Street with what looked like a gun in his hand. He chased him into an abandoned building and dragged him out of a closet, demanding, "Motherfucker, tell me where the guns are." Evans's trial would begin in December. "We all liked Evans around here," Maurice said. "We all thought he was a stand-up guy, an aggressive police officer. Most of these neighbors appreciated it," a sentiment I'd heard from others in South Shore. Evans would eventually be cleared of all charges, but Maurice said he would think no less of him if he was convicted. "That was nonlethal force," he said. "He got the guy's attention. I know what the cost of freedom is."

Conditions might be improving a bit in South Shore, but the world was still a dangerous place. Maurice took me upstairs to look at the bullets in his walls. There were two, both on the second floor, one in the family room and the other in an adjoining bathroom with an enormous whirlpool tub. Each bullet had entered through the glass just above the bottom edge of a window and embedded itself high in a wall, passing through the room on an upward trajectory that could easily have caught someone in the body or head. This had happened one night a couple of years before. Maurice had left the bullets where they were as a reminder of the facts of life, dark irregular lumps of force-mangled metal marring the creamy green expanse of painted wall otherwise uninterrupted by pictures or other decoration. The bullets had come from the southwest, the direction of Parkside and the house in which he grew up. There was always plenty of shooting out there. "I remember my father shooting out the back every New Year's" in the bungalow on East End, he said, "just to let people know there were shotguns in his house."

Maurice's daughters would be going away to college soon, and he pronounced himself done for good with marriage, so he was beginning to think about downsizing to an apartment. He had looked at some of the nicer buildings on South Shore Drive, and at land in the Dominican Republic with an eye toward waiting out Chicago winters somewhere warm and cheap. He had recently turned fifty, and he could look back at the rising arc of his path through life and see that he had done well for himself. He could turn a profit on this house, which he had gradually improved to a state somewhere between fixer-upper and fixed up, and get out of it more than whole. For now, though, it was still his castle, bullets in the walls and all.

*

When I asked Greg Mitchell—the alderman of the Seventh Ward, which includes a large chunk of southern South Shore—about the giant Lakeside development planned for the barren former site of U.S. Steel's South Works on the edge of South Shore, he told me a story about the world changing that turned into a crime story.

When he grew up in Jeffery Manor, just south of South Shore, in the 1970s and 1980s, he said, "the streets and houses were filled with kids. We obtained good educations, we had Little League, kids could be kids. Your only job as a kid was go to school, do what your parents told you, and respect your elders." Underwriting this bungalow-and-two-flat idyll was good work. "You knew what everybody's parents' jobs would be," he said. "My father worked at the post office, and if it wasn't that it was Ford, USX [U.S. Steel], police, fire department, teachers." He ticked off on his fingers those solid, reliable union jobs that had paid a living wage and enabled upward social mobility over the generations. "These families raised their children, and some of them became lawyers, doctors, accountants, financial people," he said. "Some don't come back, but those who stayed, like me, they keep it going. Crime is often the main topic of discussion, but the civic part does still exist." Sitting on a beat-up old chair in his dingy office, his blue dress shirt crisp and his novice enthusiasm for the alderman's job still evident, Mitchell presented himself as a true believer—youthful, athletic, earnest—but he also acknowledged that in trying to sustain the world his parents made, he was struggling against the tide of history. The disappearance of jobs at the Ford plant or the U.S. Steel works and of once-common Proud Union Home signs you used to see outside South Side houses are indicators that formerly familiar paths to economic security have become steeper, narrower, more unsure. Lakeside, promising to physically and functionally replace major economic and social supports of the neighborhood that were lost when the industrial order collapsed, would bring a fresh wave of investment and jobs and possibility to counter the effects of deindustrialization, depopulation, and other changes on the grand scale that had partially undone his model of the virtuous neighborhood.

"You would think that Lakeside would sell itself," Mitchell said, but the specter of crime threatened that rosy future. "You look to the east, the northeast, the southeast"—out over the water—"and it's great, the most beautiful views, but you look to the west"—inland—"and we have element there, around Seventy-Ninth Street." On the South Side you hear "the element," short for "criminal element" or "undesirable element," applied as a term of black-on-black opprobrium not only to violent criminals but also to quality-of-life perps who litter and make too much noise and wear their pants too low, wrecking things for their decent neighbors by sowing disorder and fear. As the alderman saw it, the element who gathered in force along east 79th Street—milling crews of underschooled, unemployed young men who cultivated an air of being ready to go to war over a wrong look or gesture or article of clothing, a provocation on social media, an incursion into their small stretch of run-down territory—were scaring off investment by perpetuating the area's reputation for violent crime.

As Mitchell told the story, clearing out the element would give Lakeside a chance to proceed in putting right some of the consequences of great forces that undid and remade the neighborhood order over the previous half century at a scale no alderman could do anything about. He couldn't stop U.S. Steel from going under and he couldn't stop job loss from helping to put all those young men on the corner, but he could possibly prevail upon the commander of the Fourth District to send armed officers of the law to strike a blow against fear of crime by running the No Limit Muskegon Boyz off the corner.

*

Gerald Hamilton was saying, "Forget about all these stories and statements"—about crime, he meant—"and just take a bird's-eye view of South Shore: it's one of the most ideal locations in a city you could imagine. You could put some money in Englewood or Roseland, yeah, and make it a little better, but if you had enough money and put in the work, this place you could turn around completely in five to ten years." It was a brisk sunny day in June 2013, and we were in a booth by the plate-glass windows at the L & G Family Restaurant, a diner facing the IC tracks on the corner of 75th and Exchange. Hamilton, six foot three and built thick, all in black—sleeveless T-shirt, fleece vest, shorts, sneakers—was drinking a glass of milk and shoveling up spoonfuls of buttered rice with sausage patties, the blocky muscles in his bare arms rolling under the skin. Many years of boxing, tae kwon do, and being a cop had given him the look of a guy who knew what he was doing with his hands and would not hesitate to do it to you, if you had it coming. His receding hair was clipped close to the skull, and he sported a fierce ink-black mustache. He was fifty-eight, but he looked as if enough testosterone to power several twenty-one-year-olds was coursing through his system.

Hamilton, a retired homicide detective who put in twenty-five years on the force, had been David Lemieux's partner. Everyone had called them "Hamilton and Daveed," like Starsky and Hutch or Scully and Mulder. The two had seemed an unlikely match at first. In Hamilton's telling, "He was like 'Who's this Reggie Theus motherfucker?'" (Theus was a lushly mustachioed guard for the Chicago Bulls in the late 1970s and early 1980s.) "And I was like, 'Who's this Peepee Le Pew motherfucker?'" But they had clicked and achieved renown on the South Side. "We were known as feared but fair," Hamilton said. The diner's employees greeted Hamilton as a regular, and he exchanged hellos with all the cops and many of the other customers who came in and out. Sade's "Smooth Operator" was playing on the sound system, mixing with the clatter of dishes and hubbub of conversation. Marvin Gaye's "Sexual Healing" came on next. When I'm on the South Side, I swim in a bath of old-school soul, the sound track and martial theme music of the forces of middle-class respectability. Carol Adams, then president and CEO of the DuSable Museum of African American History, waved to Hamilton from a nearby table. He said to me, "That's a very smart and important lady. Lives right around here." When I went to talk to Adams at the DuSable a few months later, William DeVaughn's "Be Thankful for What You Got," the king-high old-school summer jam of all time, would be playing in the gift shop: "Diamond in the back, sunroof top / Diggin' the scene / With a gangster lean . . ."

Hamilton said, "Excuse me, my little friend is getting heavy," and took a big weathered black handgun out of the bulging zippered pocket of his vest, which had been hanging low on that side. He put the gun on the windowsill with his keys and phone, loosely tenting his folded copy of the *Sun-Times* over it. The barrel pointed outward through the plate glass, seemingly aimed at the intersection and, beyond it, the area of South Shore known as Terror Town. Clearly visible from the street, the gun would give any passing riffraff—Hamilton's preferred term for gang members—something to think about.

Hamilton went back to drawing a lesson about money and policing from the University of Chicago's ongoing expansion into Woodlawn. "These little Gangster Disciples say, 'That is our turf.' But the university put some money in this, and then they gotta go, or the district commander gotta go, and he'll make sure it's them." As a matter of policy, he used the word "little" when talking about gangs, dismissing their fearsome reputation as puerile bluster. "These little guys in the gangs, they're so disenfranchised from the ownership of anything, they're talkin' 'bout 'We're the Murder Town Gangsters.' That sounds so scary, but that can change overnight. You spend some money, you move them out. The riffraff do only what they're allowed to do." He found it galling that there was no institution like the university to mobilize a similar combination of investment capital and policing in South Shore. "It's the biggest frustration to me," he said. "If somebody had the wherewithal and the incentive, you could do it on the cheap." The main obstacle, in his view, was not crime itself but South Shore's exaggerated reputation for crime. "With this stuff, perception is reality," he said. "It's not one of these places where you park your car and they take the wheels. And 'murder capital'? The only people gettin' killed is the ones out here at two in the morning!"

In the absence of a major institutional player in South Shore, entrepreneurial citizens would have to do it themselves. "Shit, if I hit the lottery, as my legacy I'd try to revitalize South Shore," he said. He would start by leading the way in investing contagiously in its commercial strips. When I asked what business he would start up, he said, "I'm not talking about *a* business. It's gotta come in with more, buy up a bunch, start puttin' some money where there's nothing now but vacant storefronts, liquor stores, and chicken restaurants." And wig stores, of course. A liquor store and a wig store were visible from where we sat. He had already started modestly on the residential front on his own block, 77th Street near South Shore Drive. He had bought the abandoned house next to his own and was renovating it, putting a fence around the two to form a compound, and he had his eye on a third. There were only a few houses on the short block; he was becoming a small-scale institutional player in his own right. "Spend $200,000 for a place on the North Side?" he said, aghast—not that you could get anything for that kind of money up there. "You could buy the whole block for that down here!"

A little money plus a little force—that was the formula for dealing with the element, even for a DIY revitalizer. He told me a story. "Some of them riffraff tried to set up a drug house in an empty place in my little Hamilton House area. Hypes on my block! I was flabbergasted"— more by the stupidity than by the effrontery of such a move. "I went to the commander of the Fourth District, gave him a heads-up. Then I put a padlock on the back door of the house and went in the front." He could tell me more about what happened in there, he said, but not until the statute of limitations elapsed. "When they recovered," he went on, "I told them, 'Tell your homies I'm the only gang around here.'"

From the L & G we drove out to Lakeside, the former brownfield site once occupied by U.S. Steel where developers planned to create a full-blown neighborhood with more than 13,000 units of housing, 17.5 million square feet of retail, schools, marinas, the works. But at that point (and still, at this writing) it was 589 acres of windblown prairie grass and high hopes. It put me in mind of the passage in Theodore Dreiser's *Sister Carrie* that surveys the open country around late nineteenth-century Chicago already laid with miles of streetcar lines, board sidewalks, and long rows of gas lamps flickering in the wind, all anticipating the houses and stores to be built. We were just a few blocks from Hamilton's home. He had been driving down to the spot for years, looking at the fenced-off blank space and dreaming of possibilities. "It's gonna be nice around here when this comes in," he said. "Marinas!"

Later we went cruising in his black Crown Victoria, a retired cop car with a searchlight on the driver's side. Hamilton had pulled over to the curb on 71st Street and was talking about how most black people didn't feel entitled to good police protection, when a guy in his thirties carrying two plastic bags approached my open window. He exchanged a cordial greeting with us, pronounced himself "stressed but blessed," and launched into a comparison of the bad manners of some people in the neighborhood, who said "What you want?" when asked a polite question at a store, to the high standard of public comportment in Japan, where he'd once lived. The conversation moved on to the topic of 71st Street's starkness. "These young men here on the streets need to know I *will* defend myself," said the guy. "I may be short, but I'm grown." In due course he invited us to his church, which, it turned out, Hamilton had already visited. The guy wished us a blessed day and went on his way. The encounter had been a ritual exercise in mutual recognition, two agents of militant decency hailing each other in public and confirming that they're unafraid to assert themselves.

"Ninety-five percent of people here are like everywhere else," said Hamilton as we resumed our cruise. "They just want to go to work, provide for their families, raise their kids, a good education, the usual things. Then there's just five percent or less who are tearing it all down with their antisocial behavior. These piece-of-shit motherfuckers want to mess that up."

Sometimes, especially when I was in his company, I was tempted to imagine that thirty or forty Gerald Hamiltons—backed up with judiciously apportioned investment capital and seeded throughout South Shore like Special Forces operatives tasked with raising an indigenous militia—could indeed transform the neighborhood in the five-to-ten-year span he envisioned. He represented the ne plus ultra of my Nonna's definition of good neighboring: "Say hello and cutta the grass." Modulating his greetings on a spectrum from hearty bellow to cordial nod, he seemed to recognize everybody and said hello to all: schoolkids, grandmas, cops, young men in hoodies, panhandlers, business owners, his alderman, the major-league developers working on Lakeside, strangers. And he backed up his insistence on order with a demonstrated willingness to impose it himself, though he wasn't averse to working with the authorities. If he was correct that the fear of crime rather than crime itself was the key to South Shore's continuing disinvestment problem, then his confident dominance of public space, the kind that convinces other people that it's safe to come out, looked like a model solution.

But I'm not so sure about that. The deployment of righteous force, or the threat of it, seems a less-than-adequate substitute for a social climate in which a vigorous public life and the routines of acquaintance, expectation, and suasion are enough to maintain order. Hamilton played down the fear of crime among his neighbors and claimed that he himself wouldn't be scared even if he didn't carry a gun, but he did carry one, and he was also an imposing man with a black belt and plenty of experience in physical confrontations. Other people in South Shore, law-abiding people who didn't consider themselves badasses, also told me they were comfortable in the neighborhood and that fear of crime was greatly exaggerated, but they also spoke at great length about the precautions they took and the sensitivity of their trouble radar, and none of them would have taken a leisurely stroll along 71st or 79th Street at two in the morning. Only Hamilton and David would do that, and then only if they had to, and they would think it foolish to go unarmed. Further, I can imagine that difficulties might arise within even the most well-intentioned coalition of upright citizens if some were to disagree with the purveyors of righteous force as to who qualifies as riffraff, or if some were to suggest to said purveyors that identifying people as riffraff may not in fact be the most useful response to the effects of large-scale social, economic, and cultural forces.

In fairness to Hamilton, he was not merely a purveyor of righteous force, nor did he regard as an enemy every young man who gets involved with gangs or runs afoul of the law. He hadn't settled for lamenting how messed-up kids are today; he had tried to do something about it, one kid at a time, and he'd done far more than his share. Since the mid-1970s, he'd taken in more than 110 foster children, mostly troubled adolescent boys whose lives were teetering between descent into the criminal underclass and a shot at something better. Hamilton, who said he also had five biological children and had never been married, ran an intensely male household—though he'd had a few foster daughters and helped care for their babies. A cross between a barracks and a monastery (his brother was a Catholic priest), his home offered stability, belonging, and a plenipotent father figure.

Hamilton dabbled in gang life himself as a teenager. Raised in Detroit, where his father was chief medical officer for the Ford Motor Company and his mother an assistant school principal, Gerald spent summers in Chicago, falling in with the notorious Blackstone Rangers. "It was fun and games with me," he said, and he didn't apologize for it. As he saw it in retrospect, he had the Blackstone Rangers in much the same way that his future partner David Lemieux had the Black Panthers, and both groups were at least sticking up for black people and black neighborhoods. Hamilton's version of history featured the era of the virtuous gang, "when you had to have heart to represent the hood," followed by a decline in the age of crack, when "the gangs wasn't even really gangs anymore," instead becoming "mini drug cartels." He moved on from the Blackstone Rangers to Chicago State University and the University of Illinois at Chicago, playing on both schools' basketball teams, before joining the police in 1985. He did well in the academy and, given his pick of postings, chose the Third District so that he could police his own neighborhood, working in the tactical and gang units until he made detective in 1998.

He attributed his success in life, in part, to the fact that both of his parents had ties to Mound Bayou, Mississippi, where he was born. Mound Bayou is famous for its history as a self-governing independent community of slaves and then former slaves, for its tradition of precocious insistence on civil rights, and for how well its sons and daughters have done up north. "People from Mound Bayou think different, with a more positive outlook," Hamilton told me. "My theory is that they saw mayors, lawyers, doctors who looked like them, and gained a level of confidence and inspiration different from most blacks of the South." This is a pretty fair lay approximation of neighborhood effects theory, in which a place helps inculcate and reinforce habits of mind that persist into later life and influence outcomes. He said, "I still feel the benefit now of being told when I was young, 'You don't have to think you're better that everyone else, but you know you are as good as everyone else.'"

I dropped by Hamilton's house on a rainy day in October 2015, the day after the evening I'd spent catching up with Maurice and inspecting the bullets in his wall. The house, in which Hamilton had lived since 1977, was white with bright green trim, with a basketball court in back and an American flag out front. His black Crown Vic with the police searchlight was parked at the end of the driveway by the street: *I'm home; riffraff, beware.* A spear-point-tipped iron fence, also green, enclosed his lot and the one next door, on which sat the formerly abandoned house he had bought five years before and was fixing up so that he could expand his household beyond the usual half-dozen foster children. Somebody was running a power tool in there, and a pair of hands emerged from an open window, working on the frame from within. There was a long-faced African figurine on the stairless front stoop, in the spot by the front door where in the bungalow belt you sometimes see a white lawn jockey. Hamilton stood on the sidewalk, all in black again, this time a dress shirt and pleated slacks. Now sixty, he looked as bluff and capable as ever, and surveyed his houses and grounds with evident satisfaction. What he had wasn't as grand as Maurice's holdings, but it was still his castle, a miniature city-state.

Inside Hamilton's house, a couple of young men were watching an action movie on a massive TV; Randall, a former resident, now thirty, had dropped by for a visit and was in the kitchen eating a bowl of cereal. They go through a lot of cereal at Hamilton House. Hamilton led me downstairs to his room. There was a sign on the door that read: "Old age and treachery overcomes youth, skill, and speed every time. —Old Chicago Police proverb." The walls were lined with shelves holding old-school soul CDs and action-movie DVDs. While we talked, buzzers and bells went off regularly somewhere nearby; his phone buzzed frequently and occasionally made a Klaxon noise like a submarine's dive alarm. He kept an eye on a screen that showed what the security cameras upstairs were looking at. He was always checking the time because he maintains an endless to-do list: a school pickup, a drop-off at the doctor, check on somebody else, get X from Y and bring to Z.

Like Maurice, at the other end of the neighborhood, Hamilton was feeling optimistic about recent developments in South Shore. Rumors (false, as it turned out) were going around that construction might begin soon at Lakeside, and he wanted to make sure that his foster sons, current as well as older alumni, got in on the jobs. The new Seventh Ward alderman, Greg Mitchell, seemed to have energy and character; Hamilton and his "soldiers," as he called his corps of foster children, had worked on Mitchell's behalf during the campaign. (He also lined up man-and-van work for them to assist in evictions.) Hamilton was encouraged by the launch of the *South Shore Current*, the monthly magazine expressly intended to counter the neighborhood's reputation for violent crime with depictions of it as the lively, affordable, and culturally sophisticated Soul Coast. "People just have to have a vision," he said. "People have to have a little faith. If they build it, they will come." He had friends who owned commercial real estate who were readying themselves for an upturn, including a buddy who had recently bought the old hardware store on 71st Street, Wilson Brothers, where my family once bought its nails and batteries.

He believed that crime—and the fear of crime—in his corner of South Shore was down. "There's a couple little pockets," he said, "but everybody seems to think things are on the upswing. I mean, there's cocaine to buy, don't get me wrong, but it's not crime like fightin' every day, blood running in the street. If you start making the business strips viable, they'll go away." The South Side in general might still be in trouble, even deepening trouble, but he was convinced that South Shore was finally coming back. One sign of it, he noted, was that over the previous two years "six new Caucasian neighbors" had moved into his area. "It's happening," he said. "They could go to a place with a demographic that looks like them, people at the same economic level, but they're realizing what they can get here for the money, and it means something that they find this a safe enough place for their kids." He told me about a white neighbor named Dave who took his young family for a walk to the lakefront every day. "We've become bonded," said Hamilton. "I've been to his church. I don't want to be all 'It's *white* people comin' around here!' but yeah, you know, it tells you something. I won't be around to see it all, but it's obviously a boom comin', no question about that."

When he showed me out, we paused to look over his block. As long-serving block club president, he was well satisfied with recent progress. Formerly abandoned houses had filled up, some with owners, some with tenants. New neighbors with housing vouchers had blended in. "If you're living on the fourteenth floor of the project, you've never cut a lawn or shoveled snow, but they tend to rise to the norm," he said. "There's some across the street, and we shoveled their snow the first time, and they got the idea." He pointed out a house across the street on which he had his eye. "I got seven bedrooms now, raising these guys," he said, "and we'll expand to next door, then maybe across to there." Spiderwebs and other Halloween decorations festooned a house down the block. Cars were parked in a solid row along the curb. He pointed out the place where a "little Ecuadorian neighbor" had moved in. "I was exposed to diversity in my life, coming up, so I like that," he said. "And these are good neighbors—do things for each other, help out."

Right before I left, in darker counterpoint to all this optimism and good news, Hamilton stepped back into his house for a moment and emerged with a dusty yellow metal cartridge case, identified by a stenciled label on its front as a box of .30 caliber M16 ammunition. It was full of long, ugly-beautiful bullets that looked like miniature missiles, forty or fifty of them. He had found it behind the plaster in a wall of the house he was fixing up. "Some guy who was in Vietnam probably stashed them in there," he said. "Thinkin' 'bout protecting himself." A boom, an upswing, whatever, might be on the way, but the bullets in the walls were a reminder that retired cops and cops' sons weren't necessarily the only citizens of South Shore who thought it wise to be armed.

*

Two former cops and a cop's son do not make for a representative sample of South Shore's gun owners, not that I intend Lemieux, Maurice, and Hamilton as such. But they do exemplify impulses and ideas that were widespread in the neighborhood. All sorts of people there, across the political spectrum, told me that they were in favor of law-abiding citizens securing concealed carry licenses. Val Free, the community organizer who lived in a Section 8 building in Parkside, was one of them, even though she also complained about the media's overemphasis on violent crime. Concealed carry for law-abiding citizens also made sense to Free's friend Adele Stadeker, who lived in O'Keeffe and, when I met her, was trying to organize a cotillion to teach old-fashioned etiquette to local teenagers. Neither of these two women had the income or property to identify with the haves, and neither subscribed to Maurice's apocalyptic conservatism or Lemieux's Marxian social critique, but they did share the opinion that life in South Shore might improve if more good citizens carried guns.

Something similar has traditionally held true for law-and-order sympathies in the neighborhood, though even the strong and disproportionately influential pro-police inclination of middle-class residents has been tempered by recent events. While I was working on this book, the Black Lives Matter movement grew more vocal across the nation, and the many voices in Chicago speaking out against police shootings of young black men eventually led the mayor to fire the police commissioner. There were at least four controversial police shootings in South Shore, and protests in the streets after the release of dash-cam and body camera footage of two of them. The first shows cops blazing away at Paul O'Neal, an eighteen-year-old from Parkside, after he tried to crash a stolen Jaguar through a police blockade on Merrill Avenue in Bryn Mawr East on July 28, 2016. This lethal mayhem takes place against a backdrop of well-kept houses and lawns, with officers trampling the flowers in a tidy yard as they check a colleague for wounds under his body armor while O'Neal bleeds out in custody nearby. The second video shows a typical 71st Street sidewalk encounter that escalated into a fatal shooting on August 14, 2018. Police officers who noticed a telltale bulge under the shirt of a thirty-seven-year-old barber named Harith Augustus close in on him on 71st east of Jeffery, an altercation ensues (at this writing, the lack of audio in the video released so far by the police department makes it difficult to determine what happened), Augustus reveals the holstered gun on his hip as he tries to flee, and as his right hand drops toward that hip an officer opens fire. The ensuing protests made the national news, with some in the crowd throwing rocks and bottles and some police swinging batons and roughing up protesters— including Jedidiah Brown, who suffered an arm injury and was arrested. In addition to whatever else they might tell us about the police and the black inner city, such incidents are also worst-case examples of the dynamic that has developed as the receding middle class ceases to play its once-dominant role in enforcing the neighborhood's public order. When the police try to fill the vacuum, encounters between them and the have-nots still out on the street can turn violent.

Even amid all the outrage over police shootings, there was still plenty of support in South Shore for the notion that cops need to come down hard on the element even if it means busting some heads and violating a few rights. Ava St. Claire told me, "When Glenn Evans was around, he was like, 'I'm gonna do what I'm gonna do,' and people were like, 'That's okay with us. Do what you do.'" She had a beat-up car a few years back, and the police used to stop her all the time, but the hassle of being pulled over was worth it, she said, if that was the price of a strong police presence. That St. Claire was married to a sheriff's deputy didn't make her assessment any less authoritative, nor did it make her atypical. A lot of black cops have lived in South Shore. The first headquarters of the Afro-American Patrolmen's League was at 71st Street and Jeffery. People spoke wistfully to me of a bungalow block in Bryn Mawr East that boasted at least three cops and was therefore presumed to enjoy an edge in firepower and attention to its 911 calls.

Some residents of the Jackson Park Highlands, who felt especially besieged by robbers and thieves and entitled to police protection, ranked among the neighborhood's most vocal supporters of get-tough policing. During a conference call with Evans's successor as Third District commander, James Jones, residents of the Highlands urged him to crack down harder on the crews of young men who were coming into the neighborhood from Parkside and other parts of South Shore. "We want you stop them at the border, shake them up, and send them back where they came from," one impassioned resident said. When Jones failed to wholeheartedly commit on the spot to this policy, another participant in the call chimed in to say that they were simply asking for the same service that neighborhoods on the North Side receive as a matter of course. The Highlands had long been the most integrated part of South Shore, and its white residents tended to be careful not to appear to be asking the police to profile young black men and use force on them. They were especially sensitive to black neighbors' complaints that their teenage children were harassed by the police. But some black residents of the Highlands bluntly called for the cops to come down hard on the young hangers-out they called thugs, clowns, ninjas, riffraff, or the element— and if the occasional innocent teen got rousted by mistake, that was just the price of freedom from fear of crime.

Michael Javen Fortner's timely book *Black Silent Majority* was attracting a good deal of attention in the fall of 2015. Fortner argues that in the 1960s and 1970s middle-class and working-class black New Yorkers upset about disorder in their inner-city neighborhoods played an important role in the rise of the get-tough ideology, aggressive policing, and harsh sentencing of the so-called wars on crime and drugs. My conversations in South Shore frequently confirmed that this tradition was alive and well in Chicago a half century later. Even amid the rising outcry over police practices in the black inner city, people were telling me that the problem was not enough policing, rather than too much.

Many of them turned to gun ownership to remedy the state's inattention to their welfare. A gun in the hands or home of a city dweller is a concentrated dose of force embodying the assumption that civil society won't work, the catch being that the gun's presence itself makes civil society that much less likely to work. That's why I don't believe that more men with guns—as opposed to, say, more women and men who go to meetings—will do South Shore any good. This conviction, of course, bears the marks of my own particular experience.

We had our share of break-ins, robberies, and other criminal drama. The first episode I can remember occurred when we lived on Oglesby, when I was about seven years old. The thieves broke in and stole, among other things, a walkie-talkie set. The veteran cop who sat heavily on one of our kitchen chairs said he recognized "the m.o. of a salt-and-pepper team" who were working the neighborhood. I remember digesting the new vocabulary, and noting that the tired-looking Irish cop and his younger, fitter black partner were themselves a salt-and-pepper team. Sometime not long after, I was playing ball in front of the house with my brothers when a pair of hard-looking young men, one black and one stringy-haired and white, came down the block, one on each sidewalk, cracking wise to each other on what I immediately recognized as our walkie-talkies. I never said a word to anybody about it. The lesson of the episode seemed obvious to me: people will routinely do bad things to you and get away with it, so why complain? We called the police when we had to, and they usually came, but I never put much faith in their ability to put things right. When they showed up, it was because something bad had already happened, and the best they could do was to help clean up.

Burglaries were relatively rare incursions into our fortress, disturbing reminders that the walls could be breached, as was the spectacularly awful occasion when home invaders shot up our community-minded, God-fearing next-door neighbors, who still somehow managed to repel them with their bare hands. More common were face-to-face hassles in the street, falling along a spectrum of transactions that ran from barbed badinage to out-and-out assault. On one end of the spectrum were routine and often pro forma nuisances on the order of "Can I get a ride on your bike?"—which I regarded as an insult because the speaker affected to take you for the kind of poltroon who would loan his bike to a stranger and expect to ever see it again. On the spectrum's other end were assailants like a kung fu enthusiast who came out of the bushes in textbook flying-kick position and blasted my little brother off his bike. I absorbed a few medically inconsequential but intellectually formative whacks of my own, including a blow to the head with a cut-off broom handle delivered circa 1975 by a kid wearing a pajama top featuring a motif of horses' heads. I can see those horses' heads now, and hear the sharp report of the broom handle breaking over my skull, and smell the leather tang of my baseball glove as I folded over it in my driveway and hung on, knowing that my assailant would have to give up tugging at it when the cavalry arrived in the form of my older brother and other kids on the block.

None of this, and none of the chases and standoffs and tussles that grew more serious and spread over a larger area of the South Side as I passed into my teens, ever made me crave my own gun. It might have been different if somebody had stuck one in my face, but that never happened. And it mattered a great deal that my father had no apparent desire to become a man with a gun. In potentially troublesome public encounters, he modeled for his sons an attitude that began with minding his own business—he's Sicilian, after all—but nuanced it with a tacit promise of unyielding will, a kind of confidence that managed not to come across as a challenge to anyone's manhood while still suggesting that any confrontation could become awkward or difficult for even a much more powerful opponent.

He didn't feel the need for a gun to fix what was wrong with the world, the complex of greater disorders and insecurities of which crime often serves as the iceberg's tip. He and my mother were immigrants made good, arriving with more ambition than resources and moving up in American life according to the traditional itinerary—minus the eventual move to the suburbs. Being immigrants, not to mention doctoral students as well as parents with full-time jobs, insulated them from many of the upheavals of the 1960s and 1970s. As my mother tells it, "We missed a lot of it; we were busy." Like their whiteness, their immigrant outlook and ties to the University of Chicago to some extent insulated them from South Shore, too. They were moving up, and their kids were equipping themselves to continue moving up by acquiring good educations, none of them in neighborhood schools. We didn't share the growing insecurity and precariousness of many black homeowners in South Shore, who increasingly felt squeezed from above and dragged down from below, and therefore worried about crime and bad schools not just as immediate threats but as potential impediments to their children's middle-class futures. We also didn't share Gerald Hamilton's commitment to the neighborhood as a place to save. We did try to be good neighbors in all the usual unofficial and official ways; even I took my turn snow-blowing sidewalks for the Jackson Park Highlands Association, and I rode around in a car at night a few times with my father when he did his neighborhood watch duty. But we invested ourselves in the neighborhood only to the extent that a commitment to community didn't interfere with our main project, which was forting-up in our house and making our primary commitment to school—the family business, and our path to success. You don't need a gun for that.

When we moved to a bigger house in the Highlands in 1973, we sold our bungalow on Oglesby to my parents' good friends Emil and Carol, who were among the last white buyers of the era in that part of South Shore. They involved themselves deeply in neighborhood life for the better part of two decades—helping to run community organizations, pressuring landlords to repair or sell firetrap apartment buildings where drug dealers and prostitutes did business, buying another house on the block and fixing it up to rent out—but they decided enough was enough sometime after a kid from around the way tried to rob Emil at gunpoint outside a store on 71st Street. Emil, a big man but gentle and slow to anger, surprised himself by grabbing the kid and wrestling the gun away from him. The kid took off running; the drug dealers from the corner, having gathered around to watch a white-haired Chicago Swede mix it up with one of their customers, were yelling, "Shoot him! Shoot him!" The gun turned out to be a heavy plastic fake, much to Emil's relief. The drug dealers, who apparently felt that amateur armed robberies were bad for business, gave the kid's name and address to the police, but no arrest was ever made. Emil and Carol bought an apartment with a grand lake view in a high-rise in Hyde Park.

Once, when I was a teenager, I came upon a gun in a drawer during a visit to Emil and Carol in our old house on Oglesby. The compact revolver looked to me like a toy. I didn't pick it up. Guns didn't, and don't, exert any special pull on me. However, I recognize that things could have turned out differently. After all, Emil was a grad school friend of my father's, with similar educational opportunities and upward-tending prospects, and he ended up as a man with a gun. Fear of crime and sensitivity to disorder are subject to neighborhood effects; they're aspects of inner life shaped by where you live and what you experience there. If I had stayed in South Shore instead of remaining on the East Coast after college, if I had come home to Chicago and still lived in my family's house in the Highlands, if I felt that my family's fortunes were made uncertain by the neighborhood and whatever forces were acting on it, and especially if someone with a gun had threatened me or my loved ones, I could easily have ended up deciding that I couldn't afford to go naked. Then I would be a man with a gun and I'd be a different person, writing a different book.

EQUIPMENT FOR LIVING

PULP

"Smokes in here, huh? Tie that for me, pal."

You know how sometimes at the beginning of a play or movie with archaic diction—Shakespeare, say—you suffer a moment of panic in which you can tell the actors are speaking English but you can't make sense of the lines? You may even turn to a companion and hiss, "I can't understand a *word* they're *saying*." After a minute or so, you calm down as you realize that your ears and mind are adjusting to process the unfamiliar usages, but that first flush of disorientation feels something like having a stroke.

That's pretty much how I reacted when I first picked up Raymond Chandler's *Farewell, My Lovely* at the age of twelve or so. In the opening scene, Philip Marlowe runs into a giant pale stranger on the sidewalk outside Florian's, "a dine and dice emporium" (I had to pause over that phrase for a moment to let its meaning soak in) on Central Avenue in Los Angeles. The introductory description of Moose Malloy—fresh out of prison and turned out in his finest, from shaggy Borsalino hat to alligator shoes with white explosions on the toes—culminates in one of Chandler's most famous similes: "Even on Central Avenue, not the quietest dressed street in the world, he was about as inconspicuous as a tarantula on a slice of angel food cake."

I was distracted from appreciating the virtuosity of Chandler's language by the anxiety that Malloy's catastrophic judgment raised in me. The flash getup, the combative manner, his sheer size—the doom-seeking salience of the man—all struck me as a comprehensive failure of urban technique. You go around like that, people will notice you, and

pull feeling of simultaneous recognition and strangeness formed the heart of the experience of reading pulp fiction.

*

Between crime stories, noir, espionage, adventure, Westerns, science fiction, horror, and fantasy, I picked up much of my equipment for living in pulp fiction, especially mapmaking tools and sensors for detecting overlapping orders. The more common term for it these days is genre fiction, but a lot of the best stuff I read—stories by Chandler, Dashiell Hammett, Robert E. Howard, H. P. Lovecraft, C. L. Moore, Clark Ashton Smith, Edgar Rice Burroughs—was reprinted from the original pulps, and the more recent work registered their influence. In my travels through this literature, I regularly made my way through passages that, like the opening of *Farewell, My Lovely*, struck me as clearly about and yet also not at all about the world I lived in—about black people and white people and also six-limbed green people who laid eggs and rode ill-tempered giant lizards, about places where one order impinged on another and all sorts of conflict and creative possibility and other sparks arose at the points of contact. Pulp fiction framed situations I recognized as freakish analogues and experimental exaggerations of life on the South Side.

Pulp fiction was so full of unstable situations in which one order overlapped, succeeded, or otherwise dynamically engaged another that I began to recognize such instability as a necessary precondition for generating narrative. Central Avenue went from white to black, enabling Marlowe and the Moose to meet cute. Gunfighters and settlers and Indians were sent banging around like pinballs as the frontier closed, opened again farther west, closed again, opened again down Mexico way or in outer space. Lancers and spies and planet-hopping galactic operatives propped up empires in decay, holding off massed hill tribes and rival great powers alike.

Fantasy, especially, offered endless variations of this basic dynamic of instability. At the noir end of the genre, where lust and greed and severed limbs trailing founts of smoking gore were the order of the day, a Conan story would begin with, say, our hero serving as a mercenary in the employ of a juicily proportioned, alabaster-skinned young queen

when people notice you . . . *things* can happen. I was a habitual slider-by, an aspiring master of encouraging . . . *things* not to happen, adept at finding the shadows and defiladed dead spots in any terrain, even an open sidewalk in the midafternoon sun.

And, even allowing for the literary conventions of a bygone era, I had trouble processing Malloy's militant insistence on making a big deal about having a problem with black people. I had to puzzle for a while over his first line of dialogue. Did "Smokes in here" have something to do with the lit cigar tucked away, forgotten, between his sausage-like fingers? And what about "Tie that for me, pal"? Was he too big to reach his own shoelaces? Was there some other accoutrement, perhaps smoking related, commonly carried or worn by men of the time that required tying and that he couldn't tie himself or that for some unaccountable reason he wanted to force Marlowe to tie? Finally I arrived—reluctantly, still unbelieving—at the conclusion that Malloy was expressing surprised disapproval of the presence of black people in Florian's. The novel's first sentence tells us that we're on one of the "blocks that are not yet all Negro," and as a child of South Shore I had been lightning-swift to pick up the implication that we were talking about white guys in a black neighborhood. That part I had no trouble understanding.

But Malloy's objection struck me as perverse—reacting against the presence of black people seemed akin to railing against gravity or the sun rising in the east—and for the life of me, I couldn't understand why anyone in his position, no matter how big he was, would say something in public about it, which he does not just once but several times. Continuing to marvel over the change in the clientele and management of Florian's during his absence, he calls it "a dinge joint" and a "shine box." I had to puzzle over those for a bit as well. Did the place need dusting? Were we back on shoes? Everything about Malloy threw me: his grotesque prominence of body and manner, his diction and his reckless commitment to inflammatory race talk, the way that his gravitational field pulls the judiciously circumspect Marlowe into the drama. His world resembled mine closely enough to make his judgment incomprehensible to me, and yet the plot didn't punish him for this lapse with instant annihilation, which suggested that results could vary. This push-

who rules a city-state in which a haughty brown aristocracy lords it over a restive black majority. It was just a matter of time before everybody would be slaughtering everybody else in the streets. Conan—promoted to captain of the guard by the beleaguered queen after she chanced to see him do something like dispatch a half-dozen murderous bravos by clouting them with a tankard and a chine of beef—would be in the thick of it, laying about him with notched and dripping ax atop a charnel heap of dead foemen. At the music-of-the-spheres end of the genre, where mind-fry metaphysics held sway, the royal family of Roger Zelazny's Amber lost its political and philosophical confidence as rivals from the far pole of the universe mounted a challenge to its multidimensional dominion, and Michael Moorcock's Eternal Champion cycle cast humankind as coarse insurgents struggling to displace pale, narrow-skulled ancient races in hyper-refined decline. Elves, dwarves, demons and witches, red and green and white and black and headless Martians, dragons, gods, telepathic insects, clouds of ectoplasmic force—beings of all descriptions went at it with any weapon that could be imagined, but the setup was usually recognizable as some variation on "There goes the neighborhood."

This was true even when there was no competing order in view, when there was just the one way things had always been. Conan and John Carter and their many brothers in arms were always stumbling across a remote city, cut off from the rest of the world, where things had remained the same for centuries. There was usually some kind of exchange in which a grandee of the long-lost place would ask a question along the lines of "Tell me, traveler from out of the unknown west, does Palamides the Great still rule in Armacoy?" And our hero would say or, if sensing that to say it might dangerously disturb his fey or possibly bewitched hosts, merely think wonderingly to himself, "But Great Palamides, first of his dynastic line, has been moldering in his rune-sealed crypt these thousand years and more, and Armacoy lies in ruins, as it has since the savage Zavars sacked it and put every man, woman, and child to the sword in the time of Palamides the Fourteenth." The hero's arrival in the long-lost city predictably set in train a series of events that brought the whole hermetic arrangement crashing down, revealing the creeping rot that, behind a façade of immemorial permanence, had gradually hollowed out the status quo. Even the most static-seeming arrangement proved to have been in latent motion after all, primed to collapse when an action hero came along to give it a shove.

I found it edifying, if troubling, to keep encountering the principle that the solidest-seeming ground was actually shifting and sliding underfoot, cozy familiarity forever giving way to sudden disorienting shifts in perspective. There's Marlowe in *The Little Sister*'s opening pages, cooling his heels in his office, as ever, just as I would kill long idle hours in the empty halls of my school in the afternoons, running out the clock on the day. It seems that Marlowe's in perfect private-eye stasis, but then Orfamay Quest—the murderous small-town ingenue in rimless cheaters and a hat that has been taken from its mother too young—comes calling, and it turns out that the two of them have been spiraling toward each other at a terrific pace the whole time.

*

When I looked up from whatever book I was trying to disappear into, something similar went for the South Side. There was, on the face of things, an eternal horizon-to-horizon sameness to life. The pent-up, watchful, faintly buzzing stillness of trim residential blocks and the sluggish hive of cut-rate activity along the badly faded commercial strip of 71st Street seemed like permanent attributes. There was the bus to school and the bus home, the routine of scanning for sideways-worn Pittsburgh Pirates hats before choosing to alight at my usual stop at 69th and Jeffery or stay on for another block or two and thus steal a march on the junior gangsters who sometimes trolled the boulevard for prey. There were the same books shelved in the same places in the aisles of the South Shore branch of the Chicago Public Library and Powell's used bookstore in Hyde Park. Occasionally a book disappeared or a new one appeared, but most of them stayed right where they were, exuding a sweet woody musk of decay. On weekend nights I hung out with schoolmates in Hyde Park, crisscrossing the landscape in all weathers—the Blocks to the Point, the Cove to the Midway—while addressing in stylized cant the perpetually urgent question of what was totally intense and what abjectly bogus. There were, and would always be, songs by

Led Zeppelin and Earth, Wind and Fire on the radio, and Magic Slim played Tuesdays and Thursdays at the Checkerboard Lounge for a dollar at the door and a dollar for a Stroh's. There were still, occasionally, chamber concerts and trips to the symphony or opera with my parents; and, just as I had when I was a small child, each time I would assemble my faculties as the conductor stalked out to applause and the prefatory hush fell and then the music began, and away I would go into whatever dreamscape I had prepared, like a spell, for the occasion. This was how it was because this was how it had always been. As far as I knew, Great Palamides still ruled in Armacoy.

But that was just on the face of things; down below, gears were grinding. My discovery of the relentless structural movement that makes pulp fiction go comported with a slow-forming awareness of myself as a mote crawling across the surface of a South Side that was itself in motion, shifting and changing even when it appeared not to be. There were signs that the neighborhood had once been different—a scattering of older Jewish and Irish residents who hadn't left, a dwindling handful of businesses on 71st Street that had served them in the past. The bakery where we got our strawberry-veined birthday cakes was run by a German-Dutch family who had for decades been hushing up the German side of their heritage and playing up their Dutchness, even though the time was long gone when residents of South Shore might have a problem with Germans or even make distinctions between different kinds of white people. At some point I picked up James T. Farrell's Studs Lonigan trilogy and had to get my head around the premise that it was about a white guy who had moved to South Shore to get *away* from black people. I vaguely understood there to have been many white people in South Shore at some point and had somehow formed an impression of Warner Bros. urchins in flat caps and knickers picking up stray lumps of coal along the Illinois Central tracks, but the full realization was slow in coming. It had once been theirs, and they had lost it, or given it up. It occurred to me now and again to wonder to what extent they regretted quitting on a good thing and to what extent they felt themselves to have been pushed out.

IC trains still ran down 71st Street, but the place to which they went, the concentration of steel mills and other heavy industry massed below South Shore on the East Side, was at long last going cold and falling into ruin. The details were obscure to me, but one could feel deep reverberations from down there as ponderous, slow-tipping dominos finally went over. When anything that big comes down, I vaguely sensed, it has to have consequences, but I couldn't pick them out from among the field of troubles that produced gas station lines and anxious news talk about stagflation (which caused me, trained by the frequent appearance of stags in fantasy fiction, to picture some kind of pumped-up elk). For instance, did it have anything to do with kids from my neighborhood who had gone to Lab with me switching over to South Shore High or some other public school? I didn't really want to ask, and if it came up, they'd just say, "Oh, man, you know, something with my dad and his job." South Shore's government workers seemed to be hanging on for the moment, backed up by their public-sector unions, but others looked to be slipping, caught up in some kind of comprehensive culling of the poorer-than-rich-and-richer-than-poor occurring on a scale so vast that it was difficult to get in view, let alone understand.

At the Checkerboard Lounge, the southern migrants were aging out, and their generational successors were moving away from down-home blues styles, some of them mating wailing rock-inflected guitar to thumb-popping funky bass. The younger players didn't want to grow up to be Muddy Waters, the grand old man of Chicago blues, who came around less and less often and was running out of gas in a dignified, sorrowful kind of way. The younger players idolized George Benson or Jimi Hendrix or Billy Ocean. On the radio, Deep Purple was giving way to the Police, Frampton to Devo, the O'Jays and Isleys to Jeffrey Osborne, Teena Marie, Prince, and novelty songs in which a guy just talked about himself in stilted rhyme the whole time. At school, the middle of the road was still crowded with the usual suspects wearing Grateful Dead and Pink Floyd concert shirts under the traditional flannel shirt, but new enthusiasms were showing up. There was keyboard-heavy New Wave and the floppy angular haircuts and dubiously intentional wardrobe (why own fingerless gloves in Chicago?) that went with it, and people who as far as you knew couldn't even play an instrument were suddenly in punk bands, and there were alligator shirts and Reagan and coke and other insurgencies as different waves of joiners cut themselves out of the high seventies herd.

I have names now for some of the larger-scale flows of people and capital and power and ideas that were at work on the South Side: deindustrialization and the maturing of the postindustrial service and information economy that succeeded the factories and the world they made; the final phases and aftermath of the two great folk migrations that brought black southerners to the northern inner city and white city people to the suburbs; the decline and fall of the New Deal order. These movements had swept over the neighborhood and transformed it, were still transforming it. The order I grew up accepting as the way things had always been had, in fact, been thrown together a few minutes before I showed up—was, in fact, being thrown together around me, and also already falling apart as fast as it could be assembled.

"Let's you and me nibble one," Moose Malloy says to Marlowe when they finally reach the bar at Florian's. I had to ponder that enigmatic line, too, although fluency in stoner talk equipped me to recognize it as an invitation to drink. I felt almost dizzy, watching them step to the rail and get their whiskey sours in the breathless hush between spasms of stylized mayhem in which Malloy crushes a bouncer who tries to stop him from entering and breaks the neck of a manager who tries to shoot him. Now I recognize the source of my vertigo. In the bar, as the two men nibble one, it appears that nothing much is happening at that precise moment, but all around them the world is in violent motion, spinning through a constellation of changes that the two men, broodingly lost in their own pulp thoughts, can perceive only in fleeting strobe-like glimpses.

THE DIVIDE

"On my block, literally the first five or six houses on our side is middle class," Ava St. Claire told me. "There's a gay architect, an older couple, Kellogg"—that is, a neighbor affiliated with Northwestern University's school of management—"and then us, and then, *boom*, there's a guy counting his stash. One side is *Leave it to Beaver*; the other side is *The Wire*." St. Claire, trained in both design and urban planning, created the light pole banners that went up on South Shore's main commercial streets in the spring of 2016. Some of the banners touted the neighborhood's amenities, and others bore inspirational quotes by native sons and daughters, including Michelle Obama ("Success is only meaningful and enjoyable if it feels like your own"), the former senator Carol Moseley Braun, the tech billionaire Larry Ellison, and the playwright David Mamet ("There's no such thing as talent; you just have to work hard enough"). Given the neighborhood's prominent class divide, the striving theme shared by the quotes raised fundamental questions about who gets to succeed, and the split St. Claire described on her block raised fundamental questions about neighboring. She said, "There's so much tension between the haves and the have-nots. Do I forge relationships with people on the other side of the block? Will they know when I'm not home and take our shit, or will they be my friend and protect it?" Were people on the other side of the class divide neighbors or strangers?

"South Shore may look like a high-class community," said Ulysses "U.S." Floyd, "but it's poverty here, no jobs, low education, no resources." Floyd, a former gang member of advanced middle years, supervised outreach workers at the South Shore office of CeaseFire Illinois, a branch of the nationwide Cure Violence organization, which treats shootings like a contagious disease. "It's a lot of crime here, and no resources—like no training to be a carpenter, an electrician," he went on. "And the big one is lack of community involvement." CeaseFire had staged two anti-violence marches in South Shore during the previous month, he said. "You know who came out? White college students came down from DePaul, Northwestern. Not people of my color who live around here. They scared to come out, or they don't care." He got up from his desk chair, and we looked out the back windows of his office, in a small corner strip mall at 75th Street and Cregier Avenue. Clients of the mental health clinic next door congregated in the narrow parking lot, one or another occasionally approaching the glass to peer into the CeaseFire office. Beyond them, we could see down Cregier, two neat rows of bungalows drowsing in the late June sun. "They got the grass cut, homes look real nice," said Floyd. "Look at the houses! Look at the cars! They don't care unless it happens to them, somebody kill they son. We don't have the community support, and this is a community problem. They're not organized here. You can put this in your thing"—my book, he meant—"and you can say I said it: They. Don't. Care."

Like "project people destroyed the neighborhood," "bungalow people don't care" is a tale told across a social and cultural divide within black Chicago. This divide dates back to before the CHA's Plan for Transformation in the late 1990s, back to the formation of black South Shore in the 1960s and, even before that, to the relocation crises of the 1950s (when "project people" was not yet a category to conjure with) that set black elites against poor blacks who sought to follow them into the bungalow belt from the kitchenette buildings of the Black Belt. There's variation across different tellings of both kinds of tales, which tend to sacrifice nuance and accuracy in favor of explanatory force. Some versions of the tale of the coming of the project people put primary blame on the newcomers themselves. Other versions depict them as victims of policymakers and allied business interests who shunted them into South Shore and refused to provide them with adequate services or opportunities to succeed. As for the story of bungalow people's relative lack of engagement with the poor people living in their neighborhood, some versions stress their fear and loathing or indifference, while others point out that some of those bungalow owners are living paycheck to paycheck themselves, upside down on their mortgages and downwardly mobile, too beset to address other people's problems.

However you understand its causes and meanings, the divide is evident. You can feel its presence as you pass back and forth between the bungalow landscape of homeowners and denser agglomerations of apartment buildings filled with renters using housing vouchers. You physically inhabit an avatar of the divide when you walk down the alley behind Cregier Avenue that separates the near-mansions of the Highlands from the boarded-up rear windows of HUD-administered apartment buildings in Parkside.

The divide shows up in the numbers, too. The neighborhood's median income in the 2010 census was $27,903, with roughly 16,000 households below the poverty line and 3,400 or so with incomes over $75,000. Half of the neighborhood's children fell below the poverty line, and nearly all students in its public grade schools qualified for free or reduced-rate lunches. I've mentioned before that South Shore's numbers of PhDs *and* high school dropouts significantly exceed the city's averages. Similarly, in addition to its thousand-plus Chicago bungalows, South Shore has many two-flats and houses that are larger or built in a different style, but it also has more households receiving housing assistance than any other community area. Only about 250 families directly relocated to South Shore from public housing as a result of the CHA's Plan for Transformation, but their arrival around the turn of the millennium focused the attention of many in South Shore on all of its federal Housing Choice Voucher holders, more than ten times that number. If you include the holders of all the various kinds of housing vouchers, it's more like twenty times. In 2015, 5,096 households in South Shore held a HUD or CHA housing voucher or occupied public housing, and in 2016 South Shore led all community areas in evictions.

Consider these numbers in combination with shifts happening further up the social scale. While South Shore's small percentage of high-income residents has held steady or slipped just slightly, its percentage of middle-class residents fell from 52% in 1980 to 31% in 2010–14, with a concomitant rise in lower-class percentage from 39% to 63%. Meanwhile, the ratios that track the neighborhood's relative inequality have shot up since 1980, outpacing county and national ratios. That's why South Shore's a good place to look if you want to form an advance impression of what urban America's going to be like when we have successfully completed our current generations-long project of undoing the postwar growth in the middle class that was made possible by the confluence of economic and geopolitical good fortune and a titanic exercise in social engineering. And you can see it all in one place, which is less true of white neighborhoods, where the haves are more successful in arranging to live far from the have-nots.

As rough and desperate as things can get in parts of South Shore, nobody's rushing to pour resources into the neighborhood to head off social catastrophe, especially when the situation's apparently a lot more desperate elsewhere in the city. And yet, people in quiet, green South Shore are riding out the consequences of profound changes in the form and function of city life that have produced the stark divide between haves and have-nots that is the neighborhood's most important feature these days.

It can take a bit of effort, an adjustment of sight lines and habits of thought, to cross to the other side of the divide. When you break the surface tension that helps keep you on your side, you feel it viscerally—a little shock, like the *boom* Ava St. Claire imagined in moving from one side of her block to the other. It's not that each side is invisible to the other; it's that each side has a ready-made template to make sense of the other, and people on both sides have become used to unseeing whatever doesn't fit that template. When I was talking with a young man named Aaron Brown, it came as news to him that the area in which I once lived that began not more than a hundred feet from where he had lived in Parkside was called the Jackson Park Highlands. Growing up, he and his friends had called it "the white neighborhood" or "the rich white neighborhood," even though most of its residents were black. They had vaguely assumed that only white people could live in houses so opulent and well-fortified, and after all they did see white faces there, which was uncommon for South Shore. He and his friends just put the handiest available template over the lush paradise on the other side of the alley.

Crossing the divide in the other direction, from the side of the haves to that of the have-nots, means pushing through another veil of conventional wisdom, one that's reinforced by the haves' dominance of public conversation in the neighborhood. Because homeowners set the terms of that conversation and do almost all the talking, the voices of people who are not middle class are almost never heard. For a native of middle-class South Shore like me, moving into the world of the neighborhood's poor and working-class residents can feel like passing through the looking glass.

*

On a warm spring morning in 2016, there were seventy-five or so people waiting for the food pantry to open in the parish house of St. Philip Neri at 72nd and Merrill, with more arriving. Among them were many senior citizens and several young adults, a couple of moms with little kids, a few people who were obviously drunk or high, and many who looked tired and used to waiting. Except for two white regulars, a big weather-beaten bearded man who spent his days hanging out on 71st Street and a desperately frail old woman who fainted in the sun and had to be taken home, everybody was black. Most of those waiting had formed a line along the paved walkway between the parish house and the church. Several had brought rolling grocery carts or spavined suitcases to transport their food home, some had brought folding chairs or other portable seats for the wait, and one had a wheeled molded-plastic office chair that answered both demands. Greetings were exchanged, cigarettes cadged; there was talk of the fine weather, some muted joking around. One woman near the front of the line said heatedly, "Some people got *no* manners, *no* class. This is it for me. I'm not coming back here after today." She seemed to expect a sympathetic response from a woman standing next to her, and when she didn't get it, she said, "And *you* have a *good* day," and turned away, stiff with offended respectability.

Fred Batts was giving out numbers to clients on ragged paper slips, organizing the waiting crowd into groups of ten—all there was room for at a time in the parish house's basement, where the food was. Batts, who had a forbearing, grizzled face and walked with a limp, explained things to me as he handed out numbers. The Greater Chicago Food Depository supplied most of the food, including fresh meat. The St. Philip Neri pantry was open every Tuesday from 10:00 a.m. to noon, and clients could come to it no more than once per month. Filling me in on the background, Batts told me the usual story of a wave of invaders from the projects bringing down South Shore. He didn't lump all former residents of CHA housing in that category, though, since he himself had grown up in the Cabrini-Green projects. In search of a nicer place to live, he had come to South Shore in 1967, the same year my family moved there. The neighborhood had been undone, as he saw it, by rampant criminality and drug and alcohol abuse, all encouraged and even rewarded by misguided government policies. He told me the story of the W. Clement and Jessie V. Stone Foundation giving a million dollars to the notorious Jeff Fort, leader of the Blackstone Rangers and its successors the Black P Stone Nation and El Rukns, and of Fort using the money to take over the old Southmoor Hotel building at 67th and Stony Island. The story, which was mostly true in its essence if not in every detail, encapsulated for Batts the crux of everything that had gone lastingly wrong during the Great Society years. Remarking on the number of seemingly able-bodied young men in line, he said, "Some of them robbing and stealing *and* coming here."

A man named Bobby, who said he was sixty-eight years old, was sitting in the sun with a friend near the back of the line. He said he had moved with his parents to South Shore from Bronzeville, the old Black Belt, in 1971. His parents thought that South Shore would be a better place to live, he said. "At the time we came out here, everything was green and clean. It was a whole different way of life. Through the years it has changed ten times over. They have let everybody in. It's no longer quality stores. It's a food desert. They still sell hair on 71st, and that's it. And it's no cap on owners raising the rent. It's their right, but there has to be some kind of regulation." The most egregious change, as he saw it, was the decay of community. "There's no unity," he said. "Homeowners pull together, renters squawk but they don't stand up,

homeowners lookin' at renters as part of the problem, people from projects need to find a place to live, but our youth has run amok." He made
a fence with his hands as he said, "We need to *corral* them." He insisted
that it wasn't right to let bad apples ruin the reputation of all voucher
holders. "I would like to get in that voucher program myself," he added.
"Sounds like a good deal."

Anita, who was waiting alone not far from Bobby, said she had moved
to South Shore from Hyde Park in 1965, when her father got sick with
lung cancer and had to go on disability. A friend of her mother's had
offered them an apartment in a building she owned at 68th and East
End in Parkside. The adjustment had been rough for Anita. "We didn't
have gangs in Hyde Park, and I had to run home, from boys *and* girls,"
she said. "I was an honors student when I came to South Shore, but I
became an honors in how to fight. My mother made me fight that girl,
said, 'Get back out there.'" But Anita had grown to love the neighborhood, and she had fond memories of the after-school social center, the
YMCA, police-sponsored youth programs, and other such institutions
that had filled her days with social activity when she was young. She
also looked back fondly to the time when shops thrived on 71st Street.
"I worked for a lot of stores on 71st Street," she said. "Social organizations, too." While she still found the neighborhood physically pleasant
and comfortable, she said, "I don't have anything to do with the people
who moved in, from a different class." Other senior citizens in the building at 70th and the lake where she now lived were afraid to walk on
71st, but she wasn't. She said, "I don't have anything to do with the drug
business and all that, and they see me, they know me, I'm just doin' my
errands." Like others in line, she cherished a distinction between the
respectable poor, especially longtime residents who had quietly fallen
into straitened circumstances, and the loudly uncultured criminal poor.

Anita's rendition of the story of the invasion of the unrespectable
poor emphasized their abandonment by the state rather than their
moral culpability. "When they emptied the projects out, they messed
up because they didn't show them housekeeping," she said. "They had
a concentration camp, 'cause that's what it was, and they let them out.
That's what this neighborhood is now, projects people and from the

West Side. They got the forty acres, but no mule"—they got housing, in other words, but no services and not much chance at meaningful employment. She felt keenly the decline of commitment to community and the institutions that fostered it, and she traced that decline to these newcomers' arrival in the neighborhood, but she didn't exactly blame them for it. "They did their time," she said. "Their unity in the projects was 'We take care of ourselves, forget everybody else.' So now, as far as being active, they don't do any of that." She took it as indicative of their disengagement that she never saw them at the local police district's monthly community briefings and information-gathering sessions, known as CAPS (Chicago Alternative Policing Strategy) meetings, and that elected officials ignored them because they didn't vote. "You gotta go talk to your alderman, your congressman, you got to show them you're involved, you're voting," she said. That was simple commonsense citizenship in Chicago, where poor people's main leverage was the power of electoral numbers to command respect in the city's deep-rooted systems of patronage and favor.

When the lonesome wailing of the civil defense sirens rose and fell in the distance, the crowd shifted murmurously, getting ready to move. The sirens, once a harbinger of Cold War apocalypse but now resonant of twenty-first-century worries like extreme weather and terrorism, are tested on the first Tuesday morning of every month. Fred Batts let the clients in the back door ten at a time, and they filed down the narrow back stairs. Volunteers at a card table checked in each one, making sure it had been a month since his or her last visit. A black Jesus with a modest Afro, wearing a white robe and a knowing half-smile, looked down from a painting on the wall. Posted rules prohibited cursing, abusive language, violent behavior, gang paraphernalia, weapons, and intoxication. Volunteers helped the clients take their share of fruit, vegetables, canned goods, meat, pasta, farina, and other supplies arranged on shelves and in bins. It took a couple of hours to get everyone through the line; 109 clients in all.

Upstairs in a meeting room, down the hall from a painting of a queenly black Madonna with a shirtless boy Jesus in her lap, some of the food pantry's longtime volunteers sat around a table and talked about their clients and the neighborhood. They were all of retirement age and had all lived in South Shore for decades. Jackie Drew, who had the no-nonsense manner of a guy habitually in the know, offered some numbers. Their pool of clients was 99.9% black, evenly divided between male and female, about 75% housing voucher holders. The poorest of them moved frequently in and out of the neighborhood and within it, their lives made transient by evictions and other such crises. As with South Shore in general, average income was an opaque number because there was such a wide range. "Average for us is around $14,000," he said, "but some are retired bus drivers or teachers with pensions, maybe $20,000, fifteen, and others have nothing. There are some men trying to get by on a public aid check of $76 a month." The 25% who worked tended to make the same rock-bottom salary year after year in the same kinds of contingent dead-end jobs: fast food, security guard. "They're stuck," he said, "and we're not linked to organizations that would provide services like job training to get them out of it."

Ruthie Stewart, a statuesque woman in a classic church lady's pink blouse, added, "The other services aren't there, either, especially mental health, drugs and alcohol treatment. We have a big drug and alcohol population in South Shore, and that prevents them from looking long-term." Drew added, "This is a food desert. Some people come to us just because of that. Where are you gonna get fresh produce other than here? The Arabs don't sell it"—by which he meant the convenience stores, many owned by people of Middle Eastern descent, that are known as "Arab stores." Some of the food pantry's clients had a pension or other retirement benefit, but it wasn't enough to make ends meet. Stewart said, "The food pantry still holds a stigma for pensioners. These are only the people who have overcome the stigma. I live in a senior building on Oglesby between Sixty-Seventh and Sixty-Eighth, and I see none of them here." In other words, there was even more hunger and poverty among South Shore's elderly than one could see from here.

It can feel like an abstraction to say that the neighborhood's middle class is hollowing out, but visiting the food pantry at St. Philip Neri made that abstraction very concrete. The people who ran it represented the aging-out postwar middle class who came to South Shore long ago and raised their kids there, launching them into the wider world via college and careers. They were not rich, but they were haves compared to their clients. Some of those clients, especially the older ones, had once been in that middle class or aspired to it, and still identified with it and clung to its notions of respectability, but they had fallen on hard times, often because their fixed income in retirement wasn't enough to see them through. The younger clients represented the cohort that should be replacing the aging middle but would never make it anywhere near that shrinking, increasingly remote promised land. The food pantry's volunteers understood themselves to be performing a Christian labor, shoveling against the structural tide of a changing social and economic order to help people who were left behind with little prospect of securing decent work, a decent retirement, a viable life.

As the volunteers saw it, most of the neighborhood's haves and leaders weren't doing much to help, and often couldn't even see—or didn't want to see—what was going on. "South Shore is very puzzling," said Ruthie Stewart. "You have this set of people that flourish and they kind of take over. You don't know what's going on around you." Everyday poverty disappears into invisibility when homeowners steer the neighborhood's public conversation to their favored talking points—crime, property values, development, why things aren't nicer. Jackie Drew added that nobody was bringing up the have-nots' problems at the alderman's meetings. "We talk about better street lighting, not fixing what's really wrong," he said. "Our leadership has not been good. Hyde Park gets everything, South Shore gets nothing." I heard that a lot. It was about as far as most people who participated in public life in the Fifth Ward would go in criticizing Leslie Hairston, who had been alderman for a long time and had a long memory.

Evelyn Hatch, who moved to South Shore in 1966 and started the food pantry in 1969, said she had sent all three of her children to St. Philip Neri's school. "I've been here for fifty years," she said. "Our kids was some of the first black kids over here, and we ran into some few normal prejudice." But it hadn't been so bad, she said. Everybody had found a way to get along. "It used to be a very, very good neighborhood to raise kids, and it still is good, but the change has come—maybe twice it's turned over," she went on. "You have a lot of people my age. The church is an older church now. But there's still block clubs, women's clubs—"

"No," said Adrienne Hubbard, who lived at 73rd and Oglesby, interrupting. "We were together as a block in the 1970s, but as time has gone on, the closeness has gone. My kids grew up and moved on. In the seventies, eighties, it was no such thing as not knowing your neighbors."

A polite disagreement ensued. Hatch gently stressed the persistence of community and connection; Hubbard, smaller and brisker in manner, said the days of strong block clubs and widespread neighborliness were gone. Hatch commanded a great deal of respect among the food pantry's volunteers, but on this matter they tended to agree with Hubbard. A conviction that the quality of community has declined since an elapsed golden age is so widely held that it almost qualifies as an essential component of a belief in the importance of community. This holds true not just among older people in South Shore today but among all sorts of people in all sorts of places and times. It's not just nostalgia that nurtures this conviction of community's decline; the decline formula seems to make it easier to understand and explain a difficult, changing world, satisfying a craving for an efficacious way to narrate past and present. Like Fred Batts, who blamed the neighborhood's problems on Jeff Fort and his enablers, like Bobby and Anita and others who blamed project people and West Siders and the authorities who marooned them in South Shore, like everybody with a story to tell about what had happened to the neighborhood, they were trying to articulate the meaning of that long line snaking between the church and the parish house on Tuesday mornings.

*

U.S. Floyd took me to a makeshift sidewalk memorial on the 7800 block of East End Avenue, not far from the corner of 79th Street. There was a metal stand holding bedraggled flowers and a warped rectangle of white poster board covered with scrawled condolences, signatures, and RIPs. The memorial had been out in the sun and rain for more than a week. There was a cross standing on the ground in front of the stand, with an empty Jose Cuervo bottle lined up next to it. Ten days earlier at just about this time in the afternoon, a twenty-year-old named Demetrius Archer had been sitting on a chair on this spot, hanging out. A light-colored SUV had pulled up, and a man got out and shot Archer, then stood over him and shot him several more times, making sure. Archer's murder headed a list of recent shootings on a sheet of paper on Floyd's desk at the CeaseFire office: "78th East End, 1 killed (internal); 79th Exchange, 3 shot, 1 grazed; 79th Essex, 2 shot (internal); 74th South Shore Drive, 1 killed, 1 shot, 1 grazed (retaliation)." The "(internal)" notation meant that Archer had likely been killed by a member of his own crew, the result of an intramural beef. In the blank space below the end of the list was a skull-and-crossbones doodle.

Seventy-Ninth and East End had the reputation of being a problem corner. It was late afternoon when we arrived, and the scene was picking up momentum. Older men and women came and went from the liquor store around the corner on 79th, hunting along the block for shaded spots in which to kick back with a drink and watch the show. Younger guys, many wearing their hair in braids, were starting to gather, engaging in ritual handshakes, posing along the curb for passing cars. Some of the cars stopped, windows lowered, for a word or a swift hand-to-hand exchange. This was happening on a tree-lined block of reasonably trim-looking walk-up apartment buildings, several with recently cut lawns. It didn't look like the kind of block that would host a nightly festival of open-air dereliction and criminality that lasted into the wee hours. At the end of the block, across 79th, rose up the graceful Moorish Revival hulk of the old Avalon, a long-shuttered vaudeville theater. At one point during our visit, a tour bus pulled up in front of it and a bunch of white people got out, took pictures of the historic building for a few minutes, got back on the bus, and rolled away.

I asked Floyd why building owners and residents on East End didn't call the cops every day to pressure the hangout scene to move on. "Most of 'em too scared to come out or call the police," he said. "They think something's gonna happen to them if they do." He said it contemptuously, plainly convinced that they were cowards, and that the trifling gangsters we've got these days weren't organized enough to exact retribution.

Floyd, a squat guy with gray braids and unruly teeth who looks as if he has given and taken some hard knocks over the years, greeted a couple of hangers-out by name as he made his way to the memorial. They responded cordially but moved away. "The funeral was only yesterday," he told me. "They still grievin', not ready to talk." I wondered how it felt to be the perennial raven at the picnic. Floyd's black Cure Violence T-shirt offered a reminder to all that he was there because somebody had been shot and somebody else was next. His OG manner offered a reminder that even he, a hard-core gang member for decades, had gotten out of the street life because it offered no viable future. He commanded respect because he had made his bones on the street and done his time in prison, and because in his reformed second life as a professional violence interrupter he had demonstrated his commitment to saving others. But, still, his very presence said, *You're throwing away your life out here, and you better change your ways before it's too late.*

A driver of about Floyd's age, turning across the sidewalk to enter an alley, noticed Floyd's T-shirt and called out from the open window of his car, "How do we cure violence?" The car stopped and Floyd went over to talk. The driver, who owned a store on the next street, pulled back his ball cap to reveal a healing wound on his temple and told Floyd that he had been hit in the head with a pipe the other day. He had just been minding his business, he said, and some guy had come at him out of nowhere. Floyd explained that the Cure Violence approach treats violence like a disease, detecting a developing outbreak and interrupting transmission by changing the norm. "We try to find the main person who's likely to spread it, and concentrate on stopping it there," he said. Outreach workers each have a caseload of "participants," aged sixteen to twenty-four, who are deemed by virtue of their records and associates to be at highest risk of shooting someone or being shot. Once one of these vectors of the disease agrees to become a participant, outreach workers provide conflict resolution and anger management counseling, school tutoring, job training, help with job seeking, mental health services—whatever's needed. The driver wished Floyd good luck and pulled away. It seemed to me that he'd had in mind something a little more along the lines of an eye for an eye.

After a shooting, CeaseFire operatives rush to identify anybody who might be looking to get even—a wounded victim, family members, friends, fellow gang members—and try to talk them out of it. The interrupters' authority to do so stems from having been in the street life themselves. "We try to get people who used to be with a group, what they call a credible messenger," Floyd told me. He had started off in Chatham in his mid-teens as a gang foot soldier and moved up, making a career of it. He described himself as a founding member of the Gangster Disciples. "Black Gangster Disciple Nation—that's *old* school," he said. "In the seventies, I was a king, the highest level you can reach in a Chicago gang. I destroyed communities, people, families. There's no statute of limitations on murder, so I have to be careful what I say, but let's put it this way: I put in a lot of work." He said, "I'm not proud of it," but that seemed at best a partial truth. Like many other reformed criminals who work with gangs, he took obvious lingering pride in his street credentials, and he shared with his former Blackstone Ranger enemy Gerald Hamilton their generation's wishful nostalgia for a golden age of neighborhood-affirming gangs: "When we started, we was just trying to protect the community."

But a couple of stretches in the penitentiary had given Floyd plenty of time to reflect on his street career, and he had realized that he didn't want his children, or anyone else's, to be dragged into his wake. He came to see that he had been spreading the disease of violence for four decades. Deciding that he wanted to "stop being part of the problem" and do "something positive" to control its spread, he got involved in anti-violence work and went back to school to get his college degree. When I met him in June 2016, he had been with CeaseFire for eleven years and had worked all over the South Side. He said that cuts in state funding had reduced CeaseFire Illinois from twenty-three sites to just three, all privately funded. Murders and shootings had risen significantly over the previous year, and the South Side of Chicago was generally regarded as synonymous with urban gun violence in America, but at that moment there was money for Floyd's office to operate only for the rest of the summer.

Two of Floyd's outreach workers and violence interrupters stopped by the memorial to talk with us. Jerusha Normand, known as Rue, had a forthright manner and purple dye in her tightly coiffed hair; James Sims was lean and reserved. They both had grown up in South Shore and carried themselves with the earnest confidence of young adults who have already made a momentous change of direction in life. Each maintained a caseload of fifteen to twenty high-risk participants, and they were also Floyd's social media experts, monitoring online activities for warning signs like argumentative back-and-forth, inflammatory video, and smoking-gun emojis. This gave them a way to detect incipient beefs, and it also helped them cope with the chaos brought on by a generational split in gang culture. Older participants often still identified with traditional gangs and the larger combines with which they allied themselves, principally the Stones and Gangster Disciples, but younger ones tended to hang in looser, more informal, and fragmentary cliques. Rue cited the example of No Limit, which she and her colleagues regarded as South Shore's most dangerous gang. She said, "They're still Stones, but they do what they want to do." One renegade No Limit branch had even allied with a splinter group of Gangster Disciples, the Stones' nominal blood rivals, to form the hybrid NLMB, the No Limit Muskegon Boyz. "Or look down on Seventy-First and Clyde, Merrill, Chappell, Paxton," she went on. "The Four Corner Hustlers was hangin' there, but somebody ran them off, and now you just got Merrill Boys, Pax Town, or whatever." Young people's penchant for turning even their most intimate and illegal activities into data and posting it online made it a little easier to track the shifting mess of allegiances and enmities.

Mounted on the wall back at the office were maps of South Shore marked with red dots to indicate hot spots. Most were on the corners of the neighborhood's depressed commercial main streets: 79th, 75th, 71st. "This is one of them right here," said James, gesturing around us. "Alcoholics, gangbangers selling rock, weed."

Floyd said, "We're in Beat 414," a patrol sector of the Fourth District, "and this a GD block. But look at the buildings, look at those lawns." Violence could erupt out of all sorts of fertile ground. "When I came down here after this young man got shot," said Floyd, gesturing at Demetrius Archer's memorial, "I was trying to keep people calm, and an old man came out and said he owned an apartment building right over there. He was asking what happened, so I told him. Old man said, 'If any of these people out here causes any trouble, I'll bust a cap on him, 'cause I got a gun, too.'"

This got Rue and James going on the complicating truth that not everybody pulled into violence and the street life was poor or without options. "The boy who just got killed right here came from a very nice family," said Rue. "He wouldn't go to school, he wouldn't get a job, but his sister is very educated." Herbert Wright, better known as G Herbo or Lil Herb—a South Shore native making a national name for himself as a bloodthirsty drill rapper whose videos featured his NLMB compadres crowding in front of the camera to mime gunning down enemies—also came from non-desperate circumstances. "Lil Herb family own a house on Seventy-Sixth and Euclid," said Rue. "He was—I don't want to say a nerd, growin' up, but he was a school boy. A lot of these kids have two parents at home." The standard narrative of the neighborhood's decline tended to conflate "the element" with "project people" and indeed all voucher holders, but it wasn't that simple. Kids from families leading middle-class lives, and not just those from downwardly mobile families being squeezed out of the shrinking middle, could slide into the street life along with poor ones. There weren't many resources committed to preventing this from happening. James said, "There's nothing for young people to do here—no activities and no job or training programs."

Back in the car, driving away from 79th and East End, Floyd said, "I been to a couple of meetings where people around here said they scared to march and show they face. People in Woodlawn are like, 'Yeah, let's stop this,' and they got a tradition of great community organizing. But in South Shore, they ain't out here helpin', not unless somebody kill they son. You don't see that many people with a vested interest in the community. When you try to reach out and talk to them, knock on they door, they in never-never land: 'That's not me.'" We rolled on through the neighborhood's distinctive patchwork of trim residential blocks, desolate commercial main streets, and hot-spot corners. He said, "South Shore will bite you. You see these nice houses, grass cut, picket fences, but it will bite you. It's all quiet, and then *pop-pop-pop-pop!*"

*

On weekdays when Samala Brown got home with her two young daughters after picking them up at their after-school program, the girls would change clothes, have a snack, finish their homework, and settle in for the evening. Changing clothes was an important step in the routine; Brown didn't like the thought of the outside world, even unseen traces of it clinging to their clothes, getting into the family's apartment on the 7700 block of South Kingston in Terror Town. Sitting with me in the living room—which was large but spare, with couch, love seat, and chairs pushed to the walls to leave an expanse of open wood floor—she made a gesture that took in the room as she said, "This is it for us. Most of the time, we're right here. We read; my girls love Goosebumps. We talk. We play Monopoly. We have movie nights. We spend time together, eat dinner as a family, and the girls have bedtime at nine."

It was a warm weekday afternoon in early June 2016. Her daughters were still in school. The living room windows were open, and music and men's voices, shouting and laughing, came in from the street below. The daily hangout scene in front of the building was starting up—old men and young men drinking, smoking and selling weed, passing the hours. "We usually don't even open the windows, because so much comes in," she said. "We don't talk like that. And then music and social media." Musically, she liked to "keep things as old school as possible: Marvin Gaye, Stevie Wonder, John Coltrane," and the same went for morality. Diligent industry, sacrifice for the good of the family, and the patient deferral of gratification were the household's touchstone virtues. Modesty, too. She no longer wore the revealing tube tops she had favored in her twenties, she said, and her husband, Lincoln, wore a belt and didn't let his pants sag. She disapproved of much of what her children heard on the radio, much of what came in through the windows and via computer and phone screens. So she had been aghast when her daughters came home one day singing Sage the Gemini's woman-hating "Red Nose" and doing a grinding dance that went with it, having picked it up from schoolmates' cellphone videos. She wanted to keep all that out, and she wanted to keep her kids out of the line of fire in Terror Town, all of which meant keeping them under close supervision. They spent their time in the apartment, in school, at their after-school program at the Rebecca K. Crown Youth Center, or in the car; almost never out on a street or sidewalk, if she could help it. "If I'm leavin' out of the house, it's because I'm going to work, parking in the back, or going to pick up the girls or my husband at work," she said. "We barely use the front door. Too much going on out there." The bikes the girls had won three years before in a contest at the Crown Center were still in mint condition because they were almost never allowed to ride them. Brown drove the girls to school every morning—just two blocks, but she was too worried about stray bullets to let them walk, even accompanied by her husband or herself.

Forty-three years old, petite, with tight braids and precise manners, Brown also had two adult children—a daughter who lived with the family, and a son in Natchez, Mississippi. Brown drove the daughter to 79th and Jeffery every day to catch the bus that took her to work. When her son had lived at home, she had driven him everywhere, too. "He used to play basketball and I'd go watch him, bring drinks and snacks," she said. "One time at Eckersall"—a park at 82nd and Yates—"there was a shootout while he was playing. I was so terrified. What if? I only have one son. For him to be young and male, with all that's going on. I wanted to get him away from the whole guilt by association thing."

Samala Brown was doing her best to become an example of how the housing voucher program should work: you get in the program in a time of need, you use it to get on your feet and become a more solid citizen, you get out of the program. In 2000 she came to South Shore from Englewood as a single mother of two young children—fighting with her own mother and no longer able to live in her parents' home, looking for a better neighborhood in which to raise her kids, not able to make enough money to support her young family, reaching her wits' end. "Section Eight was a blessing to me," she said, allowing her and her children to have their own place while she went back to school to get her Certified Nursing Assistant certificate. There had been days back then when she had to deny herself meals to put food on the table for her kids, but she hoped those days were well behind her. Her union job as a home health-care worker provided health insurance and other benefits, and she filled in the financial gaps by part-timing as a driver for Uber and Lyft. Her husband cut hair at a barber shop on 71st Street. If they were careful with money and their luck held, they could not only support themselves but put something aside each month toward a down payment and furniture for their own home and a rainy day fund. The objective was self-reliance.

"I've been on government assistance for a while, and I'm ready to say, 'Thank you but I don't need it anymore,'" she told me. "I'm trying to get everything together now so I won't need Section Eight anymore. I purchase a home, and somebody else who needs the voucher gets it." HUD describes its Housing Choice Vouchers program, known as Section 8, as assisting "very low-income families, the elderly, and the disabled to afford decent, safe, and sanitary housing in the private market." Rather than aiming to collect the poor as a class in massive public housing projects, it exemplifies the general tendency of the past forty years in both policy and social science to put primary emphasis on individual choice and market forces—though those with vouchers still tend to end up concentrated in a few neighborhoods, much as the projects were. In Brown's case, the policy had worked, helping to usher her into South Shore, a good marriage that had produced two more children, a chance at raising a family according to values that had become clearer to her with maturity, and one last shot at upward mobility. "Section Eight was really good to me," she said. "There was a time when I really, really needed it. I wasn't ready to be a responsible adult. But my husband is my Section Eight now. If I'm not that hungry now, I don't need the whole meal, or maybe any of it."

Buying a first house and making your move up into the middle class has long been a signature South Shore ambition, and Brown liked to indulge in the traditional neighborhood pastime of cruising through its bungalow blocks to look at scrupulously maintained houses and imagine living in them, but she and her husband were looking to make their move elsewhere, in the south suburbs. "I came from Englewood, and it's always been that Englewood had a bad reputation," she said, "and I wanted to be in a different area to give my children a chance to play outside," but South Shore, so green and enticingly peaceful-looking at first blush, had disappointed her. "I don't think it really started to get bad, in my eyes, until about two years ago," she said. "When we first moved to this apartment, we let the kids play outside. Now we only let them look outside for a weekend activity. There's people hangin' out, people selling drugs. The kids come home and say, 'Oh, they were shootin' by the school today.' Just like that, no surprise."

Brown shunned not only public space but the public sphere, public life in general. She had nothing to do with any neighborhood organizations and didn't even know if there were any, nor did she have much faith in government. "In all honesty, I'm not committed to the neighborhood," she said. "I've seen so much to change my mind. Just the fact that my babies can't walk to school."

When I asked why she wanted to leave South Shore, the condition of its public schools came first on her list. "The system has really deteriorated," she said, citing class sizes approaching forty students at her daughters' school. "And I have to keep runnin' up to the school to make sure my daughter is safe. She can't concentrate on school because she was gettin' beat up every other day. These two boys were after her, wouldn't let her be. The teacher was new, a . . ."—she hesitated apologetically, and waited until I had waved a hand to indicate no offense before she went on—". . . white lady. She couldn't keep order." The tension at school had begun to spill over into the fortified retreat of the home, affecting the daughter's mood, how she talked and acted with her parents. "It took her to a dark place, out of character," said Brown. Such a tainting of their home life was her worst nightmare. "I had to stay on them at the school," she said, "and get them to let her switch classes even though it was late in the year. I had to basically quit my job, get disrespectful and loud, to get taken seriously. I'm not a loud person, but I had to do it." She loved the Crown Center, a crisply managed after-school program for poor families that offered a well-equipped gym, a maker lab with 3D printers, a responsive staff, and a rich assortment of offerings to reinforce and augment what kids were supposed to learn in school, but the Crown Center was privately funded, not a creature of the state.

Brown's skepticism about public authorities extended to the Chicago

Police Department. "With the last three break-ins we had, the last time was in January, they came out and made a report but no evidence tech showed up—and I had really good prints because they moved the TV in the bedroom to get the Xbox," she said. "I just don't have faith in the government right now. I just want some peace. I want to just lay across my bed and if I hear gunshots, it's not all day, every day. I want my girls to be able to go outside. There's a lot of sexual assault out there." The burglaries had been an especially disturbing invasion of the bubble of decency she had taken such pains to create. "It was the straw that broke the camel's back," she said. "They took the fifty-inch TV, okay. But they stripped my bed, opened the drawers, they went through my clothes and my underwear, they touched everything. I felt violated. I felt like I can't take it anymore. I mind my business, and I will give people my last. If you're hungry, I will feed you; if you need a ride, I will take you . . ."— and this generosity of spirit had been repaid with repeated violations of her home that the authorities could do nothing to prevent or punish. She wasn't primarily concerned about the problems of police brutality and racial profiling that had become so prominent in the national conversation about race and crime. She was worried about the ineffectiveness and indifference of the police.

The Section 8 program was a third aspect of government that had an important effect on her family's life, and though she profoundly appreciated the financial assistance represented by the voucher, she chafed at the prying that came with it. Resentment of "nosey" inspection routines and hoop-jumping requirements lent additional urgency to her resolve to give up her voucher. The whole family was looking forward to moving—to getting off government assistance, to being able to walk the streets without fear and play on the block, to going to suburban schools, to having nearby karate and dance lessons and all the other lifestyle resources not readily on offer in South Shore. Brown's parents had been a sterling example of how postwar prosperity had enabled the upwardly mobile working class to get in on the perks of middle-class life. Her father had worked in steel mills, she said, and her mother on the line at the Sweetheart Cup Corporation and then at St. Bernard's Hospital for twenty-five years. They'd been the only family on their block in Englewood with two nice cars, regularly trading in her mother's for a newer model, and when Samala had become envious of a piano-playing cousin, her father had bought her a piano of her own and paid for lessons downtown. Samala now pined for this old-school version of the good life and burned to reconstitute it as best she could, and she had once believed there was no likelier place to do that than South Shore. But no longer. She might yet claw her way back up into some contemporary rendition of middle-class existence, even as getting into and staying in the shrinking middle class grew more difficult, but she was sure that such a triumph would have to be achieved far from South Shore.

In some ways Samala Brown reminded me of Minnie, the older sister who precedes Carrie Meeber to Chicago from their Wisconsin town in *Sister Carrie*. By dint of hard work, thrift, and eschewing the city's lurid attractions in favor of a spare home life, Minnie and her husband, Hanson, a silent and steady-working man "of a clean, saving disposition," have managed to pay "a number of instalments on two lots far out on the West Side" on which they intend to build a house. Dreiser was writing about the late 1880s in the 1890s, of course, when the city's great bungalow-building era had not yet begun and the West Side was still a largely undeveloped blank slate on which to project aspirations. But the Browns' situation resembled the Hansons': If their luck held and they didn't weaken, they just might achieve the dream of homeownership and a middle-class life in the face of long odds arrayed against them by Chicago.

*

Adults keep kids much more tightly under their supervision than was the case when I was growing up, and parents in South Shore who think of themselves as good parents keep their kids especially close. It's commonly assumed in South Shore, and on much of the South Side and West Side, that there's a polar opposition between time in the street and any kind of meaningful shot at a viable future, so keeping children out of public space becomes a good parent's objective. That's especially the case when a family doesn't have the insulation from the street that middle-class life can provide. Samala Brown's protective routines and her larger retreat from the neighborhood's public sphere were symptomatic of an ethos I encountered all over South Shore. One way that the neighborhood's residents express its effect on them, one way the neighborhood lives in them, can be seen in the extent to which they and their children keep to private space, minimizing the extent to which they live in public space and inhabit the neighborhood as a community. Public space and public life aren't exactly congruent, especially in the internet age, but the overlap is significant: the physical realm is still an important component of neighborhood. It's hard to participate in or even care about the public life of the neighborhood if you don't spend any time with others in public space.

Micheline Holmes, a single mother who also had a child at the Crown Center, let her son play in the backyard of the building in which they lived at 70th and Crandon, but she wouldn't take him to a nearby park in the afternoon. There were too many people there, she felt, which meant too many potential conflicts that might escalate into violence that endangered bystanders. She would put him in the car and take him to a park in Hyde Park instead. "It used to be that you could just choose to be left out of the violence, but now there's nowhere [in South Shore] that's outside," she said. She wouldn't take him up to 71st Street, either, though she would go there herself to run an errand. "I am old enough to be ready to meet my fate," she said. "Not happy about it, but ready; but I'm not ready to put a child in that situation." Keeping her son out of public space in South Shore was part of a larger regime of caution: "I don't carry cash, no cards, no fancy car. I keep it quiet, no flash." So far, she said, "I have been fortunate. I'm thirty-five, almost thirty-six, and I've never been shot, beat up, or anything, or any of my siblings."

Unlike Samala Brown, Holmes had grown up in South Shore (having moved from West Englewood in the mid-1980s when she was five), had family living nearby, and thought of herself as an engaged neighbor. "I was taught that community is my business," she said. On election days, she reminded her neighbors to vote. But the business of community, and her forays into public space to conduct it, often took the form of sorties to head off prospective threats to the safety of the private space she shared with her son. When young men hung out in front of her basement apartment, she said, "I will go out and ask them, 'Do you live here?' Then I'll ask, 'Is anybody lookin' for y'all? You seen me with my baby, and if somebody shoots at you, there's a strong possibility the bullets come in here and hit us.'" She tried to be friendly in approaching them, but if they didn't move, she would call the police. Holmes's version of the neighborhood's history included the usual account of declining neighborliness—"the community over time lost its desire to be a community," she said, ascribing the loss to a "selfishness" based in "a false sense of success" too invested in material things and a frantic insistence on being busy that left no time for others—but the decline also extended to the character and style of the neighborhood's criminals. She had been a teenager during the epochal drug turf wars of the 1990s. "Now, there is no purpose, not even tryin' to make money," she said. "Just stupid beef." As she saw it, this debasement of gangster culture put bystanders in greater danger. "If you supposed to be a gangster, *be* a gangster," she said. "These guys are cowards, punks. They shoot runnin' backward, with their eyes closed, shoot everybody."

Sitting in her basement apartment on a warm spring day, her loose housedress stirring in the wind made by a big floor fan, Holmes said, "My son has not been exposed to the problems of our community." She said it with pride, but she also regretted the necessity of cutting him off from so much of the neighborhood. "He already kind of has what we call a 'bougie personality,'" she said, putting up finger quotes. She dreamed of moving to the suburbs and sending him to Niles West High School, which she regarded as an unattainable middle-class paradise of pep rallies, clubs, band, arts, debate, involved parents, and preppy sports like lacrosse that were higher-toned than the inner-city staples of basketball and football. If they stayed in South Shore, she had resolved to find a way to send him to a magnet, charter, or exam school outside the neighborhood. And if they stayed, she said, "We will stay for the things we do now. We walk to the beach early Saturday and Sunday mornings, take our shoes off, and go in the lake. It's early, just runners and bikers out, and we go around to avoid 71st and Jeffery." They would stay for the place, in other words, not the people; the container, not the community.

As a family engagement specialist at the Crown Center, Shontell Williams was in the business of building community. It was her job to get parents with kids at the center more involved as volunteers and active partners, and to help them deal with any problems that might affect their child's performance at school. She had a small windowless office, but part of her task was to get out there and see what families were dealing with, to mediate conflicts, solve problems, and increase the collective efficacy of the network of parents whose low incomes qualified their children to attend the Crown Center. Public life was her habitat and profession. But she had kept her own sons as close as she could, which meant keeping them out of public space. The older one attended Chicago Vocational High School, a few blocks south of South Shore, and the younger went to a neighborhood school in South Shore and to the Crown Center in the afternoons. They had played in their building with kids she knew, not out on the streets. She let them walk to the store, but kept strict tabs on them. Her older son had tested these limits but willingly returned to her supervision. "He's still a house boy to this day," she said. "He tried hangin' out, up on Seventy-Eighth and Phillips, and he didn't like it. I'll call him and say, 'What you doin' right now?' The freedom we had coming up, it's all different now. You *have* to watch your kids."

Williams grew up in the Stateway Gardens projects. "My mama let us run around at Stateway and we knew everybody," she said. All the kids there went to the same school and after-school center, and everyone knew her mother. The gangs were relatively easy to understand and deal with. She said, "When I was coming up, you was either GD or BD," Gangster Disciples or Black Disciples. "Gangs got all scrambled up when we left, and they are very unorganized now." When her family first arrived in South Shore in 1998, her brother had refused to go to the store because he didn't know whose turf he would have to cross. There had been other shocks of adjustment, but they had quickly learned the lay of the land. "We was on Seventy-Sixth and Yates, and it was nicer than Stateway, and you could walk," she said. "But then I found out after a while what was going on, and it was more like where we came from. People started tellin' us, 'Y'all livin' in *Terror Town.'*" Greenery and lakefront location notwithstanding, gangsters were gangsters. "The difference was they was *out*, not in the buildings," she said. She knew more than a dozen families from the projects living in South Shore. "For the most part, they're doing great," she said. "But you have to keep your kids close. It's not about the ghetto." You had to keep them close wherever you lived.

Nobody had kept Aaron Brown close, and he ended up hanging out on the street, headed for trouble, until Victoria Brady and others at ABJ Community Services—which provides programs for public aid recipients and fosters arts-based activism—pulled him through the keyhole. Brown's family (no relation to Samala) lived in the Robert Taylor Homes until he was eleven, then moved to 74th and Jeffery, then to Englewood, and then back to South Shore, settling in an apartment building at 67th and Cregier in Parkside. "It was six of us, and just my mom, and we was bad, fighting in the house, getting kicked out of school," he said. His mother worked way out at the airport, but she had to keep coming home to deal with discipline emergencies at school. When they first moved to South Shore from the projects, it felt very peaceful. He said, "I was like, 'Where is everybody?' Nobody out." But when they came back to South Shore and ended up in Parkside, the scene was much livelier. "It was even more crackin' than Englewood," he said. "There was kids everywhere." He decided to become the toughest guy around, a project for which he was only partially equipped. He was big and strong, a deep-chested, good-looking fellow, but his nature was too reflective and warm for the role he had picked.

I mentioned that, from what I had seen of the guys hanging around on South Shore's most notorious corners, they looked bored almost all the time, droopily staring at their phones as they whiled away the tedious hours. No wonder social media beefs turn into shooting wars; it at least gives everybody something to do. Brown said, "I used to get upset when people told me it was nothing going on, on my block." He laughed. "There *was* nothin', but I was waitin' for something to happen. I feel like it was childish, now." His path off the corner began with a summer program at ABJ, at 71st and Constance on the edge of the Highlands, when he was fourteen or fifteen. He had been arrested on suspicion of participating in a burglary, and he was on probation, obliged to attend. "I didn't want to be here," he said, gesturing around us. We were talking in a classroom at ABJ full of well-used computer equipment. "I came in the first room and there was no girls," he said. "But then I came into a second room, and I realized there was a lot of girls here, so I stayed."

Back then he didn't think he had any particular talents. He said, "I was like, I can't play basketball, I can't play football, everything I touch I break," but Victoria Brady, ABJ's executive director, kept telling him that everybody's good at something. Brown finally figured out that he was good at being competitive, fired up to prove that he was the best at acting, rapping, or any other activity at ABJ. He eventually straightened out at South Shore High, working hard in his classes, and grew away from the corner, taking any job he could find and throwing himself into mentoring kids at ABJ and other local organizations. He began dressing like a citizen, too. "I don't sag, I don't wear gym shoes," he said. "I wear slacks and loafers, button-up shirt tucked in my pants." Guys on the corner teased him about it, but he shrugged it off. He said, "When the joke's over, who's doing something with they life? Then they start asking if I can get them a job, and I put my name on the line for them, and they don't even show up. A lot of them are still out there in the street."

Married and casting around for a steady-earning career, he ended up in technical school, training to be an overhead electrical lineman. When we talked in the summer of 2016, he was about to graduate. With a friend from ABJ, he had also started a small business, a hip-hop greeting card outfit that provided original beats, words, and art on demand. Once he had his certificate from the tech school, Brown planned to work 24/7 for six months straight, traveling if necessary to find companies that needed emergency electrical workers and would pay overtime rates. His objective was to amass a pile of cash he could bring back to South Shore to use as a down payment on a house. "We are *by the lake*," he said. "The property value will go up as soon as the library come," by which he meant the Obama Presidential Center, which was just appearing on South Shore's horizon. He went on, "Everybody tellin' me, 'I'm fi'n to move, I'm a move to the suburbs,' but I'm like 'This is the place.'"

*

Aaron Brown, like Shontell Williams, was one of those near-mythical "project people" blamed by residents of South Shore for such a large proportion of the neighborhood's troubles. Both of them had eventually flourished in South Shore and contributed to it as a community in ways that confounded this conventional wisdom. They were gainfully employed, paying market-rate rent without a housing voucher, and, what's more, working via the Crown Center, ABJ, and other organizations to strengthen the neighborhood's anemic collective efficacy. And Samala Brown, a paragon of bourgeois propriety even if she didn't have the middle-class income to go with the mores, was a voucher holder, one of a large group who often get lumped together with former residents of CHA projects and "the element" into an undifferentiated invading army of barbarians. It's true that these three, and Micheline Holmes, may not be typical. After all, they number among the small minority who have benefited from contact with institutions specifically designed to help have-nots make progress against the structural grain of opportunity, which tends to consign them to a hard-to-escape loser's bracket of inferior schools and poorly paid work affording little chance of security or advancement. In that sense, they may even be exceptions. But their stories, like those I encountered at St. Philip Neri's food pantry and in the company of CeaseFire's violence interrupters, suggest that the prevailing versions of recent neighborhood history might obscure as much as they explain.

When I walked out of ABJ with Aaron Brown, we strolled a bit down the 7000 block of Constance, crossing the line separating the commercial dead zone of 71st Street from the verdant residential precincts of the Highlands. Brown, when he was growing up just across the alley and the social divide in Parkside, had pressed the Highlands into service as his own personal woo preserve. "It was my quiet place to take the girls," he told me. "My mother told me girls would like you if you show them something they never seen before. So I'd be with the hood girls, and I'd be, 'Let's go look at some flowers, let's take a walk.' There's a glass house on Euclid or Bennett. I used to walk past there and say, 'This gon' be my house.' Girls used to *love* that." While we were standing there, listening to birds calling back and forth as evening fell, he gave me a quick tutorial on the meaning of the variously colored cryptic markings left on the sidewalk and street by utility workers to indicate underground gas lines, water pipes, and other hidden structures. He had been equipped by experience and training to read the neighborhood's coded ground in ways I couldn't. If I paid attention, I could learn something.

EQUIPMENT FOR LIVING

BALL

For most players, pickup basketball is all about offensive virtuosity—expressive improvisation within a community of individuals, each vying to put the ball in the basket but also subsuming that urge to the cooperative beauty of the team game. For me, though, when I played in South Shore and across the greater South Side in my teens, it was all about spoiling my opponent's virtuosity. I appeared to be a model citizen of the jazzy little commonwealth of the pickup team because I performed needful tasks that other players, fixated on the universally acknowledged priority of racking up points, didn't feel like doing. In addition to playing defense on my man with irksome persistence, I passed the ball to teammates with care and sensitivity, boxed out and rebounded, fetched loose balls, tipped away opponents' passes, and ran the court on every possession. But my motives were selfish and uncivic: I was, at best, agnostic about the greater good of my teammates; at worst, hostilely indifferent to it. My basketball self, a bad person masquerading as a good neighbor, only incidentally made his teammates' lives better by making opponents' worse. Other than wanting to win so that I could stay on the court, I didn't give a rat's ass about my team.

Intent on holding my own by dragging my man down to my level, I regarded offense as wildly overrated, mere slavishness posing as inspiration, a company man's sorry campaign to make Employee of the Month. But defense, inherently soulful and underrated, was the serious business of denying your enemies their heart's desire, which was to visit woe upon you. Defense was burglar bars on the windows of your bungalow, looking out for yourself and letting the neighbors do whatever they had to do to look out for themselves. If they wanted to pool resources and cooperate, all the better, but you had to be ready for any such arrangement to break down into a state of everyone for himself.

*

I try to expect the best of people, not because I'm particularly optimistic or forgiving but because I believe that others respond to what you ask of them. So I make a policy of treating readers, students, colleagues, friends, family, neighbors—human beings in general—as if they're capable, observant, basically decent, willing to entertain complexity, and inclined to rise to the occasion, all to encourage them to conform to those expectations. But as a kid, I learned to do the opposite on the basketball court. Think of it as a very specific kind of neighborhood effects, showing up in my ball-playing habits and psyche. Because I hung out with serious players who tended to get me into games with stiffer competition than my modest abilities rated, I was obliged to cultivate the specialized skill of playing with and especially against one's betters, a skill that's not identical to being good at basketball. I had to get by when matched man-to-man against an opponent who could outscore me so badly that it would obviously be my fault if my team lost. I didn't care much about letting down the community of my teammates, but the threat of individual humiliation bothered me. Because I didn't want to repeatedly endure this kind of public thrashing, I had to coax the worst out of the other guy. Expecting, inviting my man to fail, I had to make myself his guide and mentor in failure.

I was well suited to the task. My shortcomings as a ballplayer mostly resulted from my own failure to make something of myself. I was physically competent and built for basketball—lean and long, with quick hands and a feel for the angles and flow of a game—but I never applied myself to practicing basic skills or otherwise developing my game. I just played, like a little kid. *Ooh, basketball! Can I play?* And I had plenty of opportunities to play. My brothers played, my neighborhood friends played, many of my schoolmates played; competence at basketball was expected of a game-playing boy in that place and time, especially one who wanted to be out and about on the South Side. Playing pickup ball was one way to get around and engage with people, not just on South Shore's circuit of driveway, backyard, and schoolyard courts but also farther afield. It gave me a plausible reason to show up with a crew somewhere I otherwise didn't belong, negotiate with strangers on the sideline to claim a spot in the game, and run the court with a confidence that transmuted it from a strange place to one found on my expanding map of the world. When you put your body in motion through the world, you learn something about your place in it.

Pickup ball's other main draw for me was the opportunity to spend time inside the workings of the game. This order of pleasure resembled grooving on the lay of the land: the familiar pattern of potholes and ruts in your alley; the advance of afternoon shade in the plaza with the verdigris-streaked sea-god fountain and the three-table café to which you kept finding your way down twisting side streets in a foreign city you visited years ago. Playing ball offered a similar dynamic of sizing up the prospect and becoming adept at getting around, but I navigated among features like *Abdul wants to do everything on the baseline these days* or *The guy with the muscles appears to have a jumper and a temper*. I never found a way to appreciate victory anywhere near as much as I enjoyed being inside the narrative and sensory world of the game in progress. The only meaningful reason to win was so that I could play again and spend more time in that world.

So I played and found satisfaction within the limits imposed by my shortcomings, but an opponent who figured out that I wasn't a complete player could usually break me down simply by playing unrelenting defense that exposed my deficiencies as a ball handler and shooter, and, on offense, by methodically posting up and using his body to force me to give ground. The only way for me to stop him then would be to foul him over and over, but that would be aesthetically distasteful and could lead to serious trouble, especially for a white guy playing on the South Side.

Working around this unforgiving calculus meant persuading my man that exerting himself to destroy me might prove too difficult or embarrassing to be worthwhile. I was forced to encourage the other man to fail, in other words, not because he wasn't good enough to beat me but because he could be led to tighten up, lose his head, freak out, chicken out, get stupid, try to disappear, or otherwise suffer a failure of imagination or nerve.

*

Just before a game started, we'd figure out who would cover who: *I got this man here. You want Blue Shirt or the big man?* My man would likely be better than me, but I'd be hoping for a certain kind of opposite number: a fine athlete, eager to get free from his defender and pour in points; a guy whose pride fed on scoring in streaks and swatting away opponents' shots with a ringing finality that caused others to call out, "Face!" There were a lot of players like that around, and I felt I could do something with such a type, no matter how splendid a specimen or a talent he might be—especially if he had that tender, chesty quality that comes of masking sensitivity to shame with push-ups and manly bravado. I couldn't do much with flat-affect cobra types who just did the math and hunched to the work of putting the machine on me. So, the more visibly passionate my opponent was about playing well and looking good to himself and to others, the better my chances for bringing out the worst in him.

One thing South Shore taught me was the value of defense. My objective was not to prevent my man from doing what he wanted to do on the court—get the ball, dribble, shoot—but rather just to make it unpleasant and difficult for him to do these things. Though he could probably pile up points on me if he was willing to bend the game out of shape, patiently hogging the ball on offense to back me down time after time, such strain and scrambling against an unworthy foe could undercut his dignity. It might be safer to tacitly consent to a détente in which he would go up and down the court without doing much to risk humiliation, all the while reassuring himself that wiping the floor with me would be beneath him. My project was to turn my man into a shooter and ball handler as uncertain as I was.

I began by taking calipers to his footwork, figuring out how much room he required in order to operate smoothly. Then I moved a little bit inside that limit of comfort, then a little more—but, having found the sweet spot of his discomfort, no more than that. I didn't want to keep cranking up the pressure, edging closer and closer until we inevitably began to knock into each other and a beef ensued; I wanted to be just close enough that I was perpetually, irksomely *there*. By staying close and varying the rhythm of my intrusions to keep the irritation fresh, I could make him feel that there was an extra foot where he wanted to step, extra bulk clogging up his movements. I tried to use my hands on him as little as possible. I'd just follow, follow, follow, lining up my navel with his at a chosen distance and then trying to keep them lined up at that distance no matter what he did or which way he turned, so that he would begin to feel as if he were dragging around my body and will, my whole story, in addition to his own. I aspired to be like Jack Vance's Chun the Unavoidable, who, even after the fleet and cruelly handsome Liane the Wayfarer slips into a sorcerous portable hole to escape him, appears at Liane's elbow in his coat of eyeballs and says, "I am Chun the Unavoidable."

This was initiative disguised as its opposite, a camouflaged sort of purposefulness. What appeared to be no more than following the other guy around, agreeing to react to his decisions, was, in fact, a form of forcing him to react to mine. I knew exactly what I wanted to do on defense—preserve the chosen distance between our navels—and I did it pretty much all the time the other team had the ball, which absolved me of the burden of thinking about what to do next and placed it on him. And if his teammates got fancy, setting screens to spring him loose from the bespectacled white guy quietly dogging him around the court, that was okay with me. Shifting to a deliberate patterned "suburban" offense meant breaking with the Homeric style of heroic individualism that usually prevailed in pickup games, just another disruption of habit likely to affect his timing and poise.

It didn't always work. Adaptable opponents could incorporate the clutter of my presence into their on-court arithmetic and carry on as always. Some were superior enough or disciplined enough or literal-minded enough to simply ignore me. When I found myself up against one of these, I would have to switch tactics to take something away— grossly overplaying his shooting hand to force him to drive with his weak hand to the basket, for instance, or sagging back to concede the outside shot in order to cut down his driving angle to the basket—which meant leaving openings for him to exploit. If he knew what he was doing, he would make me pay. Sometimes I would just have to endure the schooling I had coming. But making a systematic bother of myself—a necessary departure from my normal self-effacement—was still my best hope, and it worked more often than anything else.

*

I would look for opportunities to punctuate my campaign of steady unwelcome presence with discrete nasty shocks intended to hurry my man along from mounting irritation to passive tristesse. The most dramatic and politically fraught gambit was to scheme to block his second or third shot of the game. On his first shot or two, I'd mime an honest effort to block it, holding back a bit to see what his timing looked like. On the next shot, the one I'd chosen to make an example of, I'd extend to full length and full speed, trying to surprise him with the sudden span of my bony reach. Sometimes I would catch on an about-to-be-rejected shooter's face a startled look—*The fuck you doing all the way out here with your glasses-ass-wearing self?*—that mirrored my own queasy reaction to seeing our cat, Lauren, extend herself to an improbable rib-disjointed length to claw something beyond her normal reach (in which distressingly elongated position, stiff as a board and hanging by her front claws from a curtain, she was found at the end of her days, having apparently decided to go out doing what she loved best).

There was nothing more awful for most pickup ballplayers than having their shot roundly rejected. Only the most sophisticated players in my orbit—like Walt Frazier III and Arne Duncan, advanced craftsmen with plausible futures in college ball and beyond—could appear to treat it as a merely technical matter to be coolly dealt with next time by adding a shoulder feint or shooting with a little more loft. But even these paragons of calm reason and the long view, if you watched carefully, could be seen to store away a rejection for later and seek an occasion to show up its perpetrator with an especially dazzling move or timely steal, some one-upping display of dominance. Most players, though, visibly registered rage, wounded pride, submission, or some other debilitating reaction when an opponent rose up and banished their shot, which was the essence of their game and therefore of who they were on the court.

Spectacular loss of face threatened when that shot was eclipsed and sent—in the worst-case scenario—over the chain-link fence, down the block, and through the closing doors of a city bus, passing for all time beyond the knowledge of men, in the aftermath of which the shot blocker or one of his teammates might add an obituary verdict along the lines of "Get that shit *outta* here." A booming rejection could bring on a crisis that struck to the foundations of formative manhood.

On the South Side, if the guy blocking your shot looked like me—a white boy, clearly not a serious player, wearing jeans and maybe a button-down shirt flapping open over a pocket T-shirt, and aviator glasses that when whacked would put a bloody dent in the bridge of my nose and lose a lens that skittered along the pavement so that I had to dive after it and push legs and high-topped feet aside to prevent other players from stepping on it, which often inspired somebody to suggest that I get me some Kareem goggles or contact lenses or *something*— well, that tended to magnify the crisis. When I blocked a shot someone might call out, "Face!" but it was more common that chatter would die away on the court and be replaced by a funeral-home hush of compassion for a brother's sorrow. Some opponents would automatically call a foul when I blocked their shot, on the principle that there was no other possible explanation for such a hideous anomaly occurring. Sometimes a guy who called such a phantom foul would be sheepish about it, but others overcompensated with displays of long-suffering righteousness: "*That's* a foul right *there*, man. Foulin' me every *time*," a formula that framed in advance his counter-counterargument, should I question his call, by suggesting that while I might not appear to have actually fouled him this particular time, I'd fouled him every other time, so by any reasonable standard of justice he was a duly aggrieved party. None of these guys ever quite came out and said that white people had been fouling black people off the court for several centuries, so I was never quite put in the position of coming out and saying that calling bullshit fouls on the court wasn't about to put that right.

*

If I didn't exactly disdain offense—I did love above all else in the game the sweet geometry of threading a pass between out-flung arms and turned heads to a fellow seeker pursuing the path of his own desire to the rim—I treated it as a less rigorous state of being, a morally suspect sideshow. It made me feel a little ill to be part of a team that ran opponents off the court, sinking shot after shot and whipping ever more confident passes past hapless defenders' burning ears with ever less margin of error in a mounting make-it-take-it fugue. Because for me the point of basketball was mostly to prevent the other guy from putting the ball in the basket, I saw as a study in nearly pure evil a talented ball hog like Adrian Dantley or Rick Barry or Chicago's own Alfredrick "the Great" Hughes, the kind of scoring-fixated monomaniac who would hang on to the ball for twenty seconds, dribbling and rock-stepping and setting up his defender while the other players stood around watching, before he made some well-practiced and calculatedly unstoppable move to get a shot up. To try to stop such a scoring machine was to make a stand against brigands and outriders of the imperium bent on torching your hut and carrying off your children and crops.

Back then I frequently paged through my copy of Cyril Falls's *Great Military Battles*, an oversize book full of maps showing the movements of cavalry and infantry and artillery, and of paintings in which mounted generals made Buddha-like gestures with plump white hands amid their retinues and rolling clouds of gun smoke. I returned often to the chapter on Waterloo, which seemed to make the definitive case on offense and defense. Offense was Napoleon, whose genius for the coup de main was expressed in constant attack, demanding courage and enterprise and grotesquely buoyant optimism from his men. These were marquee virtues, yes, but, especially when exercised in the service of misguided principles, they curdled into blind, force-drunk aggression for its own sake. Defense, by contrast, might be frequently drab and unpleasant, but it was how you stopped offense. Defense was the Duke of Wellington, whose greatest achievement was to deny Napoleon the victory at Waterloo, and whose schemes featured the absolute minimum of moving parts and decisive strokes because he assumed that orders would go astray, subordinates would screw up, and the troops who served under him were "the scum of the earth."

I resist the notion that what you do in games bears any meaningful relationship to what you do in the rest of life. Attributed—probably falsely—for two centuries to Wellington (that nonsense about Waterloo having been won on the playing fields of Eton), the idea was earnestly taken up by Arne Duncan and others in President Obama's South Sider-dominated inner circle, who made basketball the new golf. Their faith that basketball reveals character strikes me as naive. What you do on the court may well say something about you and the conditions in which you learned the game, but it doesn't necessarily express anything like true character. Plenty of admirable people become hotheads or pushovers or supremely irritating when they play basketball, and some of the dullest and the most reprehensible are industrious, valiant, and generous ball-players who make the extra pass and dive self-sacrificingly in pursuit of loose balls. Still, my impatience with the Obama crew's earnest jockish faith doesn't prevent me from seeing that they have a point. Like many other things about me, the way I played ball—which strongly inflects the way I still play ball—had a discernible South Shore shape to it. The assertion of self in the guise of community-mindedness and the unchar-acteristically sharp sense of meaningful purpose I felt when playing defense against stiff competition, like the political machinations nec-essary to get next game on a strange court or the exercise of deciding now and then to put the ball in the basket and then actually doing it, did seem like good practice for . . . *things*.

PART II

CONTAINER

THE LAY OF THE LAND

When people list South Shore's advantages, they tend to talk about the container—not the community but the physical setting in which it's located. I've heard and read the standard list more times than I can count: good houses and apartments that don't cost as much as they would in other lakeside neighborhoods, easy access to downtown by road or rail, a stately surround of parks and beaches, and the eternally renewed midcontinent miracle of an inland sea at the neighborhood's eastern doorstep. People have been making this list since before South Shore became part of Chicago. In 1874, fifteen years before the city annexed South Shore, an early booster described the sparsely settled region of marshy sloughs and sandy ridges as "wooded knolls and advantageous residence sites, . . . one of the best prospects of any locale about the city."

For the last half century, people have been making an equally familiar list of the neighborhood's disadvantages: too many shootings and robberies and gangs; too much petty theft, graffiti, and litter; too many undesirable neighbors; schools with poor reputations; idle or aggressive groups of men hanging out on desolate commercial strips. The word "ghetto" comes up, as does "the element." This second standard list tends to describe the neighborhood as a community, a set of people and the behaviors and relationships that connect them to each other. Assessing the pros and cons of living there, considering reasons to invest money and energy and sentiment in South Shore or to hedge that bet, often means weighing the neighborhood as a physical container against the neighborhood as a community.

This tension runs deep in the mentalities of residents, especially property owners. Deborah Harrington, who lived in a high-rise by the lake, spoke for many of her neighbors when she contrasted her investment in the container to her skepticism about the community. "I love South Shore," she told me. "Being on the lakefront is a joy and an honor, but it's a love-hate relationship. It's a troubled community. There's a lot of crime and violence in the neighborhood. There's some truth to 'Terror Town'"—as a damning label, she meant, that many in the area resent. "My home is my sanctuary," she said. "It breaks my heart, but I turn away. I don't walk around."

Harrington went on to review reasons for South Shore's troubles as a community: poor leadership, weak institutions, political fragmentation and disorganization, ineffective nonprofits, the "destabilizing" and "badly managed" influx of new residents. She spoke with the authority of not only a longtime resident but also a well-connected expert, having held policymaking positions in state government and played a leading role in the city's philanthropic network as president of the Woods Fund, which supports grassroots organizations and public policy initiatives in communities in Chicago that are most affected by poverty and racism.

Harrington made a profession and a passion of investing institutional resources in disadvantaged communities, but in South Shore even she—in her own unsparing self-description—turned away, withholding from community and neighbors the passionate investment she made in her home and in the public amenities on view from it. When I asked her, as I asked almost everyone I interviewed, to think of a story or scene or moment that captures something essential about the neighborhood, she returned to singing the praises of the container. "Looking out my window," she said. "Looking at the lake, the Cultural Center, the Chicago skyline. It's daunting and humbling." We were on the phone, and I could tell she was looking out at her view as she talked, her voice filling with feeling. "It's like I just feel honored, to have this opportunity. I'm on the ninth floor. From up here, even looking west"—inland—"looks beautiful. What better place could there be? It's a hidden jewel." I could see it, in my mind's eye, as she did: the serried towers of the Loop to the north, sometimes ghostly in the distance and sometimes glitteringly sharp and near; the man-made wilderness of Jackson Park, lit-up drives unspooling between dark groves; the neighborhoods of the South Side stretching away on three sides to the horizon; and on the fourth side the great curving sweep of the lakefront and the lake itself, the long green swells of summer and the smoking winter moonscape of wind-sculpted ice formations suffused in glowing pink by the sunrise. Her voice lost its tone of wonder as she returned from visual prospect to social prospects: "But it's troubled. This community is on the precipice"—teetering between viability and collapse, she meant. "It could very well go either way, and it's not really guided or planned, so who knows?"

*

Neighborhood is a spatial term: if object *X* is physically near object *Y*, then *X* is in the neighborhood of *Y*. But as it's usually used, *neighborhood* often connotes human feeling, community: person *X* and person *Y* engage in neighboring, and so they are neighbors who live in the same neighborhood. "Tight-knit" has become a cliché as a modifier for "neighborhood" because it compresses such connotations into a neat package. The catchphrase "city of neighborhoods" has similarly become a cliché because it builds upon those connotations a claim of authenticity and urban vitality. In a "tight-knit neighborhood" in a "city of neighborhoods," you know people and they know you, and you share with your neighbors a sentimental as well as a social and financial investment in being there. Most definitions of *neighborhood* and most analyses of particular neighborhoods by scholars, policymakers, journalists, and others emphasize the community: who lives there, how much money or education they have, how they get along with each other, how their life courses and inner lives take shape in encounters with their neighbors. The qualities of the container will come up, of course, but usually as part of an effort to define boundaries so we can decide who's part of the community, or to evaluate the condition of housing or commercial property or public space so we can figure out how wealth or power or disorder flow through this community and affect residents' relations with one another.

There's a minority tradition within urban studies that puts primary emphasis on the container. One of its principal intellectual godfathers is Kevin Lynch, who grew up in the Buena Park section of Uptown, a lake-front neighborhood on Chicago's North Side that from its early history to its border of green spaces to its mix of housing stock and social classes bears a passing resemblance to South Shore. Beginning in the 1950s and throughout the age of urban renewal, Lynch tried to determine "the image of the city" as it exists in the minds of urbanites. His vocabulary of features—paths, edges, nodes, and the like—included "districts," but by this he meant recognizable chunks of the cityscape rather than social or cultural units, nor did he connect his spatial analysis to a sociological or historical account of community. Lynch focused on the legibility of urban form, the ways in which the built environment cues a sense of where you are. He wanted to identify and, by encouraging good design, to heighten our awareness of district and metropolis, an image of the city radiating out concentrically from an individual moving through the cityscape. This tradition has mostly persisted among planners, architects, and those in the real estate business, all of whom do think explicitly about components of the container in their own right (and who are frequently accused of fashioning cold, inhumane cityscapes precisely because they may put the container's form before the com-munity's needs), but most people who think about neighborhoods for a living think of them as communities first and containers second.

That makes sense. Above all, neighborhood means neighbors, and neighboring, which is why I devoted Part I of this book to community. But I believe that we tend to underrate the container's importance in the dynamics of neighborhood—the way the container figures not just in the mechanics of property values and development but in residents' inner lives and routines.

*

The lay of the land matters—because it affects how the built environ-ment houses a community and, in its own right as a repository of mean-ing, memory, selfhood. The container is a scaffold not just for commu-nity but for identity. Deborah Harrington demonstrated as much when she described her apartment as her sanctuary. It's not just that the vista

she saw from her window situated her in the district and metropolis—
although it did, and in ways that Lynch would recognize—but that her
sense of self was caught up in it. She turned to the view from her window and, though it broke her heart, turned away from public space and
public life at street level. There's a self-portrait as neighbor and citizen
in her account of her relationship to the lay of the land.

When I consider my own relationship to the lay of the land, it similarly goes far beyond ways in which I might fit into the community's
demographics, social history, or networks of neighboring. I haven't
lived day-to-day in South Shore since the mid-1980s, but the physical
form of the neighborhood continues to give shape to who I am by providing some of the oldest, most basic templates I have to call upon in
organizing feeling and sensibility.

For instance, any exercise of calculated patience—any time I do the
math to determine that getting a small thing more quickly isn't worth the
significant risk of a bad big thing happening to me because I rushed—
takes me back to the sound of the warning bells as the traffic gates come
down along the Illinois Central tracks on 71st Street. Any time I come to
a full stop at a remote stop sign with no cop in view, or take the extra step
of putting a form with my social security number on it in the mail rather
than send it by email, I'm thinking on some fundamental level that a
slice of Italian Fiesta pizza can wait, and even the urgent desire to steal a
march on a crew in pea coats and sideways-worn Pittsburgh Pirates caps
coming up on my flank and cutting me off from the way home can wait,
because there's no screw-up more final than one that leads to darting
out onto the tracks just in time to get hit by a train.

Any time I adjust some routine to the specific strictures of a particular venue—making a lecture more informal because it's being held in a
smaller room than I expected, or deciding how there or not-there I'm
going to be as I enter a boxing gym or bar far from home—I'm exercising a faculty developed on the assortment of driveway, backyard,
and schoolyard basketball courts in South Shore in the 1970s. This one
had an ankle-threatening length of pipe sticking up from the pavement
under the basket, that one had no left corner and prickly bushes growing close up to the sideline, and on his court the Reverend Jackson did

not allow cursing by anyone other than himself. You had to adjust your game accordingly.

And all fears at any scale, from illness afflicting my children to the heat death of the universe, go back to the two-humped shape of the water crib two miles out in the lake off 68th Street, of which I conceived an unreasoning horror as a small child. I can't fully explain the fear I associated with that form—a squat round tank-like thing connected by a sinister-looking catwalk to what appeared to be a floating mill building with a lighthouse tower—other than to say that it somehow represented the horror of *process*. The water crib was clearly built for some purpose, and things happened within it according to that purpose, but because I had no idea what those things were, I somehow developed a vague impression that they involved obliteration, dismemberment, an unspeakable ablative function. Maybe the horrible results of the process were kept in the tank-like part, or maybe that's where the raw material was stored before it was fed—or *they* were fed, screaming, two miles out in the lake where nobody could hear them—into the bladed gears of the mill.

Fear, joy, caution, ambition, curiosity—the components of who I am retain at their foundations the shape of the lay of the land as I encountered it when I first began venturing beyond the reach of parents and household. South Shore provided my templates for the very concepts of home and world. I write this in a house almost a thousand miles from 71st Street, but situated on a quiet residential side street about a block from a main commercial street divided by train tracks running at grade down its middle and about twenty minutes from downtown, a recognizable East Coast copy of the physical situation of both houses I lived in when I was growing up in South Shore. This place where I now live declared itself to me as a suitable landscape of home on what felt like a cellular level when my wife and I, who were looking for a place to settle down and raise our daughters in a city that was strange to me, saw it for the very first time. It's like when my father, after he and my mother left South Shore and moved their empty nest to New York City, suddenly became passionate about taking a job in Riverside, California, which did not really make sense to me until his mother, my Nonna, remarked that the climate and landscape of Southern California's semi-arid Inland Empire reminded her of Eritrea, where my father grew up.

South Shore also provided my model for going into the world. The block of locked-and-loaded houses is not only my original idea of home, it's also my model of the base camp from which to go out in search of action, inspiration, things worth doing. I go out to the street, the library, campus, the bars, the fights, but always away from the stillness of the block where there's home life and a home base and, instead of action, the long-wave tug of large, slow forces at work over time. And then, once I've gotten the goods, I return to that stillness and hole up in the fortified house to write.

As a child I used to stand on a balcony at the Museum of Science and Industry, in Jackson Park, looking down in a state of spatial exaltation at the museum's 3,000-square-foot train set—the old one, since replaced. Created by Minton Cronkhite in 1939, the train set I loved was a compellingly outdated O-scale rendition of the country between Chicago and the West Coast, through which sixteen-pound locomotives dragged strings of clattering cars in sinuous curves along 1,300 feet of track around shin-high oil tanks and trees and a foxhole-sized replica of the Grand Canyon. For all its impressive size, the train set mesmerized me because it was also so clearly a model of its creator's being at the moment he created it—a past moment to which, despite occasional updates, the train set was permanently fixed. Going back to South Shore now puts me in mind of that train set, and not just because the wah-wah pedals and Blackstone Rangers of the 1970s are as remote now as the fedoras and Super Chief trains of the 1930s were then.

It's a complicated experience to go back, because so much of myself is built on the foundation of an internal scale model of the landscape of the South Side as it was forty and fifty years ago. Those aspects of the lay of the land that haven't changed return me to the way I was back then, so that when I'm in Chicago I experience joy or fear or curiosity not only as a middle-aged husband and father and professional with a purpose but also, disorientingly, as a dreamy child and drifting adolescent. The aspects of the lay of the land that *have* changed inspire a kind of soul vertigo, as if the disappearance of the original template for joy or fear or whatever will somehow interdict my access to these basic elements of sensibility. When I'm down by the lake, some rudimentary part of me—still, after all these years—readies itself for the sight of the double-humped outline of that water crib crouched in the sullen rolling green off 68th Street. I don't know what would happen inside me if one day it wasn't there at all, and I'm not sure I want to find out.

So I lived in South Shore, and the container plays a crucial part in how South Shore lives in me. A similar dynamic operates at the level of the community as a whole. Taking the long view, the history of the neighborhood is a story of how the lives of the people who lived there— not just the social orders they fashioned, but also their mentalities and imaginations and identities as citizens and neighbors—took form as they were poured into the vessel provided by the lay of the land.

*

South Shore lies on the northern edge of the Calumet Region, a geographical area that wraps around the southern end of Lake Michigan, encompassing the lower South Side of Chicago and northern Indiana. "Great physical forces helped shape the Calumet Area," writes the local historian Jacob Schoon. "Movements of the earth's crust raised and lowered the land, causing huge seas to slowly recede, return, and recede again. Mighty glaciers invaded from the north—not once but perhaps dozens of times." The retreat of the Laurentide glacier left behind ancestral Lake Michigan, a larger and deeper prehistoric version of our lake, which receded in turn to its current outline and left a landscape of prairies, woodlands, meadows, marshlands, sandy ridges, and wind-formed dunes along the shore. Rivers and streams drained off to either side of the eastern Continental Divide—some to the Atlantic via the lake, some to the Gulf of Mexico via the Mississippi. You can feel the earth turning through the cycle of the millennia in Schoon's account, but he is also alert to more human-scale but equally powerful forces that shaped the region. He notes that his grandfather, who was born in a farmhouse in the Calumet Region in 1873, found "a Dutch girl" to marry within his immigrant community, "as expected," and later worked for U.S. Steel and the Elgin, Joliet & Eastern Railroad.

There were Potawatomi villages, camps, and chipping stations in and around what would become South Shore, and as a Chicago child I formed the impression that they were the original human residents of the area, victims of a primal displacement that provided the ur-model for many such successions to come. Part of the reason for that naive assumption, I think, is the tribe's name. Easy to remember, enjoyable to say, it has the mouth feel of time immemorial. They were indeed violently displaced, but they weren't there first, it turns out. In the 1600s, when French voyageurs and missionaries began exploring the Great Lakes region, the Potawatomi were living in what is now southwestern Michigan. They were driven east and north from there during the Iroquois Wars to Wisconsin's Door Peninsula, around Green Bay, where they made contact with the French. Only when the wars ended in 1701 did they come south again to the Calumet Region, pushing out the current residents, the Miami.

Long before South Shore became a neighborhood, then, a central motif of its human history was already in place: the Miami found themselves saying, in the Algonquian Miami-Illinois language, something along the lines of "Got-*damn* Potawatomi; there goes the neighborhood." And it appears that the Miami, Illinois, Sac, Fox, Ottawa, Chippewa, and other tribes already in the area when the Potawatomi showed up had themselves succeeded a culture of mound-builders who had occupied the region sometime before them. Had any mound-builders still been around to see these successors come, they might well have shaken their heads and said in their own, now-lost language, "Look, the lakeside location's great, you can't beat the hunting and fishing, and I'm spiritually attached to our mounds and all, but once the non-mound-building element shows up, there goes the neighborhood."

The Indian removal policies of the nineteenth century eventually forced the Potawatomi to Kansas and other Chicago-area tribes to Oklahoma, but some groups managed to remain closer to home. The long-gone mound-builders hung around, too, in a way, by leaving their mark on the land. A map drawn in 1900 that depicts Indian sites and trails in the Chicago area circa 1804 locates a mound on 95th Street near the lake, a few blocks south of South Shore, and another at 108th and

Torrence. Schoon notes that in the early twentieth century, farmers in the Calumet Region were still plowing over and hauling away mounds, which they regarded as a nuisance.

The newcomers pushed each other out as well. The French had nominal dominion over what would become South Shore from 1673 until the end of the French and Indian War in 1763, when they were succeeded by the British, who were succeeded in turn after the Revolutionary War by the Americans, who built Fort Dearborn at the mouth of the Chicago River in 1803. Because the fort, located by the river and the lake at what is now the intersection of Michigan Avenue and Wacker Drive, formed the germ of the future city of Chicago, at that point in history we can begin to think of South Shore, at least in theory, as a proto-neighborhood.

*

By the 1850s, German truck farmers had begun settling in the area, which was then a stretch of wilderness southeast of the outlying village of Hyde Park—not yet part of Chicago and not yet called South Shore. By the 1870s, perhaps twenty family farms were scattered widely in a landscape of swamps, wooded ridges, and prairie. Deer, muskrat, and other animals were plentiful, as were flowers. Bird hunters took home bagsful of seemingly inexhaustible numbers of snipe, plover, quail, ducks, geese, and pigeons. Goldhart's tavern, on the site now occupied by the St. Philip Neri parish church at 72nd and Merrill, served travelers on the wagon trace that came up from Indiana, hugging the lakeshore until it turned inland to follow the drier ground of the ridges through oak and jack pine forest toward Chicago. A stagecoach from Michigan City to Chicago pulled by a brace of Arabian horses ran along this road twice a week, weather permitting, and Ferdinand Rohn's ox-drawn cart made the fifteen-hour round trip to market in Chicago, seven miles away.

In a speech he made to the Bryn Mawr Women's Club in 1907, a neighborhood veteran named George Clingman drew on his diary entries from the late 1870s to paint a portrait of South Shore back then as a paradise just before the fall: "The bluffs on the lake shore were thickly covered with wild crab apple trees, and in June, when in blossom, the perfume scented the air for blocks and myriads of bees were buzzing in their petals, while hither and thither darted the ruby throated hummingbirds, the ruby on their throats glistening like some great jewels. Wild flowers grew here in abundance, water lillies [*sic*], cowslips, violets, honeysuckle, columbine, Jack-in-the-pulpit Indian Moccasin, and Mandrake Blossoms were seen everywhere, while the yellow and red of the Indian Paint, scented through the light green grass on a beautiful June Morning, presented a picture in sharp contrast to the rubbish and ash heaps of civilization today. It all seems to pass before me in review like a beautiful dream."

The lay of the land became increasingly man-made as South Shore was incorporated into the metropolitan grid—and into the city of Chicago, which annexed a large chunk of the South Side in 1889, making South Shore officially a neighborhood. (South Shore backed into its generic-sounding name, as far as can be determined, because it was left over after the other neighborhoods along the city's southern shoreline got their own names.) The first streets had already been laid out there by the time the young Clingman wrote his diary entries, and train lines were already reaching into it. Each new train station served as the seed for more development, the most important one being the IC's South Kenwood (later Bryn Mawr) station at 71st and Jeffery, which opened in 1881. An influx of English railway workers helped fill houses in the area's new residential subdivisions. The decision to hold the World's Columbian Exposition in Jackson Park in 1893 inspired a boom in cheap wood-construction hotels, but also in more substantial and long-lasting homes. The establishment of the University of Chicago in Hyde Park also stimulated demand for housing in South Shore. In the final years of the century, the neighborhood grew swiftly, with stores, churches, schools, streetcar lines, and more and more houses and apartment buildings filling in blank spots on the map.

Still, the older order had not been entirely banished. The naturalist Donald Culross Peattie, who grew up in the early twentieth century in a house at what is now 76th and South Shore Drive, looked back in 1936 and saw his young self surrounded by nature, a reminiscence notably similar to Clingman's: "I remember what is now Rainbow Beach when the rainbow bathing suits were not seen there, and there was, rather magnificently, nothing but the beach. I remember the dunes there, and the gracile wild oat and marram grasses growing on them. I remember the thickets of crab apple behind the dunes, where the gnarled dwarfish stems, amid the ferocity of thorns, the delicate pink blossoms burst so miraculously in the late, wind-smitten Chicago springs. I remember the marsh behind our back fence, where Lady ferns grew, and the big prairie, where old Jim Bushnell had his farm, and the shooting-stars sprang out of the sod like an earthborn miracle in May, and the unseen ventriloquist meadowlarks whistled eerily from beyond the sloughs flowering with wild blue flag. Gulls and sandpipers calling and wheedling on the beach; flickers in the black oaks; the lisping chatter of the great cottonwoods even on breathless days, and the lashing of the big swamp willows in the storm." Like Clingman's, Peattie's portrait of an abundant, flowering South Shore in which the rhythms of nature predominate is shadowed by the development that has superseded them: "I heard these things before our street became a roaring river of motors, before the fire engines had sirens, before the church in the next block had a bell."

Though he recalls a childhood spent wandering amid natural beauty, Peattie also describes the coming of the new urban order. From the cupola of his house (a block from where Gerald Hamilton lives now), he could see east across the water, west across the "straggling and rather commonplace suburb" filling in the space between dunes and prairie, north to the astonishing twenty-story skyscrapers of the Loop that helped make Chicago the shock city of industrial modernity, and south to "the steel mills, the settlement of the Poles, and their churches." At school, he learned to do the ethnic math as one of a minority of native-born Protestants heavily outnumbered by immigrant ethnics: "every room of my school held six rows, each ten seats deep, with all the seats filled by German, Italian, Polish, Irish children in constant vendetta, united only against Teacher." These kids from millworkers' families also united in persecuting a Jewish boy, Abe, whom Peattie and the other Protestants abandoned to his fate—beatings, pelting with rocks, having his face rubbed in the dung of the draft horses that drew coal wagons through the neighborhood. Peattie catches neatly the blend of snobbery, cravenness, and clear-eyed calculation behind the Protestants' decision not to intervene: "They agreed with me that it was a disgusting spectacle. But we were only four or five against about thirty or forty; we'd be getting our noses bloodied hopelessly for Abie. I saw it was essentially an emotional affair between the Jews and the Catholics. . . ."

Peattie relates this incident as an awakening from naivete, a fall from nature's grace and into profane history. His grandfather, a Civil War veteran who had been "the first settler in this part of the city when it was nothing but dunes and oaks and sloughs, had stamped his cane in the Education offices till Ella Flagg Young got a schoolhouse up out here for Jim Bushnell's kids and the Fair children, and his," and now the schools were overrun by barbarous newcomers who showed that first settler's grandson the darker side of creation. Nature, for the young Peattie, was "the beloved," the pure and unspoiled opposite of the hard, compromised world the working-class immigrant ethnics embodied. Peattie had dutifully listened to his father preaching about "the oppressed nations of the world" and had sat through a performance of the play *The Melting Pot*, but now he "had also seen the blackness of the human heart, which I then and for long after considered smaller and more vicious than the soul of the driver ant."

*

Peattie's schoolmates were urban villagers, exemplars of the world made by the great forces that shaped industrial modernity—immigration, urbanization, industrialization—which Peattie could see converging on South Shore from his cupola. It would be as the container of an urban village, or of several such villages, that the neighborhood's lay of the land reached mature form. With one of the world's great concentrations of steel mills, rolling stock production, and other heavy industry developing just to its southeast, South Shore grew into its role as a bedroom community in an industrial city, connected by railroad tracks and paychecks and all manner of other ties to the manufacturing enterprises that dictated the city's form and function and made Chicago world-famous in the early twentieth century.

Immigrant-ethnic tribes working their way into American life moved into South Shore in the century's early decades, increasing its population to a historical high of about 80,000 by the 1940s. The Irish were one of the era's two main incoming groups, pulled to South Shore by the attractions of the container but also pushed by the great migration from the American South that caused the city's Black Belt to expand up to and beyond the edges of their former neighborhoods. Jews, the other main group, came next. In 1900, half of Chicago's population had been foreign-born or of foreign-born parentage; over the generations that followed, it was in neighborhoods like South Shore that such families worked out their long-term accord with Americanness. This process was an important aspect of what Chicago was *for*. In the urban village, the heartland of the industrial neighborhood order, newcomers were assimilated into the workforce of factory hands and the polity of machine Democrats, so that the manufacturing process of turning raw materials into finished goods flowed together with the process of turning immigrants into citizens.

The urban village's typical forms varied from city to city—the tenement in New York, the triple-decker in Boston, the courtyard building and bungalow in Chicago—but the mix of neighborhood institutions tended to be the same everywhere: churches, synagogues, schools, taverns, union halls, ethnic social clubs, athletic clubs, a network that provided a bridge between Old Country and New World. The infrastructure of manufacturing was also an integral part of the urban village, and South Shore had plenty of railroad tracks, though it lacked the typical redbrick workplaces. South Shore was a little greener and more residential than neighborhoods to its south, a little more prosperous and even genteel, and among the strongholds of the urban villagers it had pockets of more-established and more-assimilated Protestants. The Jackson Park Highlands attracted the well-to-do, as did the opening in 1906 of the South Shore Country Club at 71st and the lake.

The neighborhood began to reach physical maturity in the decades before the Second World War. Transverse commercial streets—71st, 75th, 79th—were lined with the drugstores and shoe stores and groceries and taverns and movie theaters of the midcentury Main Street. Walk-up apartment buildings predominated in Parkside and O'Keeffe, and in time more expensive elevator buildings like Deborah Harrington's went up along the lakefront. In Bryn Mawr East and parts of Bryn Mawr West, the blocks were lined with single-family houses. Some of these houses were two-flats, but many were bungalows.

The Chicago Bungalow Association provides a checklist of traits that qualify a house as a historic Chicago bungalow: built between 1910 and 1940, one and a half stories, low-pitched roof with overhang, rectangular shape (narrow at front and rear, longer on the sides), generous windows, an offset front entrance or side entrance. There are about 80,000 such houses in Chicago, blocks and blocks of them forming a half-moon-shaped bungalow belt that takes in parts of the North, West, and South Sides. It's a quintessentially Chicago experience to pass through a neighborhood of bungalows, neat and trim, and then go through a viaduct under railroad tracks and into another neighborhood of bungalows, equally neat and trim, and the only difference is that there are, say, black people on one side of the viaduct and Hispanics or white people on the other.

The bungalow may be modest in size, but it's a flexible vessel that has managed to contain a broad middle-class spectrum: factory hands, city workers, and clerks climbing up from the working class, the middle managers who supervise them, and also doctors, lawyers, professors, and other comfortable professionals who can afford bigger, fancier places in the suburbs but prefer city living. Built in bunches, sometimes so close together that the overhanging eaves seem to nearly touch, bungalow blocks give form to what sociologists of the Chicago School called "the community of limited liability": you cut your grass, your neighbors cut theirs; you protect your investment, your neighbors protect theirs; you look out for each other in a limited but meaningful way, like sodbusters on adjoining frontier farms.

In 1967 my parents, doctoral students at the University of Chicago with three young sons and full-time academic jobs at the City Colleges of Chicago (my father) and St. Xavier College (my mother), paid $22,000 for a bungalow on the 7100 block of Oglesby. They slept in one of the two smaller back bedrooms, and my two brothers and I shared the bigger front bedroom. (This house, built in 1910, was of a full two-story variant recognized by the Chicago Bungalow Association as an "other bungalow"—that is, having all the requisite characteristics of a historic Chicago bungalow except a truncated second story.) The third bedroom was an office, jammed with books. It had an unheated porch, of which I have retained an early memory: playing quietly on the rug in my winter coat with my similarly bundled brothers while my mother, wearing her own winter coat, sat at a desk tapping the keys of a manual typewriter. The boys across the street—who had no evident use for school and thought it manly good fun to throw lit cherry bombs at each other and were once caught by the cops coming out of our neighbor's basement window with stolen stereo components in hand—lived in a house much like ours, except their front door was blue. Michelle Obama grew up in the upper half of a similar bungalow in South Shore, at 7436 S. Euclid, upstairs from a great-uncle who had been a Pullman porter and a great-aunt who was a music teacher. Michelle's father, Fraser Robinson III, got ahead by fitting himself into the economic and political machinery of Chicago, working for the water department and as a precinct captain for Richard J. Daley's political organization.

The Robinsons, who moved into the neighborhood from Woodlawn in 1965, were part of South Shore's next major succession, the transition from white to black in the 1960s and early 1970s. At first, middle-class black families followed the same path taken by Protestant, Irish, and Jewish cohorts before them, moving from Washington Park and Woodlawn and other inland neighborhoods under felt pressure from the expanding Black Belt. The Supreme Court's ruling in 1948 that restrictive housing covenants were not legally enforceable helped clear the way for that expansion, and poor and working-class blacks were the motive engine pushing the middle class, white and black alike, ahead of them. South Shore's first black residents had, on average, a little more income and a little more education than the white families they replaced.

South Shore's bungalows, two-flats, and better apartment buildings filled with the black middle class and with allied working-class strivers who felt they had a realistic shot at making it into the middle: a robust cohort of teachers, court clerks, cops, firefighters, postal workers, nurses, bus drivers, unionized factory workers, middle manager small business owners. But the growth of these middle strata slowe during the 1970s, and they began to shrink and age out as the century reached its end. Meanwhile, poor people with less education joined them in South Shore. As South Shore became a solidly black neighborhood, its poverty rate climbed.

At some point in my teen years, I read about the Xiongnu, the nomadic steppe people whose movements deep in Asia supposedly set in train a whole series of migrations that pushed the Huns, Alans, Visigoths, and others westward into the Roman empire. That history made intuitive sense to me, perhaps because as a South Sider I sensed that black people without much money or power—the non-upwardly-mobile working class, the poor, the underclass, whatever label was slapped on them—were a local equivalent. When migration from the South put intolerable population pressure on their old neighborhoods in the Black Belt and they moved to the edges of Washington Park or Woodlawn in search of decent housing, Irish and Jewish families fled from those neighborhoods to South Shore. When poor black people finally made it *into* Washington Park or Woodlawn, black doctors and lawyers from there started showing up in South Shore, and in turn the Irish and Jews of South Shore lit out for whiter neighborhoods or suburbia. But in a still-segregated city, and given the mix of housing stock in South Shore, it was only a matter of time before the Xiongnu themselves showed up and settled close to the black middle class who had been trying to get away from them. There weren't all that many places to which that middle class, dug into its bungalows, could move.

*

In the canonical story of the Black Metropolis, the urban world made by the great migrations from South to urban North, migrants come to Chicago in search of dignity, opportunity, and work, especially industrial work. They pack into the kitchenette buildings of Bronzeville and then expand onto the South and West Sides, pushing against a formidable array of formal and informal obstacles, including projects and expressways sited to pen them in. South Shore began to become black as the Black Metropolis was eclipsed by the succeeding postindustrial order: the second ghetto, the signature form of which is the high-rise project. The black middle class first began moving into South Shore in part because it was trying to put some distance between itself and both the old Black Belt and the emergent second ghetto. In Isabel Wilkerson's retelling of the Great Migration narrative in *The Warmth of Other Suns*, one of her main characters, Ida Mae Gladney, ends up in an apartment in South Shore. In a way, it's the payoff of her long, upward-tending journey, seeing her on her eighty-sixth birthday sitting in a gold velveteen recliner in a place of her own, but her situation is also presented as an index of the promised land's larger historical disappointments. The image of the intrepid migrant forted-up in her neat apartment against the "crime and mayhem" outside in the streets is a classic post-1970 South Shore tableau of besieged respectability.

Black South Shore was similar in some respects to the urban village that had preceded it. Half of the neighborhood's residents in the late 1970s had been born in the South, the black migration's equivalent of the Old Country, and many incoming families were climbing into the middle class via property ownership and higher education. But their situation was also, of course, very different from that of the urban villagers. The path of least resistance for whites—up and out into suburbia—was not an option for most black urbanites, and the current conditions and enduring legacies of racial inequality in everything from education to finance to housing to employment made the slopes to be climbed steeper and greasier. So, too, did the changing economic climate, because South Shore became black just as the industrial order that had made possible the urban village, and had attracted migrants from the South in the first place, began to collapse in earnest.

A neighborhood's change from white to black is generally regarded as an all-encompassing upheaval, something like the mega-quake long anticipated by Californians: the Big One. But in South Shore—especially when we focus on the container, which except for the addition of taller apartment buildings near the lake didn't change all that much after 1940—the transition from white to black was in some ways business as usual. The deeper changes, and perhaps the ones that counted most, had to do with fundamental shifts in the city's form and function. If there was a Big One, it was postindustrial transformation. Chicago, a city that had since the late nineteenth century been organized primarily around turning raw materials into finished goods in factories, became a city organized primarily around handling information and providing services in office buildings. There were related shifts in the structure of opportunity the city could provide to newcomers, in labor markets, in the nature and availability of good work and its relationship to schooling. And, along with the continuing effect of racial segregation on everything from class mix to school quality to policy response by governments at all levels, those changes sharply affected South Shore, especially to the extent that the service sector's hourglass-shaped labor market contributed to the hollowing out of the middle class. Black workers disproportionately occupied the increasingly distended lower swell of the hourglass, where work was especially contingent and insecure, producing more have-nots to confront haves over increasingly less tenable middle ground.

Those remaining on that middle ground tended to retreat from public life. The combination of forces shaping the decline of the American middle class can all be seen at work in South Shore: the weakening of the public safety net in the name of the globalized free market and the individual; the tightening of margins in family budgets as consumer debt and job insecurity grew while wages stagnated and the power of unions waned; declining confidence in public institutions and a fraying sense of civil community; and a hardening of public discourse into an "us vs. them" politics of identity and displacement. One consequence noted by observers of this process has been greater atomization, citizens and households losing faith in government and receding from public life, turning in on themselves in the scramble to keep up—a retreat abetted by new technologies that encourage citizens to commune with their screens in little bubbles of solitude. I catch a whiff of all this in the air of South Shore's bungalow blocks and commercial strips.

But even with all these changes afoot and new pressures coming to bear, South Shore was still recognizable as a bedroom community in which the middle class, no matter how precariously situated, dictated the tone; a first-house neighborhood; a place to stage a move on the good life. And that move was still most emblematically made in a bungalow. The urban bungalow—which, like its suburban cousin the ranch house, is a machine for producing and preserving middle-classness—enjoyed a stretch of emblematic glory from the late 1940s through the early 1970s, a period when prosperity and government policies ranging from the GI Bill to labor law to a progressive tax structure underwrote the great expansion of the middle class. As that expansion slowed and then reversed, and especially after the financial crisis of 2008, the family upside down on its mortgage in a bungalow it couldn't sell if it wanted to became a common type in South Shore, an emblem of precariousness.

The bungalow people of South Shore—whether black or white, flush or desperate—have always been a minority in the neighborhood, but a large and exceedingly influential one. Seventy-five percent of the neighborhood's residents live in apartments, but 70 percent of its land area is devoted to single-family houses, 1,011 of which qualify as historic Chicago bungalows by the painstakingly precise count of the Chicago Bungalow Association. Affordable bungalows, above all other attractions of the container, have anchored the home-owning middle class in the neighborhood, enabling its concerns and voices to set the tone of South Shore's public life. That's still true today, even as the middle class shrinks and recedes. The lay of the land that achieved mature form in the industrial city before the Second World War continues to provide the blueprint for the postindustrial community's principal internal tensions—between the haves in bungalows, lakefront high-rises, and the better walk-up apartment buildings and the have-nots in the less-good apartment buildings; between owners and renters; between people with more choices about where to school their kids or shop and people with fewer such choices.

*

Throughout the major social transition that made South Shore part of the black South Side, the container, having achieved mature form, remained pretty much as it had been before. It was altered less by flows of population moving through it than by flows of money: capital flight gut-

ted the commercial strips; downtown banks redlined the neighborh
and the South Shore Bank tried to undo the damage with its prog
of "community capitalism"; and local, state, and federal governments
put money into housing in the form of rehab projects and vouchers. The
container's basic elements—the park and the lakefront, the bungalows
and apartment buildings, the Country Club–cum–Cultural Center, the
IC tracks—variously fell into disrepair or were spruced up, changed
hands or didn't, but they continued to define the lay of the land. If 71st
Street, in particular, seemed to die a lingering commercial death, it was
in part because 71st was an obsolescent prewar Main Street that *didn't*
change much in an age when people began to think nothing of getting
in the car to drive thirty minutes to a chain store offering leading brands
and convenient parking.

Think of the lay of the land in South Shore since midcentury as akin
to a climax forest. Unless somebody clears it to make way for something else or introduces extremely aggressive invasive species—neither
of which has happened so far in South Shore, where property values
haven't appreciated with sufficient speed or sustained consistency to
create the necessary pressure—this old-growth forest has a proven
tendency to keep on pretty much the way it is. And the way it is really
does help explain the state of community in South Shore. Take the lay
of the land—a bedroom community of bungalows, two-flats, walk-up
apartment buildings, and a few high-rise buildings and bigger houses,
all framed by parks and lakefront—and compile the other variables:
postindustrial transformation, the hollowing out of the middle class, the
greater proximity of black haves and have-nots in the segregated inner
city, 5,000-plus housing vouchers, lack of faith in government in the
era after the collapse of the New Deal coalition. The logical result is a
pronounced class division between owners and lower-end renters, especially those whose rent is paid by the state, that reduces mutual trust and
confidence in shared values, thus weakening community ties. Culture,
policy, and economics are all important factors in this equation, but it
begins with the mix of housing stock, the man-made lay of the land.

So, too, does an identity as someone who lives—or lived—in South
Shore. Even if I wished to accord formative primacy to the community

rather than the lay of the land, to put people above place in my account of how I turned out, I have to recognize that the community has taken shape when poured into the vessel of the container. No matter how long I live in Brookline, I am, in my social and psychological DNA, a bungalow person from Bryn Mawr East who moved up to a grander house in the Jackson Park Highlands. So I am cordial with neighbors but keep my distance, and I'm eternally suspicious of strangers on the block. I patiently accumulate the credentials and money required for upward mobility, all the time aware of others around me making their own moves in ways that resonate with mine but might also complicate or even interdict my trajectory. I'm permanently attuned to the basic fact of life that those who have less want more and those who have more want to hang on to it. And always at some sub rosa mental level, I expect the incursion of piratical boarding parties who must be repelled by householders without assistance from neighbors or government. I am a product of a landscape and a process that can be traced back at least as far as the network of trails that ran along the dry ridges between wet sloughs in postglacial South Shore, connecting Indian villages, camps, chipping stations, and mounds into a larger order—one that, as has apparently always been the case in South Shore, lasted until the next crew, pushed and pulled by the forces of history, showed up and decided that this looked like a nice place to live.

EQUIPMENT FOR LIVING

PURPOSE

When Richard J. Daley, mayor-for-life of Chicago, died a few days before Christmas in 1976, my family was making its annual visit to relatives in Italy and Spain, stopping at Romanesque churches along the way to move with spookily enlarged pupils through echoing perpetual gloom that smelled of stone and fire. The *International Herald-Tribune* and the European papers treated Daley's passing like that of a world-class strongman, in much the same way that the Chicago papers had covered the death of Chairman Mao that September. Coming just a few months apart, the two deaths became instantly linked in my mind, and, despite barely qualifying as a series, together suggested a narrative momentum. They were all going, it seemed to me — all the stocky, lumpy, shrewd pie-faced leg-breakers who had achieved the real-world equivalent of Conan the Cimmerian's ascent to the throne of Aquilonia after strangling the king with his own barbarous hands.

Daley, who had already been mayor for nine years when I was born and who died in office when I was twelve, figured prominently in the consciousness of Chicago children of my era. He was clearly more important, more tangibly powerful, than any president or movie star or sports hero. The expressways and high-rises and parks that came into being when he laid his will on the city, and the vacant lots that appeared when he sent cranes and bulldozers to clear away whatever stood in the path of his intention, were all infinitely more real than signing a treaty or miming a shootout or a kiss for the camera or managing some clever fetch of ball technique.

Daley, as I saw him, was an outsize amalgam of several types. He seemed like a character from a folktale—one of those meritocratic castle-dwelling ogres, perhaps, who had usurped by main force the perquisites of the undeserving aristocracy—and also like the kind of waterfront Mister Big fought by noir-tending comic-book heroes with no particularly super powers, like Batman or Iron Fist. He could have been an especially forbidding relative from the Old Country, a distant Sicilian cousin or a Catalan great-uncle who smelled of cigars and Agua Lavanda Puig, a man who enjoyed the fealty of underlings and was said to have done what had to be done during the war and the hard times that came after. Daley seemed akin, too, to the local cohort of men of respect whose celebrity persisted from an era with very different standards of male virtue and glamour: men like Jack Brickhouse, who sounded as if his face was darkening to a dangerous shade of red when he called the play-by-play for Cubs games; Irv Kupcinet, the saturnine gossip columnist who mumbled in Rat Pack–vintage style on radio and TV; Len O'Connor, the TV news commentator whose sign-off line, "And I am Len O'Connor," delivered with a nasal Depression-era note of challenge, sounded like something a guy who was about to get sucker-punched off his bar stool might say; and Frazier Thomas, host of *Garfield Goose and Friends* and *Family Classics* on WGN, whose air of gentle patience always seemed to me to mask perverse despairing blackout rage. And perhaps Daley was a little bit like Muddy Waters, too, another stocky, broad-faced son of hinterland peasantry who made it big in the world at large by becoming a big shot in Chicago.

There's a baby picture of my brother Sebastian being dangled by my father in front of a sign that says:

THIS IS ANOTHER IMPROVEMENT

FOR CHICAGO

SORRY FOR THE INCONVENIENCE

RICHARD J. DALEY

MAYOR

Those signs, appearing all over town, identified Daley as the maker and breaker of neighborhoods—he was both Odin, who built Valhalla, and

Surt, the fire demon who torches the heavens and all creation with his flaming sword during Ragnarok, the final battle. Daley had an aura of inevitability and ubiquity, and I sensed in a half-formed, child's way that he stood for fundamental principles one might only begin to perceive in their true proportion after stripping the sentimental window dressing from life and looking at the meshing gears of its works. He had the leverage not only to move pieces on the game board of the city but also to rewrite the rules of the game as he pleased, routinely conferring rich prizes on undeserving vassals and consigning good citizens to long-term woe—sometimes because they had crossed him, intentionally or unwittingly, and sometimes just because their alderman was in his dog-house. Even a child could see that consulting standards of decency or fair play to assess the mayor's reign was embarrassingly naive. How he did it was just how it was done. The terrible things and the great things he did were two aspects of a single atavistic potency that made him my original, authentic model of purpose and efficacy.

*

But not my only model. There was, for instance, Mike Royko, whose column appeared in the *Daily News* five days a week throughout my childhood and, after the *Daily News* went belly up, in the *Sun Times* and eventually the *Tribune*. It came as a revelation that this ball-breaking cultivator of beefs, with his eagle-beaked Slavic face and thick glasses and a slash-mouthed smile that promised a brimming stein of nasty wit chased with a jigger of sentimentality, had a job that consisted entirely of finding out about stuff and then writing about it. I became a regular reader of his column after I discovered the comics but well before I understood much of the rest of the paper. I also found him compelling because he was one of only two people I knew of who picked fights with Mayor Daley. The other was Leon Despres, longtime alderman of the Fifth Ward, but Despres seemed to cross Daley as an exercise of some self-mortifying higher principle, and to take his inevitable defeats as proof of his own moral rectitude. Although Despres was my piano teacher's brother, I regarded him as a wishful fiction dreamed up by the faculty of the University of Chicago and the listeners of WFMT.

Royko, by contrast, held Daley to account as an elected representative of the people not only because he was a journalist who got paid to do that but also because he took obvious pleasure in annoying the mayor. Royko had a gift for pissing people off, mostly by sketching deft caricatures of them as he told in acerbic column-size fragments the great Chicago story of his time: how peasants and the children of peasants came from elsewhere and made it, or didn't; moved up, or didn't; acquired wealth, power, and status, or didn't; and passed their gains on to their inheritors, or didn't. It seemed to me that Royko's ability to get away with making fun of Daley and other powerful people, his particular purpose and efficacy, had something to do with his dual citizenship in both Chicago and the republic of letters. When expected to strike from one direction, he struck from the other; when goons dispatched by vengeful overlords sought him in one place, he slipped off to the other.

And there was Mister Dunlap, another model of the passionate craftsman, this one more intimately tied to mastering the lay of the land. Before we had a name for him, he was the unknown burglar who had apparently undertaken to rob every single house in the Jackson Park Highlands. Word of his brazen virtuosity spread through the neighborhood: it was rumored that he had done three houses on the same block in one week; he had ransacked a house while the owners and their dog snoozed in blissful ignorance; he had lifted a gold chain from around the neck of a sleeping woman without waking her. I had a general idea of what he looked like because my brothers had seen someone we believed to be him. They were in a pack of neighborhood kids sitting on their bikes on the sidewalk when they heard a gunshot and then a lean, well-dressed man in platform shoes bearing a striking resemblance to Rollo from *Sanford and Son* came swiftly around the corner and doubled back up a driveway. After a few moments, a stocky, out-of-breath man with a gun in his hand came around the corner, asked which way the first man had gone, and went off after him. Only a criminal stylist of rare distinction, I felt, would burglarize a house in platform shoes.

At some point the burglar was caught and identified as Mister Dunlap. He went away for a while, but when he got out of prison he picked up where he'd left off, robbing houses in the Highlands, gripped by a magnificent obsession. I invested him with a quality of artistic purpose that I regarded as somehow akin to Royko's powerful urge to mess with the mayor. We heard, later, that Mister Dunlap had been living in an apartment on Cregier, on the edge of the Highlands. I pictured him waking up whenever burglars wake up and looking out the window at the neighborhood he had apparently sworn to pick clean to the bones, sipping ascetic tea as he considered which house to do next. Because the houses in the Highlands are architecturally distinct, each presents a different problem to a thief. That must have appealed to him, or maybe it was just that the big fortified homes were likely to have expensive things in them. He was, inevitably, arrested again and went to prison again, this time for a longer stretch. I heard he'd been caught in the act of robbery in a less fancy part of South Shore, and it struck me that this served him right for wavering in his commitment to his masterpiece, the looting of the Highlands.

And there was Kwai Chang Caine, the renegade Shaolin monk who wandered across the Old West in prime time on *Kung Fu*, earnestly trying to avoid violence but forever encountering louts with feathered thickets of seventies hair who obliged him to knock them in Peckinpavian slow motion through breakaway saloon tables and other period-appropriate wooden contraptions. He caught Indians' arrows in midflight, gently snapped them in two, and discarded them with an expression that said, "Again, with the rustic feathered darts?" He seemed content to drift and contemplate, but people were always demanding—usually right before or just after he kicked somebody's ass—that he explain what he wanted, what he was about, and he always had a satisfying answer. Some kind of American Orientalist cultural landmark was achieved in the eighth episode of the second season, in 1973, right about at the moment that it began to become apparent to the far-seeing that postwar prosperity and the attendant growth of the middle class were going into reverse, the New Deal order was falling apart for keeps, and the American century wasn't going to work out as expected. That's the episode in which Caine said, "I seek only to become a cup empty of myself, filled with oneness." Imagine Kojak or Mary Tyler Moore saying it, or even trying to understand Caine when he said it.

I admired the way Caine covered ground, going where the contours of the land or his fancy took him. He effaced himself whenever possible to reduce the friction of his passage, a policy I regarded as prudent, but he also reminded me that if you did find yourself singled out and hauled to center stage for a potentially humiliating scene, then your best bet was to double down on who you were—be it a half-Chinese drifter in the Old West or a white kid with glasses on the South Side. Soulful unbelonging, even forthright goofiness or freakiness, was always a better option than scrambling abjectly to conform to the expectations of those who had cornered you, a self-betrayal that would only cause you to hate yourself and, anyway, wouldn't save you from what you had coming. When drunken cowboys closed in on you yet again in yet another saloon, you didn't beg for mercy or try to out-bluster them. No, you sought to become a cup empty of yourself, filled with oneness, and did your best to make it to the next ad break on the strength of whatever counted as the equivalent of your Shaolin skills.

*

What I wanted from Caine and my other models were lessons in how to make a way through the world. Among caped dwellers in the city's shadows, for instance, Doctor Strange appeared to prefer the dark for purely aesthetic and thematic reasons, rather than to gain strategic advantage, while Batman concealed himself in the darkness of alleys and rooftops for more practical reasons—to evade notice and achieve the element of intimidating surprise. Among guys named Carter who saddled up odd mounts for necessary journeys, Edgar Rice Burroughs's John Carter mastered the art of riding the ill-tempered giant lizards called thoats as part of the process of fitting himself into the nomadic society of six-limbed green Tharks who roamed the desiccated ocean bottoms of Mars, while H. P. Lovecraft's dream-quester Randolph Carter mounted up on yaks, zebras, and other such creatures to traverse occult distances in search of his elusive golden city. All of them risked ridicule at least— "Nice cape, faggot"; "Tell me that's not a motherfucking *yak*"—and annihilation at worst, but there was something worthwhile to be gained in each case: advantage, belonging, a way home.

Why didn't real people I saw every day qualify for this list of models who showed me how to make a way in the world? Among my cohort, leading stoners, ballplayers, virtuosi of the mack, and other high-status types didn't offer much for me to emulate, since they were Daleys in miniature: those who took charge and advanced confidently in the direction of their desire, putting the mark of their will on the world. I looked more to the sliders-through, counterpunchers, go-arounders, and margin-skulkers who read and reacted to the conditions generated by the Daley types; but the real ones were harder to pick out and recognize against the background of the South Side than Kwai Chang Caine walking barefoot across the desert or Batman wrapped in his cape in a noir-chiaroscuro alley.

And what about female humans? Surely there were models of purpose and efficacy to be found among them, although you'd never guess it from the list I've been making so far. Setting aside for a moment Kwai Chang Caine's and Batman's fictional sisters in arms—Lieutenant Uhura, the Black Widow, *Police Woman*'s Pepper Martin, any character played by Pam Grier, and Red Sonja and Velma Valento and a regiment of similarly self-possessed pirate queens and noir vixens in the pulps—there was, in fact, a set of girls in my grade who were just about perfect in that regard. Intelligent, presentable, discerning, judiciously kind but not inclined to put up with any bullshit, they went about their business in the defensible middle ground between the Daley types who dictated terms to the world and the Caine types who slid through. Had I been considerably less dazed, I would have noticed that these girls, Monica and Masumi and Martha and others, offered ideal models for me. But I didn't. I merely appreciated that they looked and smelled nice and let me copy their French homework, although my tendency to skitter away from any substantive engagement, even a conversation in which I offered anything more than opaque wisecracks, soon exhausted their patience.

Or, keeping it simpler still, I could have just consciously emulated my immediate family: hardworking parents and grandparents and accomplished brothers who fairly bulged with honorable purpose and efficacy. And I can see now that they did serve as principal models for how to live, but at the time I wasn't ready to own up to the influence. What I thought I needed, back then, was an eye for ground and a feel for how to get across it without attracting the kind of undue attention that could lead to unspecified, inconceivable annihilation. If I had any purpose and efficacy, it was the kind that allowed me to navigate the landscape of the South Side by slipping from shadow to shadow, unnoticed or at least unremarked on, through the world made by the mayors, the players, the Mister Bigs and silverback kingpins who planned and acted and imposed their intent on the city and their neighbors.

LIMITED LIABILITY

Received wisdom on the South Side holds that South Shore has money but no organization—as opposed to Woodlawn, which has the venerable Woodlawn Organization and other such grassroots institutions, but no money. It's at best a partial truism, and of fairly recent vintage. There was a time in living memory when South Shore had not only copious resources but also an organization—the South Shore Commission and its various component area councils, each representing a discrete part of the neighborhood—that could connect leaders and citizens to each other and mobilize them in pursuit of ambitiously defined outcomes. Therein lies a tale about collective efficacy and its limits, one with potentially useful lessons for those who care about South Shore today.

This tale yields a time-tested model for success in organizing and mobilizing the people of South Shore: focus not on a broad moral or social claim to communal fellow-feeling but on a specific, highly visible piece of the container, a building or a chunk of landscape that houses an institution that matters to South Shore's agenda-setting homeowners; then show how gaining or losing that institution will serve the interests of these owners as individuals, not just as a community. This model, derived from the community-organizing victories of the 1970s and early 1980s that had long-term benefits for the neighborhood, also helps explain what hasn't worked. It offers as well a reminder that the container really matters, and may even be a key to community.

*

The story of the origin of the South Shore Commission sounds like the setup for a joke. In 1954 a rabbi, a priest, and a minister decided that the South Shore Ministerial Association needed a secular complement, control of which soon passed to lay members. South Shore already had the usual church groups, business associations, and the like, but the creators of the South Shore Commission felt a need for a civic organization expressly committed to community-building and leadership, to looking out for the neighborhood as a neighborhood. They were responding to larger changes in the postwar city shaped by interlocking folk migrations to midcentury America's two promised lands, the movement of African Americans from South to North and the suburbanization of white urbanites. As Chicago's black population overspilled the constraints of the Black Belt and as suburbia opened up to white ethnics as the place where full and permanent assimilation into the middle class could be achieved, new destinations beckoned aspirants whose sights had been raised by postwar prosperity and extended New Deal policies. For some, mostly black, that meant moving up to South Shore; for others, mostly white, it meant moving up and out from there. The old urban villages began to contract and break up.

The South Shore Commission's founders could see the ripples of change coming closer. Before the war, black residents had already started moving into Washington Park and Woodlawn, traditional feeder neighborhoods for South Shore. The influence and resources of the University of Chicago helped keep Hyde Park's white residents from fleeing as black neighbors moved in, but the resulting partial integration was an exceptional case. In other neighborhoods on the South Side and West Side, turnover from white to black—a brief period of integration-in-passing as incoming and outgoing populations overlapped, followed by swift resegregation—was the norm.

The South Shore Commission became the most powerful organization in the neighborhood. It ran a variety of programs ranging from recreation and arts to real estate development planning and building code enforcement, and its monthly newspaper, the *South Shore Scene*, was widely read. By 1966, 3,500 families in South Shore were paying dues to the commission, which had an annual budget of $90,000 and was known as one of the strongest community groups in Chicago, even in the nation. Its leading figures, a mix of successful professional and business types and their well-educated spouses, moved among the city's civic and business elites and had the ear of Mayor Daley. The people of South Shore had a reputation for standoffish self-reliance, but the commission found ways to bring them together, especially in the face of what it regarded as an existential threat.

In the 1960s, as black families began moving east across Stony Island into Parkside and, bypassing the Highlands, farther east into O'Keeffe and all the way to the lakefront, every issue that the commission took seriously—schools, crime, blight—became a dependent variable of the single monumental issue of racial succession. The commission's leaders fell along a spectrum from hard-line exclusionists, who wanted to keep blacks entirely out, to liberal integrationists, mainly educated Jewish professionals who were embarrassed by racial fear and loathing. During the commission's early years, its agenda was basically exclusionist, but by the mid-1960s, facing the fact of growing numbers of middle-class black neighbors that included a high proportion of families whose children attended public schools, the integrationist wing gradually took control and the exclusionist position grew irrelevant.

The turn was decisively marked in December 1966, when the South Shore Commission announced that "in order to achieve a stable, integrated residential community," its board had adopted an official policy of "managed integration." The announcement appeared on page one of the *South Shore Scene*, which also featured a story about new security measures initiated in the neighborhood's schools after a violent confrontation between groups of black and white students in the cafeteria at South Shore High. The commission explained that "outside forces"—including "lack of open housing in the city and suburbs, discriminatory practices by some elements of the real estate industry, and the pressures of the Negro population for more housing"—were "pressuring South Shore into becoming an extension of the Negro ghetto." The only way to intervene in that process, as an admittedly artificial "interim device until the city as a whole can effect open housing," was to keep "all real estate transactions at 50% Negro and 50% white."

Managing integration boiled down to a twofold process. First, the commission set up centralized screening for incoming black tenants

and owners to limit "Negro" transactions to 50% of the total and prevent what it regarded as the nonrespectable poor from following the
black middle class into South Shore. The screening process predictably
irritated the screened, like members of a soul group who named themselves the South Shore Commission out of ironic spite—kind of like the
southern rockers of Lynyrd Skynyrd, who were inspired by the name
of a gym teacher who disapproved of long hair. The band South Shore
Commission charted a couple of songs and appeared on *Soul Train* in
the 1970s. Second, the commission (the organization, not the band)
tried to bring the proportion of "white" transactions up to 50% of the
total by recruiting new white residents. This meant working with government agencies and other parties to interdict and punish the block-
busting efforts of real estate speculators while aggressively marketing
South Shore to white people as lovely, affordable, and not as dangerous
as they'd heard.

It was during this period of upheaval that Harvey Molotch, a doctoral student in sociology at the University of Chicago, set out to write
his dissertation about South Shore. He was more or less ordered to do
so by one of his professors, Morris Janowitz, who wanted Molotch to
prove that South Shore was replicating Hyde Park–Kenwood's model
of racial integration. The perceived success of that integration scheme
was essential to the university's reputation and well-being, and demonstrating that the model could be replicated would strengthen the case
for that success. From July 1965 to July 1967, Molotch gave South Shore
the intensive Chicago School treatment: haunting meetings of the South
Shore Commission and other neighborhood groups, interviewing community leaders and real estate dealers, reading all the news he could get
his hands on, assembling data from the census and school and hospital
records, doing head counts in bars and shops and parks to get a reading
on the day-to-day progress of integration, and shooting the breeze with
residents as he crisscrossed the neighborhood. The result eventually
became a book, *Managed Integration: Dilemmas of Doing Good in the City*,
one of the Chicago School's catalog of studies that "do" a neighborhood
in a particular moment.

Janowitz may have been a less-than-ideal dissertation director,

but he did advance at least one lastingly excellent city-related
the community of limited liability. He introduced the concept in
using the example of neighborhood newspapers to argue that the quai-
ity of community was alive and well in the supposedly anomic metropolis, although it took different forms than his colleagues might have
expected. His principal foil was the foundational distinction that Ferdinand Tönnies made in the late nineteenth century between gemein-
schaft, the supposedly simple face-to-face social intimacy of the rural
village, and gesellschaft, the complex urban social condition founded
on anonymous indirect ties to others. Rather than treating the urban
neighborhood as a survival or replica of Tönnies's nineteenth-century
village, Janowitz argued, sociology should allow for a more partial,
optional, multiple, and contingent kind of belonging, one among many
such possible belongings. If the neighborhood wasn't providing what
urbanites needed, they could shift allegiance to a different voluntary
association, like a professional group or an ethnic club; if the neighborhood was sufficiently rewarding, they could deepen their commitment to it by investing more resources in it. Janowitz argued that institutions like the neighborhood newspaper could serve as conduits and
custodians shaping this kind of community, not unlike the way print
culture would function on a grander scale three decades later in Bene-
dict Anderson's formulation of the nation as an "imagined community."

Janowitz's concept had another foil within the Chicago School, one
that went back to the founding figures Robert Park and Ernest Burgess:
neighborhood defined by the sharply bounded delineation of turf and
violent distinction between insiders and outsiders that a street gang or
restrictive housing covenant might employ. Gerald Suttles, who arrived
in the department in time to sign on as one of Molotch's dissertation
advisors, was intent on reviving this older concept in the form of what he
called "the defended neighborhood." The wave of intemperate rhetoric
and violent incidents that marked the expansion of the black inner city
into immigrant-ethnic neighborhoods during the postwar decades suggested that the concept had not lost its utility. The defended neighborhood seemed like the right label for the kind of tight little island Mike
Royko had in mind when in 1971 he famously likened Chicago's ethnic

neighborhoods to the warring states the city's immigrants left back home in the Old World: ". . . you could always tell, even with your eyes closed, which state you were in by the odors of the food stores and the open kitchen windows, the sound of the foreign or familiar language, and by whether a stranger hit you on the head with a rock."

There wasn't much rock-throwing in South Shore. There were scattered violent incidents and some tough talk in the most blue-collar sections—down on its southeast edge, nearest the steel mills, where several decades previously Donald Peattie had watched kids of Polish, Italian, Irish, and German descent pick on Abie—but, on the whole, South Shore was too middle class, educated, and liberal to go in for the rough stuff. It had also become, despite the earnest exertions of Peattie's schoolmates, a heavily Jewish neighborhood, where in the aftermath of the Second World War residents would be especially unwilling to raise echoes of the strident rhetoric of race war associated with the Nazis. White South Shore just didn't fit the definition of a defended neighborhood. For all the concerted work by the commission and various smaller groups to resist the neighborhood's transformation, the story of that transformation was a story of limited liability that turned out to be much more limited than the commission had expected.

"The efforts of the South Shore Commission and the public resources allocated to 'save' South Shore were, in terms of the primary goals for this one community, wasted." So begins Molotch's summary of his findings, putting a thumb in Janowitz's eye and appending an ironic punch line to the story about the rabbi, the priest, and the minister. Molotch found that, in turning over from white to black, South Shore remained for the most part "stable" and "orderly," with limited integration of public space but not much mixing in private and semi-private life as it moved "toward resegregation at approximately the speed which would be expected of a changing middle-class community in the mid-1960s." The commission's efforts did not manage to impede even slightly the social and market forces drawing whites to the suburbs and blacks to South Shore. Property was changing hands at about the usual brisk rate, but, except for some reshuffling of white residents into the more affluent parts of the neighborhood, almost every white household that left a home in South Shore was headed all the way out of the neighborhood and was replaced by a black household from outside South Shore willing to pay extra to live there. The commission's leaders "had succeeded in building one of the most powerful community organizations in the United States," but they never found a way "to compensate for the disparity between the white and Negro housing markets." (Hyde Park had retained its white population, Molotch pointed out, because the university's presence made white people willing to pay more—"black prices"—to live there, which harnessed market forces to the task of repositioning the tipping point well beyond the percentage of black residents.)

In its heyday, the South Shore Commission had built up a massive reserve of potential collective efficacy and mobilized it to achieve all sorts of useful things with lasting benefits for the neighborhood: school improvements, new amenities in the parks, recreation programs, urban renewal and code enforcement programs. And the commission had formulated even more ambitious plans that would never be realized: attracting a Catholic university campus to the lakefront; school redistricting schemes; covering the IC tracks and redeveloping 71st Street as a state-of-the-art bi-level shopping strip. But if the goal was to keep a lot of white people in South Shore, none of it made the slightest difference. If anything, the commission's efforts had made South Shore more attractive to the incoming black middle class. When Molotch came back for a visit in 1970, he found that the commission's leadership and membership were now largely black and that South Shore had moved significantly "closer to becoming an all black community." The commission's focus had shifted decisively from race to class in its ongoing struggle to keep out "undesirables," a term now understood to mean poor people who were black (also known as "welfare types," "Woodlawners," or residents of "AFDC buildings") rather than black people who might or might not be poor.

The commission failed to keep South Shore significantly white because, unlike the university and allied community groups in Hyde Park, it never figured out a way to harness and exploit the forces bearing down on the neighborhoods of the South Side. As long as a lot of black people were willing to pay more to move to South Shore and not many white people were willing to move there even if it was a bargain for them, there might well have been no way to accomplish that trick in South Shore. This bind was exacerbated by speculators who pressured white homeowners to sell to them at a discount by warning them that if they waited longer an impending influx of black neighbors would cause the price to fall further, and then sold the houses at a large markup to black buyers whose choices were limited by the segregated housing market.

And the commission failed because in seeking to increase and deploy collective efficacy to fight for the neighborhood, it ended up asking residents to choose community over an individual self-interest that could be pursued elsewhere. The people the commission was trying to rally weren't peasants just off the boat with nothing to go back to and nowhere else to go, a hard-ass tribe who would pull together and make a stand if they felt they were cornered. They were, rather, fighting to be left alone to be—or to become—members of the white middle class dedicated to the individualistic priorities of family, career, and upward mobility. This was the defining shape of their limited liability. South Shore had long seemed like a perfectly nice place to pursue such a social trajectory, or at least a convenient launching pad or way station for it; but it was no longer as attractive to white people as it had been in the 1930s and 1940s, and it wasn't the only option. The affluent North Side, Hyde Park, neighborhoods like Beverly out on the edge of the city, and beyond the city line the booming expanse of suburbia were, increasingly, more enticing. South Shore's white residents had choices, and many would likely have chosen something else even if they hadn't felt pushed by the arrival of black neighbors. South Shore had largely served its purpose for its third- and fourth-generation Irish and Jewish families, who, once they had moved up and out, would soon become ready to join the great nostalgic pining for the Old Neighborhood and authentic ethnic identity that underwrote the heritage movements of the 1970s and after, the cultural epoch defined by the touchstone narratives of *The Godfather* and *Roots*.

The story of South Shore, the quintessential quiet green place to live in the city, is in great part the story of being middle class in the city. Is it to the credit of the South Shore Commission that it shifted from a policy of keeping South Shore white to one of keeping South Shore middle class, which meant accepting integration? That might make its leaders and members seem a little more enlightened, or at least more realistic, and perhaps they are partially redeemed or excused by the fact that the black residents who took over the commission in the 1970s continued along this same policy line of defending South Shore as a middle-class bastion against interlopers from below. Or perhaps not.

South Shore's transformation offers a reminder that neighborhood is a cause for which you can feel great passion but will almost always sell out if you're pushed hard enough at the right time. That's what makes the neighborhood of limited liability a more powerful explanatory concept than the defended neighborhood, to which a quality of wishful sentimentality often clings. Family and nation might be worth sacrificing and even dying for, and any tour of South Shore today will show that the defended *house* is a vibrantly useful concept. But no matter how committed you are to your neighborhood, that commitment is limited, and you'll move on if the perceived rewards of moving are high enough or the penalties for staying severe enough. And the more resources you command, the more choices you have, the more easily the bond to neighborhood can be broken. People with choices and something to lose don't risk it all to go out in the street and throw rocks. They call the cops, they call whomever they might know downtown, they look around for somebody to sue, they talk about digging in and holding the line in solidarity with their neighbors, the more intemperate among them use phrases like "never, ever" and "over my dead body," and then they leave.

*

There's a twist to the story about the rabbi, the priest, and the minister. In the 1960s, the South Shore Commission organized and mobilized a great deal of potential collective efficacy but still utterly failed to realize its impossible dream of keeping South Shore white. However, in the 1970s, as the commission weakened and faded into irrelevance and eventual collapse, with no comparable organization rising to take its place, South Shore's shifting and temporarily integrated ad hoc crews of leaders managed to amass and shrewdly direct smaller-scale doses of collective efficacy to accomplish three big wins that had long-lasting effects. Neighbors got together to stop the South Shore Bank from leaving the neighborhood, to force the city to convert the defunct South Shore Country Club into a public amenity, and to shut down one of the city's most notorious tavern strips.

I felt the immediate and lasting effects of these victories. I still have my first passbook, from the South Shore Bank, in a box somewhere. Its raggedly printed entries detail my modest but steady accumulation of money I collected from odd jobs, gifts, and my Spanish tooth fairy, who left dollar bills and orthographically wry notes—her laugh went "jeh jeh jeh"—in my mother's foreign cursive. I don't know much about money, but I do know how to save it, a habit I formed early in life by making two- and four-dollar deposits I was resolved to fight to defend if anybody tried to take them from me on my way to the bank. Tucked away, too, in vivid memory, is a halcyon moment at the defunct country club: idling in the shallows of Lake Michigan on a sunny August afternoon with just my eyes and ears above water, like a crocodile, as Muddy Waters led one of the final iterations of his great band with grandfatherly aplomb through a set of favorites on an outdoor stage behind the old main building. It's one of my primal synesthetic experiences of music and the cityscape, one of those perfect early highs that the addict is always trying to reproduce. And somewhere deeper in memory, not so easy to recover, is a peripheral half-awareness of local taverns going away all at once. My formative sensitivity to change over time, the embryonic historian in me, got an early jolt from the extinction that took the Old Style signs and hot-parked Impalas and LeSabres with the knob on the steering wheel to facilitate gangster lean, the watchful men in three-quarter-length leather car coats and the mincing women in tippy heels and boldly unnatural wigs, the wafts of for-lovers-only balladry and cologne-over-liquor-and-sweat reek drifting out through scarred, propped-open doors. After the taverns went, it was quieter on the nearby tree-lined blocks, and there was less broken glass strewn around in the morning, and there were fewer calls to the cops about scuffles in the street and car crashes, and fewer drunks sleeping it off in gangways or doorways. It was quieter, too, on the commercial blocks lined with even more empty storefronts than before. They took on a sere quality reminiscent of the Greek ruins in the Valle dei Templi at Agrigento, where as a little boy I climbed with the lizards over sun-blasted Sicilian stones.

These are all memories of living the consequences of the collective efficacy exercised by my neighbors in the 1970s. Each of these victories—the bank, the country club, the taverns—had lasting effects on life in South Shore, and each came about because community groups set their sights on goals consonant with the container-oriented limited liability that residents, especially those with the most resources and connections and choices, were willing to invest in their neighborhood. These community groups were smaller and more narrowly defined than before. As the South Shore Commission receded in importance, block clubs and area councils representing discrete subunits of South Shore became the prime exponents of community feeling in the neighborhood. The Chicago School had terms for these more intimate tiers of local association—respectively, the face block (the two sides of a block facing each other across a street) and the nominal neighborhood (the smallest scale of discrete area that has its own name, like the Highlands or Parkside)—which now took greater precedence than the notion of South Shore as a whole.

South Shore's new black residents settled in and sent their kids to the local schools and made use of the parks and beaches and fading shopping streets, rebuilding and revising the networks for collective action that had been disrupted by the rapid departure of so many previous residents. Because the new order, which included many more poor people than before, divided along class lines dictated by the mix of housing stock—more apartments and poverty in Parkside and O'Keeffe, for instance, and more bungalows and middle-class owners in Bryn Mawr East and West—it was subject to block-by-block and even intra-block variation that could limit the ability of an area council or block club to represent a cohesive constituency of mutually obligated neighbors. But the 1970s was also an era of racial integration-in-passing, especially within the ranks of South Shore's leaders, whose partnerships across racial lines strengthened the movements that produced the era's big collective-efficacy wins.

The first and most important of these was helping to prevent the departure of the bank situated at the central intersection of 71st and Jeffery. In 1972 the South Shore National Bank, a neighborhood institution since 1939, applied for federal permission to move downtown to the new Standard Oil building. The bank argued that it could make more profit there, as South Shore no longer provided a suitable banking environment. It blamed its falling deposit levels on rising crime, a declining business sector, and an incoming black population that was younger, more mobile, more likely to feature two working spouses, and less likely to save money than the white population it was replacing.

There were two challenges to the bank's request to move, one by a competitor and one by the Stop the Bank Move Committee, operating under the aegis of the declining South Shore Commission. Among the commission's board members was Bob Keeley, a lifelong South Sider and veteran community organizer and teacher who had lived in South Shore since 1956. Keeley, who is white and who then lived at 73rd and Paxton in Bryn Mawr East, recruited local residents with authoritative credentials—a banker, a professor of management—as well as politicians ranging from aldermen to Senator Adlai Stevenson to argue for the bank's importance to a neighborhood trying to stabilize after a major social upheaval. They also refuted the bank's case point by point, demonstrating, for instance, that the decline in deposits was the result of its own failure to keep making the kind of loans it had when the neighborhood was white. The bank stayed and was taken over by an interracial ownership group—Ron Grzywinski, Milton Davis, Mary Houghton, and Jim Fletcher—with fresh ideas about community development banking in the inner city.

The bank, eventually renamed ShoreBank, and its parent entity, the Illinois Neighborhood Development Corporation, became internationally famous for taking a creative and successful approach to community development, using lending and other financial practices to provide the material basis for a viable inner-city urbanism. If a neighborhood in transition could be stabilized, the bank's new directors believed, then market forces could begin to work in its favor, rather than tearing it apart. In practice, banking with the goal of neighborhood stability and development meant more than reversing the effects of redlining by other banks that had made it so hard to get conventional mortgages, business loans, and other sorts of credit in places like South Shore. It also meant planning and financing extensive building-renewal projects in Parkside, O'Keeffe, and other parts of the neighborhood, systematically funding and providing management assistance to black franchisees and other such business owners, and taking on the challenge of reviving South Shore's commercial streets. Until it was done in by the combination of the financial crisis of 2008 and a perception in the Republican-dominated Congress that it was somehow a pet of the Clintons and President Obama and therefore politically unqualified for the bailouts that other financial institutions received, the bank invested about $750 million in South Shore (out of a total investment in Chicago of nearly $3 billion) in the form of loans to businesses, churches, and nonprofit organizations; loans to purchase or rehab single-family homes or apartment buildings (the bank financed 18,195 multifamily units in South Shore); and consumer loans.

The bank gradually spread its influence throughout the neighborhood. It played a supporting role in both the country club and anti-tavern campaigns, used its newsletter (which had a pitch-perfectly 1970s name, *The Bread Rapper*) to help keep locals abreast of upcoming meetings, donated staff time and work space to community groups, and otherwise involved itself in the organizational life of the neighborhood. Milton Davis, president of the bank and a resident of South Shore, testified against demolishing the old country club building, served as an honorary chair for the "local option" campaign to close the taverns, and served a term as president of the South Shore Commission. Davis and Grzywinski and other major players at the bank developed deep connections throughout the neighborhood, and the bank grew so involved in so many aspects of neighborhood life that it was perceived as having taken on the mantle of the South Shore Commission, which ceased to exist in the early 1980s.

Stop the Bank defined the model of how to mobilize collective effi-cacy in South Shore: pick a piece of the container to fight for, push for the proper institution to be housed in it, and base the argument not primar-ily on the common good but on the individual self-interest of residents who may well be more invested in the neighborhood-as-container than in the neighborhood-as-community. The arguments made by Keeley and his allies proved at least somewhat meaningful to the Office of the Comptroller of the Currency, but, for the purposes of drawing a lesson in community organizing, they proved extremely persuasive to fellow residents, who were inspired to pitch in for the greater good by offer-ing testimony. The basis for making common cause was an assumption of middle-class priorities—property values, respectability, propriety— shared by the growing black majority among South Shore's leaders and the fast-shrinking but still influential white minority.

A second major victory of the period, forcing the city to turn the defunct South Shore Country Club into a public amenity rather than demolishing it or selling it off, also conformed to the model. Since opening in 1906, the club had been a resolutely exclusive institution to which blacks and Jews, no matter how affluent, could gain entrance only as kitchen help or caddies. Its fortunes waned in the 1960s as the neighborhood changed around it and the club-joining class departed for far suburbia, and it closed in 1974. The club's buildings, grounds, and beaches occupied fifty-eight choice lakefront acres at the eastern end of 71st Street. Word circulated around the neighborhood that the Park District, which had acquired the property, was planning to sell it to developers who wanted to build high-rises there, or to the Nation of Islam, which said it wanted to build a hospital. Once the Park Dis-trict had been persuaded to hang on to the property, it then had to be prevented from tearing down the country club's once-elegant Medi-terranean Revival–style main building and replacing it with a standard concrete-block fieldhouse.

Motivated neighbors, including some who tended to value the con-tainer over the community, could reasonably be expected to go to war for a lakefront park that was on everyone's short list of South Shore's most attractive advantages. The long campaign to save the club wasn't quite a mass popular movement, but it was more inclusive and broader-

based than the work of the handful of experts who undertook to save
the bank. A series of neighborhood groups that formed to stop the Park
District from destroying the club eventually coalesced into a broad-
based organization, the Coalition to Save South Shore Country Club
Park. The coalition and its predecessors arranged for plenty of citizens
to show up and speak at public hearings, a show of force and unity that
impressed representatives of the Park District and other city agencies.
Phyllis Betts, who wrote her dissertation in sociology at the University
of Chicago about black activism in South Shore in the 1970s, was struck
by the militant voices of middle-class respectability that she heard at
public hearings. "One of the things that has continued to stand out in my
mind for all these years," she told me in 2015, "was black activists taking
real issue with the Park District's plans to put basketball courts and bar-
beque pits there." They also objected to a plan to create a scaled-down
pitch-and-putt golf course, of a kind widely considered beneath the dignity of serious golfers. Betts said, "Their attitude was, 'You think that's
good enough for us? Basketball and hot dogs and pitch-and-putt?'"

The decade-long campaign forced the city to create and sustain a
public amenity that combined green parkland and cultural program-
ming. In the early 1980s, as the struggle dragged on, the property hosted
the Jazz Comes Home concert series at which I had my music-and-
cityscape moment of crocodile ecstasy in the lake's shallows. The South
Shore Cultural Center formally opened in 1985, with the coalition refor-
mulated as its citizens' advisory council, and since then it has hosted
programs and classes in music, dance, fitness, culinary arts, and more.
A ballet school has operated there, the South Shore Opera Company has
performed there, and the restored main building has hosted all manner
of meetings and galas, including Barack and Michelle Obama's wedding
reception in 1992 and, more recently, public hearings about building the
Obama Presidential Center in Jackson Park. The Cultural Center has
long been the neighborhood's most gracious amenity, a "hidden jewel,"
as Deborah Harrington said while gazing down at it from her lakefront
high-rise window.

The local option campaign, which did away with about thirty taverns
on a four-block stretch of 75th Street east of Yates, was even more
broad-based than the effort to save the country club. On November 5,

1974, the day when showing up counted for everything, 1,627 citizens voted in favor of turning ten precincts dry, overwhelming the 418 who voted against it. But the local option movement still conformed to the privatist South Shore model of activism: clearly defined features of the container (storefronts on a specific stretch of 75th Street and also parts of 71st Street) were occupied by the wrong institutions (taverns and associated liquor stores), with the result that individual residents' middle-class status was threatened by the crime, disorder, and other less-than-respectable behavior concentrated around the taverns.

The problem was embodied, as one resident put it, in "Superfly individuals, bums, and wineheads," who represented both a practical and a symbolic threat to the neighborhood's middle-class character. A letter to the editor of the *South Shore Scene*, its author scandalized by a tavern advertising the appearance of an exotic dancer known as Body Meat, claimed that the strip attracted patrons from the West Side, Gary, and other locales that were generally viewed as ghetto (the letter writer didn't use the word, but didn't have to) in a way that South Shore wasn't. Proponents of the dry vote pointed out that the 75th Street tavern strip was the worst in the city for complaints of theft and damage, that drunken roisterers regularly jumped on passing cars and got in fights and passed out in gangways and alleys, and even that mail delivery was rendered "unsteady" by the convenient availability to mail carriers of strong drink throughout the day.

The organization that arose to do away with the taverns, the Committee for a Safer South Shore, grew out of the Bryn Mawr East area council, representing a part of the neighborhood well-endowed with bungalow blocks. The campaign worked out of the South Shore Commission's offices, with black activists taking the lead and the handful of white participants keeping a low profile. The coordinator of the committee—Bob Keeley—and its office manager were white, but its spokesperson and most of its members were black, which made it easier to reject the tavern owners' attempt to cast it as attacking their civil rights. The tavern owners presented themselves as black businessmen under assault from intolerant puritans, but they had misjudged the relative importance of race and class in South Shore's public discourse and had little success in arousing sympathy.

The public debate about the local option campaign was also a discussion of how life should be lived in South Shore, of what South Shore was *for*. The tavern owners—in addition to trying to shift blame for disorder and crime from their patrons to "junkies," who "don't drink"—mounted two arguments that offered social and cultural visions of South Shore. One argument cast the neighborhood as a place of racial solidarity where black culture was appreciated. (The photographer Michael Abramson, celebrating that very segment of black urbanism, was at that time taking some of his finest pictures of Superfly individuals and Body Meat types who hung out in South Shore's taverns and other South Side night spots.) The tavern owners' other argument advanced the notion that South Shore needed places where adults could go to relax and talk.

The tavern-abolitionists, who largely ignored the "it's the junkies" argument, dismissed the black solidarity and black culture gambits as cynical maneuvering and countered the adults-need-a-place-to-relax line of reasoning by stressing that South Shore was above all a respectable residential neighborhood. Their commitment to this identity was so complete that they would willingly accept even more empty storefronts in order to preserve it. Only three of the ten precincts voted dry actually contained parts of the 75th Street strip; residents of the other seven were voting preventively to make sure that the tavern owners, some of whom had already been pushed from 47th Street to 75th by the University of Chicago's urban renewal projects, did not relocate closer to them. If adults wanted to relax and talk, they could do it in their living rooms or backyards, or while engaged in wholesome recreation in the park, or if they really needed booze and music in a bar, they could find that in another neighborhood. This view, this vision of the limited but still potent liability that bound self-interested individuals together into a community, easily prevailed on election day.

*

Among these big wins of the 1970s, there was a notable failure, which had similarly long-lasting consequences and offered a pointed reminder that residents' limited liability did not necessarily extend as far as activists hoped it might. In 1977 a community-development-minded consortium called the Phoenix Partnership bought a three-block stretch of the north side of 71st Street east of Jeffery from Allan Hamilton. Backed by the South Shore Bank, the partnership intended to revitalize the commercial strip by filling thirty-five storefronts and twelve second-floor office spaces with thriving black-owned businesses. Steve Perkins, who had been one of the first hires by the bank's new management, headed the group. Carol Adams, recruited by the bank to direct its research arm, the Neighborhood Institute, was one of the partnership's original investors. When I talked with Perkins in 2014 at his office at the Center for Neighborhood Technology, a nongovernmental organization based on the North Side, he said, "The conventional wisdom was that commercial districts in new black communities after racial change had always gone to hell in a handbasket." In his youthful optimism, he had set out to reverse that logic by orchestrating a blend of bank loans, pressure on the city to improve the streetscape, management assistance to small business owners, and rallying of the community to support local merchants. "We spent an enormous amount of effort trying to make it happen," Perkins said, "but it never did."

Perkins came to believe that the Phoenix Partnership had undertaken an impossible task. South Shore was over-endowed with storefronts—1,200 in all, many of them small—and its old-fashioned shopping streets with limited curbside parking and aging buildings were of the kind being eclipsed all over the country by suburban malls. South Side shopping centers like River Oaks, Ford City, and Evergreen Plaza were having a similar effect on 71st Street. "For business to be successful in an obsolete real estate structure," Perkins said, "there has to be a reason for people to shop there, and not at big box stores." Usually, that reason has to do with ethnic belonging. The most vital commercial district on the South Side in 2014, he pointed out, was in Little Village, where Spanish-speaking customers went to shop in Spanish and outsiders went to soak up the atmosphere. There's also an upscale neo-bohemian version of this kind of shopping district, a "cool and interesting" place, as Perkins put it, where residents and visitors alike go to stroll and linger. The black version of cool and interesting has tended not to work as well, Perkins said. People who aren't black tend to avoid such places, and as a general rule the black middle class has proven to be particularly unwilling to shop in local neighborhood stores selling what are perceived as second-best goods. "You have this extremely brand-oriented, status-oriented consumer group that doesn't want unique and different or some kind of ethnic theme," Perkins said. "They want conventional middle-class consumer items, national brands, of the kind you get in a mall." So the failure to fly, at least so far, of funky little shops in South Shore should have come as no surprise. As Benet Haller of the city's Department of Planning told me, "Usually, the more acculturated a population is, the lower the percentage foreign-born in it, the less neighborhood retail they're going to support." The middle-class American norm is to get in the car to shop at name-brand national outlets, and nobody's more acculturated to that norm than middle-class African Americans.

The Phoenix Partnership's plan conformed to the model of successful collective-efficacy campaigns in South Shore in some ways, but not in one crucial respect. It identified a specific piece of the container and tried to fill it with desirable institutions, but it failed to recognize that asking shoppers in South Shore to patronize scrappy local businesses they could reach on foot rather than name-brand competitors they could reach by car was asking them to choose neighborhood over middle-classness. This exceeded the limits of their liability, especially as homeowners increasingly retreated from the neighborhood's public life. Appealing to their sense of black solidarity by asking them to support local business owners didn't help at all. It might even have hurt.

In 1981 the bank finally cut its losses and parted with Perkins, over his strenuous objections. "I lost a friend over that one," Ron Grzywinski told me. Perkins eventually managed to disinvest from South Shore, selling off his properties and moving out of his house at 73rd and Luella in 1992. Not only had he been forced to give up on 71st Street when the bank had given up on him, he said, but his wife "didn't want to be the only white lady on the block anymore." After two decades in South Shore, he didn't like the neighborhood's direction. "The class war hadn't really heated up yet when I was there," he said, "but the schools were already terrible, and South Shore High was already full of young men wearing their character armor." Recent visits had not given him confidence in the neighborhood's future. "I was driving around Seventy-Eighth, Seventy-Ninth a couple of years back, and I was appalled," he recalled in 2014. "It looked like the West Side. Whatever gains were made by the South Shore Bank and its various affiliates have been wiped out." The popping of the housing-market bubble in 2008 was "the last straw," he said. "They bet on the neighborhood and the neighborhood went down and they went down with it."

Perkins had described himself to me as "willing to dedicate what's left of my sentient life to trying to help Chicago's black community fig- ure out a viable future," and South Shore still seemed to him poten- tially "the most savable" of all the neighborhoods on the black South Side, given its housing stock, location, and transportation network. But, he said, "South Shore has no institutional or governmental capacity to solve problems." That's not necessarily always the case, and it certainly hasn't always been the case, but consider the empty-supermarket- building fiasco that began when the Dominick's at 71st and Jeffery closed in 2013. The supermarket was in the strip mall financed by the South Shore Bank as its Plan B for 71st Street after the Phoenix Part- nership failed. The effort to fill the vacancy adheres to the model of successful organizing in South Shore: focus on the container, pick an institution that homeowners care about, appeal to their self-interest. At this writing, a Shop & Save is finally slated to move in; but even if that does happen as expected, it will have taken five long years to fill this prominent dead spot at the neighborhood's heart. As the middle class recedes from public life in South Shore and the divide widens between haves and have-nots, even organizing efforts that follow the time-tested model may not work so well.

EQUIPMENT FOR LIVING

MUSIC

The radio was a squat menhir with a face panel of brown plastic fake-wood and pebbly-rough knobs that had to be adjusted just so with a flutteringly delicate touch to coax a station's signal at the proper volume from the ambient static. The built-in tape player opened with an abrupt uncalibrated *whunk*, but I had just a few oddly assorted cassettes—Spyro Gyra, Jimi Hendrix, Herbie Hancock, Atlanta Rhythm Section—cast off by my older brother or other kids on the block, so I mostly listened to the radio: WXRT; WJPC, the J in which stood for Johnson, I knew, but was it the Afro and Ultra Sheen *Soul Train* Johnson or the *Ebony* and *Jet* Johnson?; WVON, "Voice of the Negro"; WDAI, which became WLS-FM; WSDM, "Smack Dab in the Middle," which played Donna Summer's "Last Dance" over and over on its final day of existence and then played Cat Stevens's "Morning Has Broken" to mark its rebirth as WLUP, a rock station. The radio, its display giving off a faint cold glow in the darkened room, stood on the bedside table, facing me as I lay with my head on the pillow. My younger brother's bed was on the other side of the table. He often slept with his eyes partially open, slivers of white showing. At bedtime I turned the radio way down, drifting off to the murmurous voices and faint wails that came out of the hissing distance.

Having the radio on all night was part of a grand project of exploration, an unarticulated intent to go out into the wider world and see what people were up to, that I would have disavowed if accused of harboring it. It seemed presumptuous, dangerously forward and self-exposing, to aspire to map the world, and yet I felt a potent need to know what was out there. So I stored safely below the level of conscious desire the expectation that in my travels-to-come I would learn how each element of what I heard and saw, however individually puzzling, connected to what might turn out to be a dawn-breakingly elegant whole, a map of the big picture that afforded perspective and understanding. I relied on the radio as if I were a castaway or trapped behind enemy lines. Over the air, occasionally transmitted in plain speech but more often in enigmatic code, came fragmentary instructions, cautions, bulletins, field reports, chart readings offering guidance to navigation in the outer and inner worlds.

A deejay would announce that the Isleys, say, or Mahogany Rush would play the Aragon Ballroom next month, welcome confirmation that the figures inhabiting the radioscape were also people of flesh and blood, wearing vertiginously flared pants, who came to town from time to time and could, at least in theory, be tracked down and perhaps even interrogated as to their role in . . . *things*. Such points of information could be gathered and held in reserve, to be slotted into the emerging overall design of . . . *things* at some later date, when all had been revealed. But where did the Brothers Johnson's orange birds and river cousins dressed in green fit into the picture? Why did England Dan and John Ford Coley keep insisting that they were not talking about Bolivia? And what crucial information was being conveyed by other means— semaphore? mime? ultrasonic pulses?—during the long stretch during which Peter Frampton's band vamped on the groove of "Do You Feel Like We Do"? The radio was trying—the world was trying—to tell me important things ("Bob Mayo on the keyboards! Bob Mayo!"), but I wasn't equipped to decrypt all the messages.

I had to estimate and extrapolate, and often to guess, which I did with variable confidence. I was, for instance, pretty sure that I knew what Yes was saying. They seemed cosmically ill, as if prevailing conditions on this planet caused them to be in perpetual anguish. Gaunt and caped and stroking cunningly fashioned instruments of esoteric design, they sent complex distress signals back to their home world after crash-landing on this one. Moving beneath the clamor of Jon Anderson singing like a defrocked member of the Venusian Boys Choir, Steve Howe piling on the harmonics and baroque licks, and Rick Wakeman challenging

Keith Emerson for the title of heavyweight champion of keyboard over-kill, the subtext of every song was something like "The situation is dire. The light is distressingly bright, and the alien atmosphere poisons our minds so that we suffer oppressive visions. We must constantly change key and time signatures to vary the flow of sound waves over our sensitive nerve endings. Wakeman has grown moody and distant; he plays two keyboards at once with no regard for others' suffering. There are flying elephants. The mountains come out of the sky and they stand there. Send help soon. Over."

But the distress of, say, Maria Muldaur was more difficult to decipher. "Midnight at the Oasis" seemed a mostly straightforward Orientalist desert fantasy (except for "Cactus is our friend," which I didn't like the sound of), but something about her tone suggested there was more to it. Behind the façade of playful beguilement, her voice was shot through with a sobbing, half-swallowed quality of—what, exactly? Sorrow? Regret? Panic? Was this "sheik" she was addressing some kind of cruel tyrant? It seemed to me that she was having a hard time maintaining a cheery front that she had learned to counterfeit so as to lessen the hardship that was her lot in life after making a terrible mistake, perhaps involving giving up her passport.

There was a lot of that kind of thing on the radio, where everybody seemed to be afflicted with a despair over having chosen unwisely—the wrong person, the wrong pill, the wrong turn. Even when they got what they wanted, the getting was suffused with sadness. Billy Paul got to be with Mrs. Jones, yes, but their routine of meeting every day at the same café at 6:30 and then going their separate ways seemed heartbreaking. And what about Mr. Jones? He had to suspect. Mostly I wondered what *he* was doing at 6:30 every day. Probably brooding over a sticky-sweet drink in some place on 75th Street with Z. Z. Hill on the jukebox and an atmosphere redolent of Kools, Colt 45, and tropical-scented personal grooming aids manufactured by the Afro and Ultra Sheen *Soul Train* Johnson's Johnson Products Company (not to be confused with the *Ebony* and *Jet* Johnson's Johnson Publishing Company). Such a scene had a kind of grandeur, but it was a grandeur constituted principally of woe.

In addition to offering a gallery of models of how to be a person in the world, with a new one arriving every few minutes as the next song came up, the radio extended the map of that world around and ahead of me, marking out a tracery of routes and destinations. I had thoroughly explored my own sections of South Shore from an early age, gotten used to going back and forth to Hyde Park on my own by bus and bike and on foot, and gone on longer-haul lakefront biking expeditions with other kids, but the first time I can remember going downtown on the train without an adult was to buy a record I'd been hearing on the radio. I was in sixth grade, and the record was *Chicago IX*, a greatest hits collection that stayed at number one for many weeks. "25 or 6 to 4" led off side one; even these horn-playing, easy-listening gentle woodland creatures reported staring blindly into space in a catatonia of fearful regret, a condition that seemed to haunt every venture into the wider world and communiqué from it.

And yet it seemed worth the attendant risk to find out what was going on out there. The radio put other destinations on the map that became reachable in my high school years, among them concert venues like the Uptown and the Aragon—which offered notoriously toasted and unruly crowds six-hour shows and thousands of folding metal chairs, handy to swing two-handed by the legs or to hurl, hammer-thrower-style—and the big new outdoor arena at Alpine Valley in Wisconsin. And when the high-school-era reaction against standard-issue hits set in and it became imperative for persons of discernment to go beyond mere kid stuff and the conventional grid, there would be blues at the Checkerboard Lounge in old Bronzeville, jazz at the Showcase downtown, an occasional junket to Symphony Hall or the opera with tickets somebody's parents couldn't use and cans of beer tucked into coat pockets and sleeves. The smuggled cans, heavy and cold against the skin, got shaken up in transit, so they had to be opened with care after the house lights went down, and with a fake cough to cover the distinctive metal-and-fizz sound of breaching the can's seal.

*

The arrays of preset buttons on the radios of rental cars I've been picking up at Midway Airport over the past few years are riddled with wormholes leading back to my age of exploration. On the rock stations, they never tire of flirtin' with disaster and getting the Led out. On the dusties stations, native South Sider Minnie Riperton is still hitting her dogwhistle high notes and swearing that no one else can make her feel the colors that you bring, and Teddy Pendergrass is still pleading for trust and understanding without ever quite going on record as categorically stating that he has not, in fact, been running around with Mrs. Jones. And the lite stations, purveyors of sonic wallpaper for office and home, are playing songs like the Little River Band's "Reminiscing" and Ambrosia's "How Much I Feel" that I hated intensely when I was a kid and to which I'm now strangely drawn. It might as well be a slow Tuesday night in 1979.

As I pull out of the airport lot and start east on 55th Street, heading for the lake, I shuttle among the stations playing the well-ridden warhorses of my childhood, jumping past ranchera duranguense and Dirty South hip-hop and everything else that has proliferated on the radio since I lived in Chicago. Some part of me resists being manipulated with the music of my childhood by format programmers, but when I'm in Chicago I'm too vulnerable to musical nostalgia and they usually win. That music has become an atlas of place and time, a device for wayfinding into the past. If, say, "Always and Forever" or "Fool in the Rain" comes on, I return to bittersweet memories of fuzzy-sweater dances and palsied flights of inexpressible Byronic inspiration. When I was fifteen or sixteen, I would walk around for hours under a slate-gray sky musing on "I run in the rain 'til I'm breathless, when I'm breathless I run 'til I drop." All these years later, the remembered pleasure of adolescent infatuation with the song layers together with the fresh pleasure of finding that I still go for it. *Hey*, I think, *that's still a pretty good song*—and I can not only forgive but enjoy Johnnie Wilder Jr.'s drifting out of tune on "Always and Forever" or Led Zeppelin's ill-advised whistle-blowing fake-salsa break in the middle of "Fool in the Rain."

With soft rock, it's different. The songs that generate the most powerful and uncontrolled time-traveling momentum are not the ones on which I grooved deeply as a kid but instead the gossamer America's Top Forty hits that reeked of gonging boredom and the forlorn hope against hope that there was more to life than this. There was never anything less going on than when "How Much I Feel" was on the radio—as close as you could get to nothing at all being on—and nobody was around and there was nothing to do and there would never be anything to do, ever. When one of these spiked madeleines comes on, it's as if I'm comparing scars or tales of dangerously foolhardy hijinks with an imaginary coeval. Bob Welch's "Sentimental Lady"! I can still recall the burning passage through my system of that sulfurous cocktail of bad juju. Or Paper Lace's "The Night Chicago Died"! Jesus, that one nearly killed me. And Gerry Rafferty's "Baker Street"! I can barely stand to recall how, sitting on my neighbors' stoop on an achingly slow Tuesday night with their radio playing, I would hear that song's tweedling intro resolve into its signature sax riff and wonder if I was going to make it all the way through the thing one more time without being utterly destroyed by its payload of weapons-grade ennui wrapped in a velvety outer coating.

I drive east on 55th through West Elsdon and across the tracks into Gage Park, and on across Kedzie, California, and Western, the mix of pedestrians and businesses shifting from Mexican and Central American to black, then across Damen and Ashland, another big commercial street every half-mile, with Back of the Yards on my left and West Englewood and then Englewood on the right. I cross Racine and Halsted, passing more boarded-up and empty buildings fronting the tree-lined, potholed boulevard; more empty lots with high prairie grass where buildings used to be; more chain-link and wrought-iron fences around the occupied buildings. I go under the tracks and over the Dan Ryan Expressway and across State Street into Washington Park, through the green belt of the park itself, and into Hyde Park—university buildings, busier streets, suddenly a lot of white people—and then out the other side and into the green reaches of Jackson Park, bending south along its curving drives to close in on South Shore.

These days I'm coming in from the airport, but in my late teens and twenties I did most of my traveling back and forth between the East Coast and Chicago by car, which meant that I was usually coming in at night through Gary and the far South Side, high up on the Skyway with a steel mill or two breathing fire in the distance—the last of a near-extinct race of dragons. I was almost always riding shotgun in someone else's car, since I didn't own one, so I would be well situated to find the right music on the radio or tape deck to accompany our approach.

I was already by then thinking of Chicago as the place to which I return when I am chipped and dinged by the world, in need of a spell of contemplative retreat. That feeling has grown stronger with the years. Returning to Chicago is going back to the original stuff that matters, not the analysis of the stuff or the pitching of that analysis to an editor or the wondering about who has a contract to write about the stuff or who's getting reviewed where for writing about the stuff—the whole tangle of considerations surrounding all the many sorts of professional moves I make on the stuff for a living. I want to just go, and be there, and fill myself up with the stuff itself.

*

My first job after graduate school was at Lafayette College, in Easton, Pennsylvania, a town in the Lehigh Valley that, like its neighbors Bethlehem and Allentown, hadn't yet figured out what to do with itself after the factories closed. The college, which looked exactly like what I thought college was supposed to look like, crowned a steep hill overlooking the rest of the town, which looked like what a former mill town in Pennsylvania was supposed to look like. I'd be out at night, coming back up College Hill from a bar in the desolate downtown, thinking about the book I was trying to write about the Checkerboard Lounge and *The French Connection* and other teenage enthusiasms, the classes I had to teach, the students who didn't know how to try harder, and my own inability to show them how to. All the things that I'd agreed to care about by accepting the position and the career and the life that went with it were pushing around in my head, tipping me off balance. So I'd imagine pointing the car I now owned west and taking off away from it all.

I'd picture pressing on through Pennsylvania and into Ohio by dawn, filling the car with gas and myself with eggs and coffee at a truck stop somewhere out past Sharon, the urge to reach Chicago flooding me with energy that eclipsed the urge to sleep. I could call my girlfriend back in New Haven, my wife-to-be, from the road. She would understand, I assured myself, although if I didn't turn around after a day or two and get back to my job, she would soon begin to wonder if she'd made the wrong choice after all. I'd make Indiana by noon, and not too long after that the East Side of Chicago would swing into view around the nether curve of the lake, with its mounds of slag and ballast left out in the rain and ruined factories like titanic car chassis rusting on cinder blocks.

The moment I had most sharply in mind was coming down off the ramp of the Skyway onto Stony Island Avenue and into the South Side, the wide street spreading away under the overcast, angular figures at the curb sliding by. In this moment there would be just the right song on the radio, something I had helplessly loved or hated when I was growing up, something that therefore now lent itself to the most potent time- and space-warping conjurations. I wanted, instead of taking College Avenue up the hill to Lafayette and then going left on Cattell and left on Parsons to park in front of my rented half of a side-by-side duplex house, to be taking a right off Stony Island onto 71st Street, into South Shore; and I wanted "If You Don't Know Me by Now" or "Kashmir" or Bobby Caldwell's "What You Won't Do for Love," or, hell, "Reminiscing" or Gary Wright's "Dream Weaver" (another one that scorched my insides like Greek fire when I was eleven) playing on the radio when I did.

When I was a kid, inclined to daydream and drift, listening to the radio raised a simultaneously yearning and heartbroken feeling in me that was a lot like being in love. Because I had never been in love, I didn't recognize the feeling, and anyway I had nowhere to put it other than in the cityscape. So that's what I did with it. I poured the feeling into the container of Chicago—the wide empty streets, the bungalow blocks, the lots going back to prairie, the beer-signed lounges and streetlight-spotlit corners and the darkened groves of the park, the clang of the warning bell as the crossing gates went down along the train tracks.

When I come back to Chicago now, it's like an experiment in what it would be like to have always remained the person-in-theory I was and never have become the person-in-practice I turned out to be. Since I left home, I've found or dug channels along which heartbroken yearning and other strong feeling can run. I can tell my wife and daughters about it; I have brothers and parents with whom I share a lengthening past; I have friends and colleagues who will probably know what I'm talking about—also a handful of trusted editors and a literary agent. One thing I now know to do with strong feeling, one thing I didn't know how to do then, is to tell a reader about whatever inspired it. But coming back to Chicago—or being caught in a vulnerable moment by a soft-rock hit of the 1970s—returns me to a time before that complex of purpose and meaning took shape and became available to me, when I had no clear sense of a path to acting on or even articulating the inchoate urges that meandered through me. From my base camp in South Shore, I made my way through the city, careful to deny any immediate sense of mission but vaguely assuring myself that it would all turn out much later to have been part of a coherent plan that made good sense. I can see now that there was more substance to that lazy, evasive promise than I gave it credit for at the time.

When I return in the flesh or in a song, I'm revisiting the landscape in which I cached all that feeling, and in which I first began to act in a deniable, indirect sort of way on the impulse to see what people were up to, what they made of their world. That impulse has acquired sharp edges and matured into a calling, but it was indistinct then, which was how I preferred it. I wasn't ready for anything like a calling. I had very little idea of what I was doing when I set out into the city, guided by the radio; but it turns out that whatever I can claim now in the way of purpose and meaning comes from those seemingly aimless first steps, the first tentative marks I made on the nearly blank slate that would become my map of the world. Every time I hear a song that was on the radio then, I find myself back at the starting point—a little daunted by the echoes of old fears and confusion that the rush of memory awakens, and maybe a little renewed, too, or even inspired, by the prospect of beginning, again, from the beginning.

LOST CITIES

A broad flight of stone steps descends from the rear of the Museum of Science and Industry into the lapping waters of the Columbia Basin, which connects to the Jackson Park lagoon and, via the 59th Street Harbor, to the lake. This is the kind of evocative scene that cries out for a giant toad-thing to come bloated and squelching out of certain unspeakably ancient ruins secreted in the watery depths and mount the steps to slaughter shrieking victims until a pulp hero arranges for one of the museum's massive caryatids to topple athwart the obscene batrachian's sloped skull, then plunges a yard of cold steel through its gelatinous vitals. No such ruins or monsters came to light when a work crew temporarily drained the lagoon in 2015 as part of a project to restore Wooded Island, which sits in the middle of it, but they did find guns, ammunition, knives, axes, car parts, a whole car, a streetlight, tents, Christmas trees, and of course shopping carts. There's a long tradition of throwing things into the lagoon. In 1924 Leopold and Loeb, looking for a good place to dispose of the frat-house typewriter they had used to write a ransom note about a victim they had already killed, threw it off the footbridge at the north end of the island. Fourteen years later the ashes of Clarence Darrow, the lawyer who saved them from hanging, were scattered over the lagoon from that bridge, which is named for him.

Against all reason, I half expected news stories about items turned up by the dredging of the lagoon to make some mention of the pipe I tossed into it thirty-five or so years before, on a cold, clear morning in late 1980 or early 1981. I remember the little pipe's brass bowl catching the thin sunlight as it tumbled end over end, trailing bright smears of afterimage as it arced down to disappear with a hollow *splash-plop*. I had made a serious chemical mistake on the previous evening, and my aching bones felt as if overnight they had been carved by demons into fluted arabesques so fragile that one more wrong move would cause them— and perhaps also the dying planet across the face of which I crept, bug-like, in the winter glare—to collapse into dust. I had slept in Hyde Park at the apartment of a school friend I will call Peter, and on the walk home through Jackson Park, I had decided that I was done forever with getting high. This resolve lasted only a few days, as it turned out.

When I look back on things I did as an adolescent that caused me to say to myself *This is a bad idea* right before I did them, Peter was usually involved. He exerted a force field that dispelled caution, relentlessly pushing a good time into scary excess. In his presence, the dire logic of chaos and ruin that shadowed the apparent order of daily life seemed to gain strength, developing a terrible momentum as it rushed into the light. Back in sixth or seventh grade, we were at his apartment one day after school, spraying paper airplanes with Lysol and then setting them on fire and throwing them out the window. Upon leaving my hand, one of them traced an improbably tight downward parabola, arcing with great purpose and increasing speed as if piloted by a madman, and flew, cheerily aflame, through the open window of the apartment downstairs. Hundreds of people lived in the two-towered, seventeen-story building, built two years after Leopold and Loeb killed Bobby Franks, which commanded fine views of Jackson Park and the lake. I lingered by the window, dully contemplating the possibility that the burning airplane could at that moment be nestled in curtains a few feet below us, long tongues of fire beginning to rise from the bunched fabric to blacken the ceiling beneath the carpeted floor on which we stood. I vaguely assured myself that everything would probably turn out all right, and we went off to eat a box of Rold Gold pretzels or something. I don't recall even mentioning it to Peter, who in some occluded way I chose to hold responsible for attracting whatever sinister force had guided the burning plane through the window.

Peter's gift for compounding pharmaceutical and mechanical risk, paired with a clean-cut, helmet-haired look that suited him for a supporting role in a cereal ad, made him exactly the kind of guy who kids in my neighborhood had in mind when they described white people as crazy. In another couple of years, a typical inspiration for him would be to steal his parents' car so we could use it to steal a tank of nitrous oxide from the hospital, and if he could get somebody else's girlfriend to come along and share in the excitement, which would ideally have a corrosive effect on her monogamous commitment to that somebody else, even better. It was mostly in Peter's company that I departed from workaday dope-smoking to sample more advanced forms of damage. In the end, during senior year, I had to fall away from him before I could finally muster the sense and will to leave the stoner realm behind as I readied myself to leave home for good.

That makes the stoner realm one of my lost cities. Once, it overspread the land I lived in. I was one of its shaggy citizens, and one signature of the era was that their number embraced all kinds of types: college-bound achievers as well as dead-enders, jocks alongside bookish types, the popular and the marginal and all gradations in between, adults and middle schoolers, and heads of all colors—though being a stoner was regarded as a white thing in much the same way that basketball was regarded as a black thing. The stoner realm's citizenry went about with a pent-up, bouncing gait, hands jammed deep in jacket pockets, talking head cant in highly stylized accents based on models already lost in the irrecoverable past of the sixties. They were perpetually on the look-out for a nice spot to smoke up in peace: the Point, the Blocks, the far reaches of the park, the rooms of certain kids you knew or sort of knew whose parents were supposedly cool, although it never seemed to quite work out that way and you ended up outdoors in all weathers. Such spots were prominent features in a geography that also included record stores, head shops, concert venues around town, and more distant places that were rumored to be stoner paradises: California, Hawaii, and, weirdly, Wisconsin. This was long enough after the sixties that getting high had been thoroughly stripped of political or moral or generational valence. It was just a thing to do—an *excellent* thing, totally in*tense*—that happened not to be legal. You could just choose to be a head, one of millions, and it meant next to nothing. Soon heads would be falling away in large numbers to pledge allegiance to New Wave, punk, metal, hip-hop, cocaine, Valium, Izod, Reagan, computers, weight lifting, or some other such cause, but while the stoner realm flourished, it gave me a convenient way to fit in at my school in Hyde Park and, in South Shore, afforded me an easily assumed persona when I needed one. What was that white kid doing walking around on 67th Street after dark? Just a stoner; no need to devote any more thought to him.

When I left the stoner realm, it faded and thinned in retrospect until it formed a filmy remnant through which I pass now and again in the world I inhabit today. Once in a while the dimensions intersect, perhaps because Yes is caterwauling enigmatically in 13/8 time on the car radio or because when looking at Frederick Law Olmsted's preliminary plans for Jackson Park, I spot the germ of a copse I used to cut through during my long walks home with a head full of smoke. When such intersections happen, I feel a little jolt: a flash of recognition, the simultaneous sense of a veil's brushing touch on my skin and of dense-packed layers underfoot.

Density is a defining quality of cities, and lost cities are a form of it: the proliferation of superseded and decaying versions of the city that are layered under by newer ones. Whether the lost city has physically ceased to be or you've just moved on and left it behind, whether it's objectively or subjectively lost, either way it's a good idea to keep in mind the stickiness of neighborhood effects. Lost cities are in one sense spent, exhausted, but as they recede into the underlying structure of a place, they can still exert an influence on what comes next—subsequent landscapes, stories, ways of knowing the world or being in it. To move through a city, in the material world or on the page or in the mind's eye of memory or fantasy, is to simultaneously inhabit any number of lost cities, each exerting its own ghostly neighborhood effects.

*

I spent a lot of time in Jackson Park, playing pickup football and baseball, attending day camp, shooting the occasional salvo of bottle rockets at golfers, and brooding over what the peerless Chicago neighborhood writer Stuart Dybek called "the long thoughts." Part inner-city steppe, part enchanted forest, dotted with romantic ruins, the park was a 543-acre solitude that I regarded as home ground.

Its layers felt most accessible, its stillness most expressive, late at night. Having taken leave of the evening's company in Hyde Park and set my sights on South Shore, I'd cross wide, empty Stony Island Avenue on the diagonal at 59th Street, with the twin towers of Peter's building at my back. Approaching the dark tree line, I'd feel for the right gap through which to enter. Beyond, deeper within the greater darkness of the park, the glow of streetlights lining the drives pinkened the sky. I'd pick my way through murky groves, navigating by keeping the lights of Stony Island on my right and those of Cornell Drive on my left. Occasionally a late-night crew, up to something mysterious, would pass nearby, and I'd go to ground or hurry away in the shadows. I'd pick my moment to trot across Cornell, momentarily exposed, then continue south and east in woodland gloom again, skirting the parking lot on which the statue known as the Golden Lady turns her back, where cars cruised in circles on the hunt for business or trouble or something else I couldn't provide.

This part of the walk took me through the site of the White City of 1893, the Columbian Exposition's idealized model in plaster of the industrial age. The pavilions that lined the lagoons turned the park into a fantasy land out of classical antiquity, and the engines and dynamos and other machines gave it the feel of a steampunk Olympus. Extending to the west along the Midway Plaisance were arrayed carny attractions like Ferris's giant wheel and Houdini's escape act, and also a schematic map of the peoples of the world, favoring the exotic: Little Egypt dancing the Hoochee-Coochee, singing Fijians, Hindoo jugglers, Bedouin warriors, and, down at the far end, Buffalo Bill's Wild West Show. I picture the young Edgar Rice Burroughs, there during his summer vacation from military school to show off a prototype horseless carriage for his father's American Battery Company, nearly running down the aging Frederick Douglass, who interrupts his inveighing against the exposition's racial politics and the U.S. government's treatment of the Black Republic of Haiti to shake a fist at the damn kid in his proto-flivver. The exposition's surviving relics include Wooded Island and the surround-

ing lagoon; the Museum of Science and Industry, its original tempo-
rary gesso exterior replaced with 350,000 cubic feet of durable Indiana limestone; and the Golden Lady, a one-third-size replica of Daniel
Chester French's 100-foot statue of the Republic that had presided over
the exposition. The little sister stands with arms upraised in imitation
of the long-gone big sister's proud gesture of benediction over a city
that vanished.

The exposition's model of the industrial city and the world system
centered on it is the South Side's Atlantis. Other lost cities may be older
but none is as definitive, as pervasive. As a native of Chicago, you may
grasp, intellectually, that there were many phases of human settlement
prior to the industrial city. But industrial Chicago so completely enjoys
the status of ur-city, of template and basis for all that follows, that sometimes it feels as if when the Laurentide ice sheets receded, they revealed
industrial Chicago already fully formed and populated, streetcars and
freight trains putt-putting here and there as in the Museum of Science
and Industry's giant train set—all the moving parts, mechanical and
human, going about their business of turning raw materials into finished goods.

Those late-night walks home also took me past a more recent lost
city in Jackson Park, off to my left in the darkness on the other side of
the lagoon: the Cold War city, represented by the defunct Nike anti-
ballistic missile base that opened in 1955 and closed in 1972. The missile
silos, capped and sealed, were buried under a part of the park called
Bobolink Meadow. The command center had been out on the Point,
a spit of land jutting into the lake that featured prominently on stoners' map of the South Side. The testing of the city's civil defense sirens
on Tuesday mornings offered a weekly reminder to panic a little about
death from above, and there were more sustained episodes of panic in
1968. Gary Huber, a retired soldier who served at the base, told me that
during the Democratic Convention riots, extra troops were brought
in to repel rumored imminent raids by the SDS or the Yippies or some
even more nefarious crew of crazed, love-spouting Ostrogoths bent
on seizing nuclear warheads. Huber said he had also been briefed on a
plot to dose the city's water supply with LSD. And then there were the

Blackstone Rangers, whose turf began just across Stony Island Avenue, and who were reputed to have the numbers to go head to head with the National Guard.

Put the two lost cities together, the White City gearing up to dominate the world and the Cold War city perpetually fending off existential threats from enemies foreign and domestic, and they tell a story of foundation and empire giving way to the growing fear that even the most robust-seeming order won't last. The entropic facts of life dictate that just by virtue of *being* order it wants to fall apart, and must be shored up and defended even to the brink of self-destruction. But on those nighttime walks, I wasn't yet putting together the lessons taught by the park's lost cities. They were just out there in the dark, gently pulsating with obscure significance. Nor was I yet equipped to learn such lessons when as a little boy I attended day camp in a field separated from the missile base by only a ragged scruff of trees and undergrowth. Searching for a foul ball or making an end run in a game of Capture the Flag would bring me once in a while to the base's perimeter wire, sending a cool prickle up my neck.

In recent years I grew curious about what physical residue might persist from the missile base, its silos sleeping beneath the park's green surface. Perhaps this lost city's capacity to reach out from beyond the grave to shape lives wasn't just symbolic. Perhaps it had a tangible chemical or even nuclear component. On summer weekdays in my elementary school years, both when the base was operational and after it closed, I played all day and sat on the grass in a circle to eat my spaghetti omelet out of my plaid-patterned red lunchbox within a few hundred yards of the base. There was no doubt that remnants of a lost city could get into one's head and linger there, but could trace elements of its material form get into one's cells and linger there? My criminal ignorance of chemistry, abetted by overfamiliarity with the logic of pulp fiction (here I cite the toad-thing from the lagoon), made it seem at least possible. I filed a FOIA request for studies conducted by the U.S. Army Corps of Engineers, which had been charged with ensuring that the closed base did not become a threat to the park and the people. Reams of reports duly arrived, filled with maps in which lists of dire-looking chemical names and notations about "exceedances" were linked by arrows to locations in the park. I sent it all to Philip Landrigan, a renowned pediatrician and epidemiologist who is a leading expert on environmental threats to children's health. He wrote back to say that he thought that the Army Corps had done a pretty good job of monitoring and remediating the site. "For the most part the material that they are excavating appears to be standard-issue urban fill dirt," he concluded. "The only materials that may relate specifically to the missile base are the solvents. I see residues of industrial Chicago here, most especially the polycyclic aromatic hydrocarbons that represent soot probably from the burning of coal, but no particular signature of the Nike base." So the chemical-nuclear horror scenario didn't pan out, trumped by the defunct factories of Chicago's Atlantis. If I carried trace elements of a lost city in my cells, it was the same old industrial city of which every child of Chicago bears the imprint in one way or another.

Once across Hayes Drive on my walk home, the Golden Lady and the ghosts of the White City and the Cold War city receding behind me in the night, the park felt darker, closer. I'd be in long-haul rhythm by then, covering ground, firmly thumping my heel down on the turf with every step. I'd cross unlit stretches of grass and cut through narrow gaps between patches of brush, still keeping off the paved paths. I'd pass the locked-up marina, which usually caused me to wonder if boats get stolen just like cars, and if joyriders crash them or bring them back. Then I'd cross Marquette Drive and enter the homestretch, my feet finding the path worn across the golf course by cross-cutters like me. I'd see golfers in the daytime, and I understood that they enjoyed walking around and hitting the ball and not being at their jobs, but I didn't understand why there was a golf course here. It had something to do with the marina and the Golden Lady, I assumed—something that felt historical, lingeringly persistent, atavistic. I was grateful, in any case, for the expanse of grass and trees and water on the border of my neighborhood, the open territory where nobody lived, the way home.

Jackson Park always felt like Nature to me, but of course it was second nature, a triumph of artifice. Digging, draining, sculpting, clearing, planting, shifting dirt to flatten here and build up an eminence there, shaping the raw materials against the backdrop of the lake, Olmsted's workmen had executed his magic on a mostly treeless parcel of land dominated by sand hills along the lakefront and boggy sloughs inland. The lagoon and Wooded Island, conceived by Olmsted as a place of respite from the frenetic delights and crowds of the exposition, were man-made. The island and its meditative Japanese garden, set within the White City, rendered in miniature Olmsted's idea of how a park functioned in a city—as a carefully fashioned place of recreation and recovery from the mechanized pace, noise, stress, and cold money logic of industrial modernity. Olmsted's genius was to augment and remake the materials at hand to serve that high social and moral purpose, not to return them to the state of nature. (This seems like the right moment to note that, according to a well-informed Army Corps source, a Park District employee has compiled a highlight reel of human sex acts captured by critter cams on Wooded Island.)

So, one more lost city in Jackson Park: the undeveloped, pre-industrial, pre-Chicago landscape of prairie, scrub, swamps, wooded ridges, and lakeside dunes that once extended all along the lower curve of Lake Michigan. That landscape wasn't entirely gone for good from Chicago—I used to look out from the IC train at vacant lots along the tracks near 71st Street and see the high prairie grass that had reclaimed them moving in the wind—but there wasn't much of it left in the urban garden that was Jackson Park. The old landscape had been layered under, along with any number of man-made successors.

If I take this walk again in a few years, for old times' sake, the park will very probably have acquired additional layers that add up to a major transformation. The Obama Presidential Center (OPC), with its plans currently calling for a 235-foot main tower and extensive grounds and the closing of Cornell Drive, is slated for a 19-acre chunk of the park between Stony Island Avenue and Wooded Island. The Park District has approved a separate plan to combine the Jackson Park and South Shore Cultural Center golf courses into one championship-level course designed by Tiger Woods's company, TGR Design. Together, these projects would end up semi-privatizing huge chunks of the park, drastically limiting the range of public use and making it harder for the park to do for all comers what an Olmsted park is supposed to do. The golf course plan, slowed down to let the OPC get through the approval process first, would make the more significant change in the character of the park. Even the old golf course never felt exactly like the rest of the park to me. It felt like a golf course, an alien landscape several times removed from Olmstedian recreation. Combining and expanding the existing courses will push the whole southern reach of the park further toward being something that's not quite the park.

The result might well turn large stretches of Olmsted's park into a lost city in its own right, layered under a generic landscape of fairways and bunkers that might as well be anywhere. Jackson Park's history amply demonstrates that a park can serve different purposes and still retain its character, but some of those purposes, like those that led to the Columbian Exposition and the Nike missile base, can more drastically alter a park's character and inhibit its ability to be a park. Whenever anybody expresses concern about the golf course plan at community meetings about the OPC, they're told that the two projects shouldn't be considered together, but the golf course upgrade, more than the OPC and especially *in addition* to the OPC, could perhaps tip the balance against Olmsted's park.

On the final leg of my night walk, the path across the golf course crested a small rise, dropped away from it, and ran across a flat stretch to another rise, then a final dip. At the park's southern edge, I would put my hands on the top of the chest-high chain-link fence that used to be there (since replaced with a higher one) and vault over without breaking stride. Leaving the park, I'd continue on the diagonal across 67th Street and then down the chute of Euclid, under streetlights once more as I passed the dark stately houses of the Highlands. When I got to the high-shouldered brick house with no front door on the 6900 block of Euclid, I would remember to disarm the alarm before I unlocked the door, and to rearm it once I was in. I would find something in the refrigerator and see if there was anything on late TV, padding around the sleeping house, snug inside the castle with the drawbridge pulled up. But, really—walking down Euclid with tight-shut houses on either hand and the street all to myself, a freight train calling on the IC tracks in the distance, the park a vast darkness behind me haunted by ghosts of its former selves—I was already home.

*

To reach the portal to the next set of lost cities, come with me across the neighborhood to 79th and East End, the corner where U. S. Floyd took me to Demetrius Archer's sidewalk memorial, near Stony Island Avenue and the far southwest edge of South Shore. Thanks to the artist Mitch Markovitz, who lived in South Shore in the 1950s and 1960s, I spend a lot of mental time on this corner. Mounted on the wall in the hallway outside my bedroom, where I see it every day, is a framed poster of an oil painting he did for the cover of Caryn Lazar Amster's book *The Pied Piper of South Shore*.

It's an evening scene in which a father and two small children, seen from behind and below as if by another child (or perhaps, less benignly, by something slinking up on them), look at the display window of the Wee Folks toy store. The little girl points; the father, solid and slope-shouldered in a short-sleeved white shirt, stands patiently between the girl and her brother, holding each child by the hand. The outlines of the cars along 79th Street and the bus across the street identify the era as the 1950s or early 1960s. Beyond the bus stop the Moorish-fantasy Avalon Theater is all lit up, and indistinct adult silhouettes cluster by the box office. The setting sun floods the sky with dark oranges and reds, and long shadows reach up the pavement and gather, deepening into night. The low-angle point of view and the rounded shapes of the father and bus give the scene a gentle child's-eye quality of nostalgia and innocence that resonates with the two kids' wonder at the toys in the store window. But there's also a tang of menace in the shades of descending night, the dark moving figures in the distance, the hint of predation in our view of the well-lit and unaware family's defenseless backs from low down in shadow, and a lurking vaguely human shadow on a wall between us and the family. And the Old Style sign, streetlights, elevated train, and Skyway ramp sharply etched against the blood-orange sunset all suggest a bigger, harder, scarier world beyond the bar of light cast on the sidewalk by Wee Folks. The combined effect is as if Edward Hopper had illustrated a South Side version of *Goodnight Moon*.

Markovitz has caught perfectly the tone of *The Pied Piper of South Shore*, a memoir published in 2005. It's the definitive ode to one of South

FIG. 2. Cover illustration for Caryn Lazar Amster's *The Pied Piper of South Shore*. Courtesy of Mitch Markovitz.

Shore's principal lost cities, the immigrant-ethnic urban village. The author's parents ran the Wee Folks toy store until her father, Manny Lazar, known as "Mister Wee Folks" and beloved by generations of children in the neighborhood, was killed during an attempted robbery in 1970 by a young black man named Darrell Cannon (who in later years, after parole and then another long stretch in prison, came to prominence as a victim of police torture). The killing, like other such bitterly remembered incidents during the upsurge in street crime of that era, is presented as the great final wrong that broke the shell of prelapsarian

South Shore, allowing the goodness and decency and sense of community to drain away down the gutters of a fallen neighborhood. The first chapter of Amster's book is entitled "The Day the Laughter Died," and she quotes a former customer as telling her, "The day 'Mr. Wee Folks' was shot was, for many of us, the day that South Shore died." In Amster's telling, Wee Folks and its proprietor represented "everything that was good about our South Shore neighborhood and postwar America: honesty, sincerity, a willingness to work hard, and love of all people, regardless of race and religion."

Reasonable people can debate that final virtue—though Manny Lazar may have been kind and decent to all, it's hard to argue for racial tolerance as a notable hallmark of South Shore's or postwar America's history—but its inclusion signals a balancing act essential to the book's portrait of the neighborhood. Looking back on South Shore's transformation, Amster is careful to walk the line between regret and recrimination. The teller of a story like hers typically feels genuine grievance but doesn't want to come across as a bigot who blames Them for everything that went wrong. So such stories often navigate between the acceptance of difference compressed into conventional universalist sentiments like "deep down we're all the same" and the kind of potentially inflammatory distinctions implied in "there goes the neighborhood." Amster tacks toward acceptance, describing the first cohort of incoming black families as "good people who enhanced our neighborhood's ethnic and religious diversity" and aligning them with the urban villagers' norms: "The new families moving into our community wanted what we wanted: a decent place to raise their kids, good schools, and good neighbors. They wanted to walk safely to the grocery store and sit on their front porches, watching their homes appreciate in value."

If these new neighbors didn't wreck the idyll, who did? She places primary blame on block-busting real estate speculators who exploited residents' unreasonable fears of blackness, but she holds herself and her neighbors responsible for harboring those fears in the first place. "We were gullible and they were relentless," she concludes. "We were cowards and they grew rich." Framing her story within the sweep of an immigrant history that makes the nightly gunfire in transitional South

Shore resonate with the gunfire of Eastern European pogroms that terrorized the shtetl, she's willing to understand the urge to flee that seized her neighbors and her own family, who had already moved to suburban Glenwood a few months before her father was killed. She stops well short of excusing that urge to flee, but leaving her own kind on the hook doesn't let everyone else off it. She's apparently talking about knuckling under to speculators when she asks, "Didn't we Jews learn after the Holocaust that we can't let people push us around?" But the question also leaves room for another blameworthy faction: among those feared by the Jews of South Shore were black gang members, who joined white block-busters as the transitional neighborhood's leading villains. "There goes the neighborhood" always lurks implicitly behind "deep down we're all the same," even—or especially—when "deep down we're all the same" is deployed to explicitly disclaim "there goes the neighborhood."

Amster's book maps her lost city in loving detail, exemplified by an appendix that makes a door-to-door inventory of businesses on 79th Street in the 1950s and 1960s, noting the quirks of each long-gone deli, millinery shop, dentist's office, or beauty salon. The book is a monument to South Shore's last days as a predominantly Jewish and Irish urban village, an avatar of one of the industrial city's most myth-encrusted features. Reconfigured in nostalgic memory as the Old Neighborhood, immortalized in popular narratives like *The Godfather* (which is all about what a terrible mistake the Corleones made when they left the Lower East Side) and in political and historical discourse, the urban village is a ripely remembered generational way station on the path from the Old Country to the suburban middle class. In the mid-twentieth century, as late-industrial Chicago enjoyed the benefits of the postwar consumer boom—which, in retrospect, looks more like industrial urbanism's dead-cat bounce—South Shore had the feel of a thriving urban village, or a collection of urban villages. You can catch an Irish version of that feel in something an elderly former neighbor told me: during the 1950s and early 1960s, she said, parishioners "would hold a coffee for the nuns at St. Philip Neri, and they'd give them a new station wagon."

The Pied Piper of South Shore is part of a robust literature that looks back at this moment, almost all of it written after the villagers left. Together, these backward-glancing stories map a lost city that's remembered with both sweet nostalgia and bitterness over its passing. There are other self-published South Shore memoirs like Amster's: Gerald Lewis's *South Shore Days 1940's and '50's*, L. Curt Erler's *Southside Kid*, Dorothy Sinclair's *You Can Take the Girl Out of Chicago . . .* , Gladys Keenan Henry's *The Innocent Days*, and Gerry O'Brien and Bob O'Brien's *The Heart of Chicago's South Shore*, a massive compendium of first-person anecdotes recounted by dozens of former residents. Amster also edits a monthly online newsletter that collects reminiscences, circulates news of class reunions and death notices, and otherwise takes its audience of senior citizens back to the urban village of their youth. Here, too, a nostalgic tone prevails, but more astringent notes do occur. One George Petros wrote to Amster in the spring of 2016 to complain that biographical sketches of the Supreme Court nominee Merrick Garland, a former resident of South Shore, noted his family's move from 79th and Jeffery to suburban Lincolnwood without making "any reference to the conditions that drove them out. All of us former South Shore residents know that Whites and Jews were ethnically cleansed from our neighborhood by rampant Black criminality."

Extending beyond South Shore to surrounding neighborhoods, similar tales of the urban village and When It Changed include Louis Rosen's semi-nonfictional *The South Side*; Ray Hanania's *Midnight Flight*; and C. J. Martello's long-running "Petals from Roseland" column in *Fra Noi*, Chicago's Italian-American magazine, which practically comes with its own love theme by Nino Rota. Roseland also produced the band Styx, which contributed an operatic prog-rock suite to the literature of nostalgia for the old South Side in the form of a triple-platinum concept album about the destruction in 1956 of the Paradise Theatre—a sister venue to the Avalon, both of which were the work of the architect John Eberson—in West Garfield Park. And then there's Alan Ehrenhalt's historical paean to Chicago in the 1950s, especially its urban villages, which is of course entitled *The Lost City*.

These accounts remind me of the ongoing conversation among the Asmarini—Italians who, like my father, lived in Eritrea's capital city in

the 1930s and 1940s. There aren't many of them left, but they remember their time in Asmara with ever more intense longing, a variant of
the old mal d'Afrique that has infected former colonists for centuries.
My father's mother, my Nonna, was one of them. To hear her tell it, the
sun was particularly golden and salubrious in Asmara, and the fruits
and vegetables had a unique succulence. Men and women of modest means worked hard and dressed for dinner in her lost city, where,
despite war and hardship, life was good when she—when everyone—
was young.

A similar and equally understandable rosiness of hindsight animates
stories of the Old Neighborhood. In them, Irish and Jewish South Shore
and other white-ethnic neighborhoods like it on the South Side are
remembered as places of ideal fellow feeling. Kids ramble in the safe
and busy streets, going down to 71st, 79th, or one of the other vibrant
shopping strips for a matinee double feature, a francheezie (a hot dog
split down the middle, filled with cheese, and wrapped in bacon), or a
chocolate phosphate. Strict but wise and loving teachers, coaches, nuns,
priests, rabbis, and other responsible adults dispense wisdom and discipline in fine schools and other places of moral instruction filled with
upward-striving students whose wrongdoing never gets too far beyond
mischief. A few colorful rogues pursue thrillingly illegal capers without
doing any real harm to the social fabric. Nobody has much but everybody gets by; dads work, moms keep house, and the evocative aroma of
(you fill in the name and ethnic food here, but for argument's sake let's
say:) Mrs. Passman's blintzes wafts across a landscape filled with regular
folks who deeply know and feel bonded to each other as members of a
strong community.

But the specter of the inevitable breakup lingers over this love story's
rosiness. If everything was really so perfect in the urban village, why did
the villagers start leaving at the sight of the first few black neighbors?
All the hot sentiment that flows through such stories tends to obscure
the hard social-historical fact that—like the Lazars, who had already
moved to Glenwood and were commuting back to 79th Street to run
Wee Folks—they were already on their way out of this lost city anyway,
no matter how much they idealize it in memory or blame block-busting

speculators, gangs, muggers, junkies, or other villains for driving them out. The industrial city was coming to the end of its run, and the logic of upward mobility in midcentury America increasingly led outward. But you can read the extensive body of accounts of the end of South Shore as immigrant-ethnic village, and from them you can reconstruct the landscape of the neighborhood in excruciating detail, and you will never encounter similarly detailed information about the life in suburbia to which the neighborhood's residents went on. The literature exists to look back to an idealized urban moment that Amster and others, aware of their own wishfulness, call "Camelot" with a mix of self-mocking irony and real longing.

Camelot has the ring not just of the Kennedy era but of the language of fable, of narrative on a grand scale that fuses myth and history. That kind of language shows up in the literature of neighborhood as people try to make sense of the world-shaking events and life-shaping forces at play on them. Here, for example, are excerpts from Dale Pelletier's account of South Shore's transformation in the late 1960s and early 1970s: "What happened? Why did everyone have to move? Why did everyone flee so quickly? . . . You read in history books about all those great civilizations or eras that came to an end, and the historians debate the causes. The St. Philip Neri/South Shore civilization was coming to an end. . . . South Shore hit an iceberg, and the ship was sinking. Fortunately, everybody made it to the lifeboats. We took our possessions and started over in the suburbs."

He's feeling for suitably dramatic language to communicate what it's like when forces beyond your understanding cause your neighborhood and the only way of life you've ever known to undergo drastic change, seemingly all at once. An undertow of regret and shame moves through his account that resonates with Amster's. Pelletier goes on to lament "the 'what might have been,' the 'coulda, woulda, shouldas,' the 'if onlys' had South Shore stayed afloat." He puts the blame for its sinking on abstractions like "the gods of change" and "some kind of giant cultural cosmic collision," but he and other writers in the genre can also be more tortured, beating themselves up with the question of why they were so foolish and cowardly as to give up their idyllic South Side villages without a fight. It's a reminder that these are stories about the sorrows of success, about what was lost as well as what was gained as you moved up and out.

What about the world they left behind in their socioeconomic wake? The view from 79th Street offers some answers to that question. You know that scene in *Blade Runner* in which the private eye of the future enters a photograph and probes around in it for clues? One can do something like it with Markovitz's painting. In recent years I have regularly visited the block it depicts, stopping for a look at the vacant building that housed Wee Folks. The only business showing any sign of life on that end of 79th Street was the liquor store across the street from the old Avalon Theater. It was plain to see that South Shore's main streets never recovered from the evacuation of capital that occurred when the urban villagers left. But the story has more layers than that.

On a rainy day in February 2016, I met Jerald Gary at the Avalon, which he bought for $100,000 in 2013. Gary, who headed a company called Community Capital Investment and went by "J" (which caused rumors to circulate that Jay-Z was buying the Avalon), was in his early thirties, but he could easily pass for a high schooler when he wore a hoodie, as he was when I met him. He unlocked a side door, and I followed him inside the shuttered theater. The heat wasn't on, and we put up our hoods against the chill. Making my way in the gloom through a warren of backstage spaces, I could hear water falling steadily from leaks in the roof. That sounded ominous, and I was expecting to see a disaster when we got out onto the stage and I had my first look at the auditorium, but it was in remarkably good shape. The red plush seats, 2,250 of them marching row upon row up and away into the darkness of the balcony, looked plump and clean and ready to be sat on, and the rich carpeting was not obviously stained or moldy. The theater's thick Orientalist filigree of Moorish Revival architectural detail, featuring an Arabian striped-tent effect around the stage and minarets rising up toward the auditorium's starry-sky ceiling like the skyline of old Baghdad at midnight, was for the most part in good repair. The theater had been restored in the 1980s by previous owners, the co-founders of Soft Sheen Products Company, before falling into the hands of its most recent owner, a former suburban police chief who had defaulted on the mortgage and been convicted of fraud.

The largest theater in Chicago south of the Loop, the Avalon began life in 1927 as a vaudeville house serving a local clientele of largely German, Irish, and Scandinavian descent. It was converted to a movie theater after the Great Depression, became a church in the 1970s, and was then intermittently used for live events, standing vacant for more than a decade before Gary bought it. Along the way, it was renamed the New Regal Theater in memory of a famous Bronzeville venue that was demolished in 1973. Gary had rechristened it yet again—it was now the Avalon Regal Theater—and he had big plans for it. To be put back into service, it needed roof work, an elevator upgrade, bathroom renovations, mechanical updates, and acoustical work. He said he thought he could get it all done for a million dollars, a sum he could plausibly raise. The figure struck me as wildly optimistic, but, unlike previous owners, he was not under enormous pressure to turn the theater into a revenue-generating proposition as fast as possible. Because he had not gone profoundly into debt to acquire the property, he could afford to run into a few unexpected obstacles, and to be patient.

He planned eventually to buy up the whole face-block, opening a restaurant in place of the liquor store, so that patrons could park just once to conveniently combine dinner and a show. "South Shore needs sit-down restaurants," he said. "The city did a study of the South Side that shows it's undersupplied with every kind of business except alcohol, where supply exceeded demand by $80 million." He intended to use the theater's multiple spaces—the vast main auditorium, a richly ornamented lobby with mosaic tile murals that could serve as a smaller venue—to mount shows of different kinds and sizes. As he envisioned it, neighborhood arts groups might use the smaller space for free, more established arts groups would pay a partial rate, and moneymaking propositions like a concert tour or a corporation seeking to stage a gala event would pay full freight. "You drop pebbles, you get ripples, other pebbles drop, you get intersecting ripples," he said. "The Obama library, Theaster Gates's Arts Bank"—a gallery, archive, and community center in an old bank building—"at the other end of Stony Island, Lakeside, this place, they're all pebbles."

The Avalon's rebirth was all in the future at that point. The only sign of occupancy was a drum kit set up in the middle of the otherwise empty main stage. Gary liked to come to the Avalon to play the drums and mull over his schemes. But he did have a plan to start making some money out of the place. He was having holographic projection equipment installed so that he could begin presenting virtual shows by some of the many entertainers who had played the Avalon and Regal in the past: Curtis Mayfield, Richard Pryor, Nat King Cole, Billie Holiday, Duke Ellington, Count Basie. He was working on an inaugural show featuring Jackie Wilson and Redd Foxx, with plans for additional acts intended to exploit nostalgia for an era of black entertainment stretching from swing to soul. When it came time to book live acts, survivors of that golden age's latter phases—Patti LaBelle, say—could plausibly be expected to fill the house with black boomers and younger folks caught up in their vortex of nostalgia for a golden age of upward mobility and civic life. Chicago's own Museum of Holography had created a potential problem by complaining that the company with which Gary was partnering didn't create true holograms at all but was in fact using an inferior 2-D technique called a Pepper's ghost illusion that dated back to the nineteenth century. Still, whether the projections he planned to show were Pepper's ghosts or genuine holograms, they would be potent visitations from yet another lost city: the Black Metropolis.

A product as much of constraint as of aspiration, the Black Metropolis is not remembered with quite the same rosiness as the urban village, but, still, its thriving small-business sector and nightlife, its vertical integration of classes and flourishing civic life, its resonances of stylish respectability in old photographs of men in hats and suits and ladies in dresses, and its vibrant culture ranging from house-rent parties to Muddy Waters and Dinah Washington to Gwendolyn Brooks and Richard Wright are all fondly recalled. You'll hear old Bronzeville, home of the original Regal Theater, brought up in arguments for the value of self-segregation as a strategy of black self-determination.

What comes after the end of the great migration story? South Shore, which became black as the Black Metropolis reached the very end of its development, is a good place to ask that question because it doesn't fit neatly into the available pigeonholes for inner-city neighborhoods and narratives. It's not the projects and it's not really gentrifying, and there are arguments over whether it should count as the ghetto. So it affords a less conventional angle from which to consider what, besides the second ghetto and black suburbia, comes after the Black Metropolis.

Jerald Gary answered the question as a young businessman who grew up around the way—at 79th and Evans, not far to the west of Stony Island. As he saw it, the half century of disinvestment from the South Side that began with the twin demises of the urban village and the Black Metropolis left desolation but also opportunity. Reinvestment will be very gradual, he believed. "It's a fifty-, sixty-year process," he said. "This isn't Harlem or Brooklyn. You can't even buy property in those places anymore. That's New York, it happens fast there. Here, most places, it's slow, but it's happening, and you can still buy the whole block for $100,000." Institutional investors had already spotted the potential bargains in places like South Shore, snapping up residential buildings and commercial property and holding on to it in hopes of an eventual payday. When I asked if that meant they were waiting for white people to move back to South Shore, he said, "White *money* is already here, because the returns are better here, but white *people*, not yet, really." Reinvestment would take long enough, and white people's fear of the South Side would wane slowly enough, he believed, that there was time and room for black South Shore to recover, gradually integrate, and prosper entrepreneurially from that process without losing the connection to the past that his theater and its holographic entertainers represented.

There was potential in South Shore, and he had plans to develop it, judiciously dropping a pebble here and a pebble there. During our tour of the theater, we stopped and talked for a while in the vestibule, where a row of doors to 79th Street were secured with heavy rusted chains and padlocks. I could hear men calling out in front of the liquor store across the street. As he discussed the neighborhood's unrealized economic possibilities, Gary was moved to quote Adam Smith: "It is not by augmenting the capital of the country, but by rendering a greater part of that capital active than would otherwise be so, that the most judicious operations of banking can increase the industry of the country." Gary said it reverently, with scriptural fidelity to the original, though his interpretation of it was more thematic than literal. In that passage in *The Wealth of Nations*, Smith considers how banking can make other businesses more efficient—by, for instance, making it less necessary for a businessman to keep some of his wealth "unemployed" in the form of ready cash. Gary saw investing in real estate in an undercapitalized, underemployed community as akin to Smith's notion of converting a nation's "dead stock into active and productive stock to help increase very considerably the annual produce of its land and labor." And if in doing so he turned a large profit for himself, so much the better. It wouldn't bring back the Black Metropolis, but bringing back ghostly memories of that lost city for fun and profit might help restore life to 79th Street.

*

The best spot for ectoplasmic people-watching in South Shore is the raised wooden platform of the Bryn Mawr Metra station at 71st and Jeffery. This is the old Illinois Central station that formed the principal bud from which the neighborhood grew in the late nineteenth century and early twentieth. From there, you can watch the ghosts, and the lost cities they represent, converge. Ferdinand Rohn comes with his celebrated ox team, Christian Seip works his twenty-five acres on the southwest corner, Charles and William Seigler leave their father's farm to become policemen. Bessie Goodwin, Mrs. Downs, and Jessie Mann come and go from the German Settlement School on the southeast corner, where they taught the local children on weekdays; Messrs. Wunderlich, Urlich, and Keller taught there on Sundays. Travelers on the Michigan City stage, the one drawn by two Arabian horses, climb aboard after stopping at Goldhart's Tavern, just southeast of the intersection, where the church of St. Philip Neri is now. Then come the railway workers who built the station; and the pioneering developer Frank Bennett, who built a tract of houses on the prairie just west of the intersection; and George Bour, whose real estate office was at one time the only business establishment on 71st. There are more recent ghosts, too. The officers and volunteers of the South Shore Commission, for instance, come and go from its office at 7134 S. Jeffery. Next door at 7124, once the headquarters of the Afro-American Patrolmen's League, you can see the organization's founders, the young Buzz Palmer and Renault Robinson (both very much alive at this writing, but their youth is long gone), the AAPL style of checkerboard-strip police hat perched atop a modest afro signaling the tricky confluence of black and blue solidarities that they navigated in the late 1960s and 1970s.

And then there's the literary contingent of ghosts. From the platform you can look down Jeffery Boulevard to catch a glimpse of Studs Lonigan, the protagonist of James T. Farrell's trilogy of novels published in the 1930s. Studs, a prewar incarnation of the sucker-punching neighborhood troublemaker who lives for the approval of the pack, lives on Jeffery just south of 71st, if I read the novels' landscape right. He runs with an Irish crew of the kind to which Richard J. Daley belonged in his youth, but give him a makeover and an updated vocabulary, including gestural innovations like the repertoire of finger-throwing gang signs that became so popular in the 1970s, and he could pass as a semi-committed member of the Disciples, Stones, or other latter-day gangs. It's kind of uplifting to realize that they're all brothers under the skin, hands figuratively joined in a cross-generational and cross-racial tradition that links antediluvian rushers of the growler to contemporary street-corner pharmacists.

Studs makes a scrappy, doomed exemplar of the South Side Irish. Farrell, in keeping with the literary tradition of Chicago realism, bends the naturally upward-tending arc of that tribe's immigrant story into a downward slide toward failure: Studs collapses under the combined pressure of the capitalist disaster of the Great Depression and internal contradictions that divide him against himself—especially, as the Popular Front leftist Farrell saw it, the tension that comes of aspiring to individual success and refusing to recognize the communal ties inevitably attaching him to other members of the working class. Broke, broken, and mortally sick at the end of *Judgment Day*, the last of the trilogy, he staggers off the train at Bryn Mawr and drags himself down the block toward his deathbed. Like so many characters in Chicago neighborhood novels, Studs, and the way of life for which he stands, has been ground up by the relentless action of business as usual in the city. That's how Chicago's literature tends to roll: bear in mind that Farrell was writing in an era that laments for the urban village regard as a golden age, well before anyone could reasonably foresee the immigrant-ethnic neighborhood becoming a lost city.

Now, turn to look down 71st to the east from the Bryn Mawr platform, and, half a century later, here comes the essayist Gayle Pemberton, picking her way through the ruins of the Black Metropolis. In her essay "Waiting for Godot on Jeffery Boulevard," she describes a Saturday morning walk on 71st from the lakefront to Jeffery in the early 1980s, past heaped garbage, shuttered storefronts, and menacing male idlers. Reaching Jeffery, where there are more signs of life but also more young men "with plastic bags on their heads" messing with passersby, Pemberton enters a shoe repair shop. Inside, a group of middle-aged men are extolling the verities of the book of Genesis. She wonders how they can talk so complacently about God's creation when "just outside the door was desolation and death." Pemberton wants the men in the shoe repair shop to "act in the face of the ironies of black American life, . . . to stop preaching to the converted and get out in the streets to do some small thing, like suggesting to young men that obsession with one's genitals stunts one's growth and that curls, though no doubt pleasing to their wearers, look like conked, greasy Afros to a whole lot of people—potential employers, for instance." She makes 71st and Jeffery into ground zero of a biblical devastation visited upon the black inner city, the kind of plague that drives young men violently mad and turns old men into maundering weaklings. The essay proceeds to the deaths of men—her father, Paul Robeson, a friend who died of AIDS, a friend who died of alcoholic despair—and the evergreen subject of violent crime: her mother has been stabbed by someone who broke into her house in Kansas City. Enough is enough; the mother is moving. At the end of the essay, having retraced her steps to her sister's lakefront apartment, Pemberton concludes that "something out there today is too much for me," puts her head back, and cries herself to sleep.

I recognize this reaction to South Shore's desolate public spaces, but I also recognize that Pemberton looks at them from an angle that emphasizes isolation and despair. When she took her walk, South Shore was blessed not only with a coterie of active citizens coming off recent big wins in the exercise of collective efficacy but also with the results of one of those victories—the central presence, right at the corner of 71st and Jeffery, of the South Shore Bank, committed to sustaining black South Shore. I'm not overly patient with readings that assign importance to what's not in a text, but in this case any reader who knows that intersection will notice that Pemberton would have walked right by the bank on the way to her encounter with desolation. Pemberton details the landscape with care in making 71st and Jeffery stand for what's wrong with the black inner city, so it's not trivial to leave out of this wasteland the central presence of what was by then arguably the neighborhood's most important institution.

When I asked Pemberton about the bank's invisibility, she said it had not been the result of an oversight. "My sister worked there, and she was not treated well," she said. "The bank is a cold place, because money is cold. The bank maintains itself, whatever happens to the neighborhood." In that sense, the South Shore Bank might have made the perfect centerpiece for her essay's cold, sinking South Shore. "I felt that South Shore is a neighborhood by territory, but it has no feel of a neighborhood," she told me. "Where would you put the town green in South Shore? It's split like a zipper by the tracks. I've lived in places where a street like 71st will have a set of players you recognize, but it just never felt that way to me. I never saw people. It was a place where life was lived indoors, where the curtains were heavily drawn. There was a fearfulness out of proportion with what felt scary in the street. The blinds were drawn to their own safe neighborhood." That last image captured the essence of South Shore for her. She said, "My sense is that people don't know their neighbors," and perhaps they don't want to know those neighbors, because "everybody makes different sorts of sacrifices to be there, and everybody's reluctant to find out what the sacrifices are their neighbors made." South Shore, she believed, was haunted by a question: "Can you go far enough? It may well have to do with having had a place to get to, and getting there, and that not being it, the reality of one's kids still being black, no matter how nice the house you give them. I've felt that in every parlor I've sat in, in South Shore, except my sister's." Summing up the neighborhood, she said, "It's about holding on tenaciously to a class place," as opposed, in her view, to a collective sense of community—which wasn't that far from one of Farrell's main themes in the Studs Lonigan novels. "Whatever people have in common," she said, "they're not willing to share."

Turn around on the Bryn Mawr station platform and look west to see Tommie Simms, the hero of Bayo Ojikutu's novel *Free Burning*, coming eastbound on 71st in pursuit of his mother. She's on foot, he's in a car; desperate in their separate but linked ways, they're unable to do much of anything for each other. Tommie's a midlevel office worker who gets yanked out of his information-handling gig at an insurance company in a downtown skyscraper and into the drug-dealing street life in South Shore. It's "last hired, first fired" again—not only as a service worker but as a member of the shrinking middle class. His mother, who used to work on the line in a Ford plant farther out on the South Side, has been reduced to a marginal state somewhere between barfly and bag lady. It's getting harder for both generations, the industrial-era mother and the postindustrial son, to hold on to Pemberton's "class place" in *Free Burning*, which was written in 2002-2004 and published in 2006 but reads like a primer on what would shortly be coming in 2008. In contrast to the Old Neighborhood narrative's version of decline, which is really about the sorrows of making it in America, this is a story about *not* making it, about the fear of being pushed back into second-class citizenship by institutional racism and pulled back to it by underclass neighbors.

The great fear expressed in stories like this, and more generally in South Shore's version of the politics of respectability, is that the urban world made by the black middle class that expanded so promisingly in the New Deal era, and by the black working class that confidently believed it had a realistic shot at making it into the middle, will itself become a lost city. This complements the fear that gentrification will impinge from above. Either way, whether the bungalows fall into prairie-grass-choked ruin like a chain of sacked frontier forts or get expensively renovated and fill up with white hipsters who ride fixies and keep organic chickens and cultivate an inauthentically acquired appreciation of Quiet Storm slow jams, the worry is that in the future people will say, "Can you believe Michelle Obama grew up in that house?"

This kind of anxiety can supercharge the language of black decline stories, making it every bit as apocalyptic as the language of white flight stories. Here's a snippet from a letter handwritten on yellow legal paper by a South Shore resident named Hattie Wilburn in 1998: "It is as if the gates of Hell opened, and these people were let out. I had to ask again, where did these people come from? And, lo, I was told they came from the projects, the CHA. And as they tear down more of these projects, we can expect more of these people to be relocated in our neighborhoods." The *Tribune* story that quoted Wilburn's letter took pains to note that the people she was complaining about had not, in fact come from a housing project, but that detail didn't prevent her from using biblical language as mock-epic as Dale Pelletier's falling civilizations and sinking *Titanic* to tell a story about the coming of the project people.

From the platform of Bryn Mawr station you can also see the ghosts left behind by white flight, going in and out of Mr. White's long-gone shoe store as children who will grow up to be the adult characters in David Mamet's play *The Old Neighborhood*. This time the decline and fall is played as farce, not tragedy. As both an instance and a parody of nostalgic longing for the Old Neighborhood, it's more like *The Sopranos* than *The Godfather*. Mamet runs a series of satirical riffs on laments for the urban village, expertly pouring salt in the open wound of shame and regret. In the play, a fortyish man named Bobby returns to Chicago and visits with family and friends. Their seemingly tangential talk about the usual Mamet subjects, like who was or wasn't a fag or why their parents hated them so much, keeps circling back to the topography and meaning of their Old Neighborhood, which is Jewish South Shore. Mamet, born in 1947, lived there, on the 6900 block of Euclid, in its late heyday. Looking back at it over a widening gap of social distance and decades, Mamet's characters see desolation: "Oh, Bobby, it's all gone," says one of them. "It's all gone there. You knew that. . . ." This comes after an extended discussion of the broadly symbolic Mr. White's broadly symbolic shoe store—so, recalling Pemberton, we're back on shoes and desolation at 71st and Jeffery.

Mamet's characters pick at the scab of an idea that marks South Shore and its literature: that an apparently passionate commitment to neighborhood masks a deeply felt right to disconnect from any sense of collective peoplehood except as a safely distanced nostalgic curio. A character named Deeny comes closest to laying out the stakes of this logic in a typically flailing speech about human disconnection and what she calls "the stupid *molecules*." Musing on what it means that experts keep breaking down "whatever the smallest unit is" into even smaller units, she brings the play's last act to a climax: "And you say, 'this is ending.' Well, then there's *another* thing. And that will take its place. And sometimes that's okay. But then, sometimes, that's just cold comfort. *Isn't* it?" Deeny's riffing on a first principle of neighborhood life: if one dispensation is coming to an end, then there will be another to replace it. The world we know will come to an end, but it will also not come to an end, because all that scenery-chewing noise about disconnection also turns out to be itself the stuff of connection, identifying the characters to one another as members of an inner-city tribe's diaspora. To say "it's all gone there" is not only to rehearse a routinely distancing account of succession and decline, it also invokes a hot, intimate feeling that can bind one to others and not just to the memory of a long-lost place.

The Old Neighborhood is mean but wickedly incisive, and it makes me laugh. It helps, of course, that Mamet's people aren't mine and their lost city didn't feel urgently alive to me when I grew up in South Shore. I was aware of the urban village, and I could certainly make my way to remnants of it when I needed a birthday cake or a matinee, but the urban village meant almost nothing to me, its story having ended before I showed up, and its remaining artifacts were curiosities. Identifying your neighborhood by parish rather than community area has long been a standard authenticity-establishing routine in Chicago, especially if you have a resonantly white-ethnic name like mine, but St. Philip Neri parish meant just about nothing to me.

In a larger sense, however, even if the urban village and the Black Metropolis were largely exhausted, their legacies influenced the neighborhood world that shaped me. The lost cities of South Shore had a persistent effect on everything from the lay of the land to job opportunities to enduring local notions about how to make and dig beauty. And the literature of South Shore, as I discovered it in fits and bursts, was richly loaded with old but still meaningful ideas about how to be a man or a woman, what counts as good work or satisfying play, how a place changes and how we live the consequences of those changes. On the greater South Side, I found my way to older layers of Chicago at the Checkerboard Lounge on 43rd Street in Bronzeville, a lingering outpost of the Black Metropolis where I got the bulk of my blues education, and the persistent bits of immigrant-ethnic village life in the Taylor Street area, where we got our olive oil, sausage, and other Italian staples. Lost cities don't die—they layer under.

*

It's in the nature of lost cities to multiply densely. I can't explore them all here, though they tempt me. There's mystical South Shore, for instance. In Michael Bertiaux's *The Voudon Gnostic Workbook*—a massive volume so rigorously nutty that just leafing through its pages can make me feel as if my long-ago chemical mistakes are coming back to haunt me—he notes that he moved to Chicago in 1966, having already "set up a temple for the practical operations of cabalistic and voudoo work in the South Shore area. . . ." He soon shifted his center of operations to Hyde Park, but for a while "fields of invisible energy" radiated from his headquarters in South Shore, adding the conjuring city to the neighborhood's roster of lost cities. It's part of the bigger story of Chicago's salient role in the publication and dissemination of the literature of magic. Or consider Theaster Gates's Stony Island Arts Bank at 68th and Stony Island, which at any given moment offers portals to many lost cities. The record collection of the deejay Frankie Knuckles archived there takes you back to the South Side of the late 1970s and 1980s as a cradle of house music. In the spring of 2016, there was an exhibition of work by Noah Davis, *1975 Paintings*, featuring paintings based on photographs taken by the artist's mother when she was a student at South Shore High. And the Arts Bank building itself opens a way to the days when it was the home of the Stony Island Trust and Savings Bank, through which money flowed into the neighborhood along courses that are now dried up but still traceable in the cityscape.

The flow of capital creates and forecloses possibilities, burying some

iterations of the city under fresh layers—turning them into lost cities—
and generating others as tantalizing mirages, possible future cities, that
may or may not ever take solid form. Gayle Pemberton's Saturday morning walk took her right through the Phoenix Partnership's failing plan to
revive 71st Street, a plan that was already well on its way from visionary
scheme to lost city. The late Henry English's vision of sidewalk cafés
and fashionable shops, the South Shore Commission's bilevel plan of
1967, and all the other unrealized schemes to revive 71st Street are even
more immaterial, a series of veils through which Pemberton passes with
at most a fugitive, anonymous sensation of their insubstantial touch.
Jerald Gary's vision of a revived 79th Street, with its lively theater, thriving restaurant, and bustling foot traffic, is similarly immaterial at this
writing—a future city that might become a lost city that never really
existed. And the same goes for Lakeside, which at this writing is once
again a giant blank space after McCaffery Interests bailed out of its plan
to develop an entirely new neighborhood that it had already mapped out
in careful detail. I know that lost Lakeside from planners' and architects'
renderings of its streets and buildings. I've been there, wandering along
its virtual streets between white blocks of schematic buildings, and yet
so far it's a mirage.

On an October afternoon in 2015, I sat with Calvin Holmes, president of the Chicago Community Loan Fund, and listened to him map
another plausible future for 71st Street. We were in his apartment in a
building on 67th Street that commands spectacular views of Jackson
Park and the lake. The apartment, he noted, was worth less than when
he had bought it eighteen years before. Real estate prices were still
severely depressed in South Shore, which created possibilities, given
rising prices elsewhere along the lakefront. He thought the market had
finally hit rock bottom, though, and would begin to recover. A banker
with a background in urban planning, he envisioned a booming South
Shore anchored by a revived 71st Street. "Main Street South Shore is
possible," he said. Taking as a model the development of Columbia
Heights, a demographically comparable neighborhood in the District
of Columbia, he said, "If you had a master plan and designated 71st
as something beyond a TIF"—a Tax Increment Financing district, a

development tool that allows government to redistribute tax revenues within a defined area to attract business, invest in infrastructure, and broaden the local tax base—"to create a high stack of subsidy capacity, you could repurpose, reutilize, and upmarket."

The heart of his plan was a dense hub around Bryn Mawr station at 71st and Jeffery, with four new mid-rise residential towers on the corners flanked by national and regional retailers: Target, Bed Bath & Beyond, a supermarket. Moving out from the hub in both directions would be "chainlets, more regional to local," and on the margins toward Yates and Stony Island would be "truly local businesses." Other pieces could be arranged around the spine of a revived 71st Street. "With the right kinds of incentives," he said, "Stony Island could be Big Box Alley." A trauma center at Jackson Park Hospital was a long shot (the University of Chicago eventually opened one), but some other sort of standout specialty could improve its reputation, and La Rabida, the children's hospital in Jackson Park, had "some possibilities." A neighborhood brand could be built around athletic events like a half marathon, triathlons, a basketball tourney in the park (and, in time, high-profile tournaments hosted by the Tiger Woods–upgraded golf course), and of course there was the ripe prospect of Obama's presidential library. With the right marketing savvy, housing in the Jackson Park Highlands and O'Keeffe could be sold "on the sheer quality of the building stock," and that would bolster the residential market in the rest of the neighborhood.

As I listened, the future city Holmes was building took shape in my mind. He made good sense, especially for an optimist, and he knew how to make money talk to money, sorcerously gathering and shaping the converging notional flows of it. I could see business commuters coming out of their new mid-rises in the morning and walking no more than a hundred yards to catch the Metra train downtown. When they came home, they shopped along 71st, stopped for a drink or a bite there. I've been in places like that; his plan could work. This particular future city could come to be, or pieces of it could, if the money flowed down the paths Holmes mapped for it. Or the money could take a turn down an unforeseen path and none of it could happen, making it just another lost city you can see, if you know how to look, from the platform of Bryn

Mawr station. One moment it was there, already built, in my mind, and the next it had already begun to evanesce, fading to transparency.

When the real estate man Allan Hamilton said, "The world is always coming to an end in South Shore," he was apparently taking the long view. Asked in 1969 by a *Daily News* reporter to comment on the rapid social transformation then underway in the neighborhood, Hamilton said, "You know, when the Irish came to South Shore, the English thought the end of the world had come. When the Jews came, the Irish thought the end of the world was here. Then when the blacks started coming in, there was the end of the world again." He meant this observation as cultural criticism as well as social commentary, urging white people to calm down and realize that their new black neighbors cared at least as much about property values as they did. "The merchants," he claimed, were already calming down as they realized that "we are black now" and that black people's money spends as well as anybody else's. Having told this strategically hopeful story and underscored its inclusive and far-seeing moral for his target audience, the many business owners on 71st Street who were his tenants, Hamilton went on to sell off his family's extensive holdings on 71st—to the Phoenix Partnership, among other buyers. A half century later, the street still shows the enduring effects of the Hamiltons' creative efforts and also their sudden departure. Even as Hamilton spoke to that reporter, even though he still owned large chunks of the street, the 71st Street his family had helped to build had already begun to become the lost city it is now, layered under other 71st Streets, other cities, other stories, other possibilities realized and unrealized.

CONCLUSION

69TH AND EUCLID TO 71ST AND OGLESBY

On a summer evening in 2016, I set out walking from my old house on the 6900 block of Euclid to my old house on the 7100 block of Oglesby. A chorus of birdcalls rises in response to the fading light, and the houses of the Highlands recede into romantic gloom, remote and solitary. Cars are parked in driveways behind security gates, lights on behind barred and grilled windows. I feel the familiar click and airlock effect as I pass the Bourellys' old place, cut through the cul-de-sac, and turn left onto 71st Street.

Imminent sundown imparts an extra charge to the atmosphere on 71st. Hangers-out are taking their places and hailing each other, working up an initial buzz, looking for the action to begin, all of which inspires those getting back from work or running a last errand to head for home with a little extra urgency. If you're not one of the night people, it's time to get inside and put the chain on the door. A shirtless old man with achingly prominent ribs and spine sits in the gutter in front of a beauty supply store with a cop standing over him. The two are talking calmly, but a small crowd has begun to gather. I usually draw no more than a glance or a "How you doin'" on 71st, but this evening I catch a couple of stares and one guy mutters, "Motherfucking white man," to a companion—though he says it conversationally, apparently expressing wonder rather than hostility, as in "Look at that, a motherfucking black swan."

*

Residents of South Shore have been telling me unprompted stories about sightings of white people on the street, typically describing these occasions like glimpses of fairies in the gloaming or a near-extinct species on the rebound. In 1998, when I was just beginning to poke around the neighborhood with this book distantly in mind, Darryl, who grew up in South Shore and lives in my old house on Oglesby, told me, "I see white people walking around sometimes, and I'm like, 'Where are you going?' But they're coming back, they're coming back." Back then, the return in force of white people to South Shore seemed a farfetched fantasy, but now it's part of a popular narrative of imminent gentrification that turns sightings into omens suggesting the play of large unseen forces. Ava St. Claire told me, "Every once in a while I see a beautiful white guy on Seventy-First at seven p.m., then never again. Where did he go?" Julia Hunter told me a story about a flurry of police activity drawing her and a friend up to 79th Street one night, where they were distracted from the spectacle of lights and sirens by a sort of vision: a well-dressed white woman who came out of nowhere, walking down the street. "She was, like, model-beautiful, and she was going with such confidence, like she belonged here," Hunter said. "And we were thinking, 'Where is she *going*? We should follow her.'" One South Shore resident with a prominent position in city government plays a game with a friend in which they count white people on the Metra train and try to imagine where they might be going. This official told me, "When we see a white woman with a stroller, we'll know" they're coming back in earnest. A real estate speculator wishing to speed along such a turnover might, in fact, consider hiring young white women to push strollers up and down 71st Street.

The semiotics of walking while white in South Shore has changed since I lived there. In the 1970s and 1980s, my visible presence served as a reminder that there were still a few white people left in the neighborhood, curious remnants of a bygone order. That would have been a misrecognition, since my family had arrived in 1967, along with a lot of black newcomers, and never knew South Shore as a white-ethnic village. These days, I'm more likely to be misrecognized as a harbinger of an emerging order, an outrider of the expected invasion of white people and their money. Especially when I stop on 71st to scribble in a notepad, I wonder if passersby think I'm pricing commercial properties. When I do it on a residential block, well, I'm too old to be one of those young pioneers known to be quietly snapping up houses, but maybe I'm a gay architect, or a parent looking for a bargain property to gift to hipster offspring recently launched in postgraduate life.

Whatever kind of portent I am taken for, false or otherwise, nobody's particularly interested in giving me a hard time. As the sociologist Matthew Desmond has pointed out, white people tend to draw exaggerated courtesy in black neighborhoods, not the melodramatic hostility they are taught to expect by Hollywood. Some residents give them extra credit for being there at all, and the police pay special attention to their welfare. In the eyes of those few young men inclined to mess with people, I am, as Ian Frazier once observed about himself, too old to qualify as a threat or prospect. They usually mess with other young black men, probably the most messed-with demographic in America, and I fail that test on two of three counts. A bungalow-dweller named Katrina, whose manner radiates an unmistakable warning not to mess with her, told me, "I don't have a problem walking around South Shore, but then I'm from Flint, Michigan," famously one of the Rust Belt's hardest-boiled places. I send the opposite set of signals. Out on the street in South Shore, I fall into my old habit of studied neutrality, moving with purpose but emitting a minimal field of low grade white noise that jams attempts to read it as either aggression or diffidence.

*

There's the familiar click when I turn the corner from 71st onto Oglesby and enter the atmosphere of the bungalow block, the houses looking shipshape and durable in the deepening shadows. Darryl's dog, Bella, is barking in the backyard of my old house. That yard is separated by a fence from the neighbors', where when I was a little boy, a crimson-eyed albino German shepherd mix named Bigot used to foam around in a permanent fury. Back then the Thigpens lived there. The father was black and southern, and the mother was Canadian and white. When the dog's snarling and leaping at the fence grew too frenzied, the mother would come out on the back steps, trailing cigarette smoke, and say "Bigot" in a low, flat voice that calmed the dog for a little while.

Darryl's in his backyard, and when I come up to the gate to say hello, he shushes his dog and invites me to have a beer with him on the deck. I've been dropping by to check in with him for the better part of two decades, and the yard has grown ever more lovely over the years. When I lived there, it was just a patch of grass and a rusty swing set on which my brothers and I tore around, but Darryl and his wife, Tonia, have made it a transcendently lush and tranquil spot. Well-tended flowers, hanging plants, and the immaculate little lawn burst with life, and by the opaque slatted cyclone fence separating the yard from the alley are trees grown full and tall that weren't planted yet when I lived there. A stone gargoyle on the corner of the garage roof peeks out from the deep green leaves of vines that grow thick over the brick structure. Bella lies down next to a portable woodstove, growling intermittently, as Darryl and I take seats on the spacious deck's cast-iron furniture to drink beer and talk about the neighborhood. Darryl, who's a couple of years older than I am, grew up in South Shore and went to school at Bryn Mawr and South Shore High. He started out as an apprentice typesetter at the Chicago printing giant R.R. Donnelley & Sons, kept up with the technological times, and now handles data for a government agency. Tonia works at an upscale clothes store on the Near North Side. Darryl tells me about the young white couple living in the Thigpens' old house. "They had a cookout the other day with the other white families who live in the area, three or four of them," he said. "I call them the Pioneers. They invited me over but I was like, 'No, you have your party.' They're cool. I mean, I work with white people, I'm cool with them, but my neighbors are *cool*."

Full dark arrives as we talk. The rich smell of growing things suffuses the soft evening air. From 71st Street we can hear the warning bells of the crossing gates going down as a train approaches, then the gentler cattle-like sound of the train's bell as it glides through at a stately pace. Shouts, whistles, sirens, the sounds of an evening well underway, float with great clarity into the backyard's bubble of private space. Sooner or later there will be the popping of gunshots in the distance. It's all rain pounding on the roof of an attic bedroom that feels the cozier for its proximity to the weather. Darryl tells me that Tonia, who has good sources, hears that the Obama library will definitely end up in Jackson

Park. "Something's happening," he says, knowingly. Investors buying buildings, pioneers making their move—it feels like a junior version of the boom in the early 1890s occasioned by the announcement that the Columbian Exposition would be held in Jackson Park. He believes that only a fool would sell South Shore property at the current depressed prices. Hang on to what you've got, he counsels.

*

In the year that follows, the Obama Presidential Center's projected opening in 2021 will rapidly become a big new fact of life on the South Side, bringing the promise of rising property values, jobs, economic development, school improvement, and other kinds of revitalization for the surrounding neighborhoods—and also renewed anxieties about displacement and gentrification. Obama will ask Arne Duncan, the Hyde Park native who served as his secretary of education, to co-chair the volunteer board in charge of ensuring the distribution of these benefits to South Shore, Woodlawn, and Washington Park, the assumption being that Hyde Park will already be getting more than its share. When I talk with Duncan (with whom I attended Lab and day camp in Jackson Park) in October 2017, he will describe the OPC as "a once-in-lifetime opportunity" for the South Side, a chance to "break the wrong way spiral and create a virtuous cycle." One important component in that process could be Obama's principal ambition for the OPC: that it functions as a center for training the next generation of leaders, both international and local. It could thus provide one way to address both South Shore's generation gap in leadership and its anemic public life. "It feels odd to me to tell South Shore what institutions it needs," Duncan will tell me in his office on the fortieth floor of a downtown building, looking out across Maggie Daley Park at the South Side sprawling away into the distance, "but are there twenty young leaders out there who with some training and help could figure out what institutions are needed and build them?"

Calvin Holmes, the community banker with an apartment on 67th Street and a scheme to remake 71st Street, will become a member of the board chaired by Duncan. Holmes will explain to me that they can work with the state, county, and city to "thwart displacement" by designating a conservation area to preserve extant units of assisted housing, creating zoning set-asides for affordable residential and business space, encouraging homeownership among people of modest means by setting up shared-equity housing on the community land trust model, and buying up still-cheap tracts and placing restrictions on capital gains when they're resold. "We have to do this well in advance, which means now," he will tell me; "the window's already closing" as property values in northern South Shore rise in anticipation of an OPC-related boom. When we speak in October 2017, in fact, Holmes will report that his apartment is finally worth a bit more than he paid for it in 1997. Strategic redevelopment of existing neighborhoods for the benefit of their current residents will be his goal, as opposed to wholesale clearance and gentrification. "Even if the lower segment of the community doesn't have the volume at the table," he will tell me, "we can maximize the argument for them."

As we sit amid pleasant bustle in Majani—a new vegan soul-food restaurant that will open at 72nd and Exchange, part of a growing foodie network in the neighborhood—Holmes will tell me that when he moved to Chicago, he chose South Shore because of the possibilities of community it suggested, not just for the attractive container and the bargain real estate prices. "I value the sense of inclusiveness, of all types," he will say. "And I value the quality of Afrocentrism, and not just in the political sense. I value being recognized and regarded as normal, not being seen when I walk down the street as different and remarkable." But he will go on to acknowledge the class divide. "We don't live in the same properties together—on the same block sometimes, but not in the same properties," he will say. "I don't know any low-income people in the neighborhood as friends. I see people I know at work events, at fund-raisers, at social gatherings of people with my educational and professional background." Between South Shore's cohort of middle-class, educated transplants to Chicago like him and its many transplants from other neighborhoods living in assisted housing, "nobody went to junior high or high school together."

Duncan, too, will note the importance of the class divide that under-

mines community. "Nobody's speaking for my guys," he will say, referring to the jobless and undereducated young men in an anti-violence
program he will direct, "and there aren't leaders they know and respect."
That lack of representation will contribute to South Shore's weak showing among neighborhoods competing for the OPC's bounty. The general
perception will be that Woodlawn, better organized than South Shore or
Washington Park and also most squarely in the University of Chicago's
sphere of influence, will get most of the benefits and also run the greatest risk of transformative gentrification. "South Shore's not punching its
weight," Duncan will tell me. Referring to one of the violence-plagued
West Side community areas where his program will be heavily involved,
he will say, "I wish to God that North Lawndale had South Shore's challenges. South Shore has it pretty good, considering."

*

Darryl and Tonia bought their house from Emil and Carol, who bought it
from my parents. Neither couple had kids, and they had time and money
to put into the house. My parents had no spare resources to devote to
being house-proud, and we lived in the bungalow as a serviceable container for lives more fully realized at school and at work, which in my
family's case was also school. But now it's a 2,172 square foot pocket
castle with burnished hardwood floors and elegant touches throughout, like the raised floor of the study off the dining room that makes for
a perfect easy-chair view of the backyard and the garage gargoyle. As
a machine for generating and reproducing middle-classness, this bungalow is still running smoothly and showing no signs of wearing out.

I've been in the house a few times in recent years, raising the ghosts
of old memories and especially of old dreams. On the upstairs land-
ing, crossing to my parents' room after waking in the night with a high
fever, I once encountered a diaphanous lamb that trailed after me, bleat-
ing eerily, afloat along the carpet like a plastic bag in a light breeze.
In the folds of the pulled-back curtains above my bed lived a gorilla
that emerged at night to grab me by the spine with impossibly strong,
long-nailed fingers, and there was no point in telling anybody about it
because the gorilla hid so well in its curtain-fold lair and they wouldn't

believe me. I had a recurring early grades nightmare in which a red fire-alarm box and Klaxon of the kind you see in old school buildings were mounted on the wall of our basement under the stairs, the alarm blaring so loudly that I couldn't make out what the panicky announcer on the radio was shouting about. I suppose it was in part a Cold War dream, fed by news of war and atomic competition, radio tests of the emergency early warning system, the air-raid siren tests on Tuesday mornings, and the missile base in Jackson Park. But I think it was also a South Shore dream, fed by riots, break-ins, confrontations in the street, dire talk of urban crisis, and other signs of social upheaval.

Why shouldn't neighborhood effects show up in the most intimate, unquantifiable realms of selfhood? As a kid, I was South Shore in miniature in the sense that my quiet, homey exterior belied the fear and violence that pervaded my inner life, sleeping as well as waking. There was the dream in which the bus home from school changes its route and misses my neighborhood, and I am the only passenger left as it noses down increasingly alien and forbidding streets on its way to a depot far away on the West Side; and the one in which I'm in the kitchen of the house on Euclid late at night and somebody is rattling the locked door to the basement stairs from the other side. I used to dream—still do, sometimes—about assaults on our house by indistinctly seen intruders, against which I was forever trying to seal the perimeter. Doors would not lock or would turn out to be too small to fill the doorway, windows would fly open for no reason, or I would get one door locked and when I went to close another, somebody would unthinkingly open the first one.

Sometimes the dreams began with me looking out from a second-floor window as a terrible, final momentum developed outside. A car had been abandoned slantwise and set afire in the middle of the block, and a mob had gathered. Somebody was down and getting a beating as looters trooped out of the house across the street with booty in hand. Then I would hear a noise downstairs and rush to the breach. I'd find myself trying to walk or bike on 71st Street between Oglesby and Euclid as night fell, and I wouldn't be able to get through the packs of angry people roaming the streets and roiling crowds blocking intersections. I'd keep detouring, trying to find a way around, until I didn't recognize the streets at all or ended up in Brooklyn, or Easton, Pennsylvania, or Middletown, Connecticut.

And is it weird, or just an indicator of an ingrained shared sensitivity to the flow of change in the place we come from, that my brothers and I discovered recently that over the past twenty years all three of us have independently had unsettling dreams in which South Shore is being overrun by unseen white people? Like my brothers, I realize in these dreams that the strange upscale housing developments of an advancing invisible gentry have turned the neighborhood's landscape unfamiliar and obscurely threatening, and I can't find my way back home.

*

Talking with Darryl on his deck, I am revisited by a very early memory of a winter storm that caused an enormous tree limb to fall on the swing set that once stood just about where I am now sitting. I woke up one morning to find an essential piece of my familiar landscape transformed into a fantastically compelling new hybrid structure of twisted metal and elaborately forking branches, all covered and surrounded by deep snow. I played on it day after day, overjoyed and a little terrified, trying moves I'd never attempted or even imagined before. A great force had swept over the neighborhood and changed everything. The lay of the land would never be the same, and therefore life would never be the same. As I climbed around and explored this new dispensation, I could feel myself growing stronger, more daring and capable and purposeful, more subtle in my understanding of how to make a way through the tangle of things. But underneath the novel environment and the altered me shaped by its effects were the persistent layers of what had been there before. When the spring thaw and the cleanup were done, I discovered that, though the world had changed and I had changed with it, everything was also still what it had always been.

ACKNOWLEDGMENTS

I first started thinking about this book in the late 1990s, and in the intervening two decades more people than I can thank by name have helped me write it. Between current and former residents of South Shore, experts in many fields, fellow journalists and writers, students, archivists, librarians, editors, friends, family, people with whom I grew up and went to school, audiences at various lectures and conferences, and more, they add up to a neighborhood's worth. Though I am grateful to all for helping me write the book, I'm responsible for how it came out, and I'm aware that some may feel ambivalent about being thanked. I have done my best to be accurate and fair and to do justice to a neighborhood I love and to its residents present and past, but not everyone who graciously consented to speak with me or pointed me to a source will be entirely happy with the book's composite portrait of South Shore. It's in the nature of neighborhood to inspire different accounts of a place and its meanings, and when those different accounts meet they sometimes strike sparks off each other.

I won't repeat here the names of the many people quoted in the book, but I thank each and every one of them from the bottom of my heart for giving generously of their time, stories, and thoughts. Wherever you see quotation marks in the book, they indicate a debt of gratitude on my part to the speaker. Among those not quoted, I owe special thanks to Jubril Adeagbo, Angela Barnes, Christie Beigh-Byrne, Tom Belanger, Alex Bourelly, Victoria Brady, Thomas and Deborah Bump, Charles Cherington, Noreen and Gilbert Cornfield and my old friend Tom Cornfield, Milton Davis, Richard Davis, Shelley Davis, Stuart Dybek, Doug Earp, Mary Earp, Chris Erikson, Joyce Gibson, Caroline Gillette,

Paulette Grissette, Mia Henry, Mary Ellen Holt, Jasmine Jackson, Isaiah James, Sashai Jasper, Raymonda Johnson, Bob Keeley, Arleyn Levee, Karen Lewis, Rhonda McMillon, Sandra Mohammad, Edie Moore, Evan Moore, Makayla Moore, Lisa Page, James Polk, Sue Popkin, Billy Powers, Adolph Reed, David Reid, Eric Allix Rogers, Abdul Salaam, Louise Schiff, Raven Smith, Alisa Starks, Mary Steenson, Tonya Trice, Frank Veraldi, Madeleine Walsh, and Janice Wells. Darryl and Tonia do appear in the book, but I owe them special thanks for making me so welcome in their house, and for pleasant evenings at Tom's.

My regular conversations with my Brookline neighbor Robert Sampson have been essential to the progress of the book. He has given freely of his data, field knowledge, advice, connections, and moral support— all vitally important, all profoundly appreciated. He and other social scientists have welcomed my intrusion into their disciplinary neighborhood with open minds and collegial goodwill. I thank in particular Phyllis Betts, Bob Bursik, Kate Cagney, Marcus Casey, Wendy Griswold, Theodoric Manley, Harvey Molotch, and Richard Taub. And I thank Jared Schachner for his crack analysis of census numbers.

David Rowell, Alex Star, and Susan Rabiner all read the manuscript in its early stages and helped me figure out what kind of book I was trying to write. Barbara Epstein and Jim Throgmorton got me started with an invitation to talk about South Shore in Iowa, where Bob Beauregard offered commentary and cautions I have kept in mind. Beryl Satter—fellow alum of the 6900 block of Euclid, among other places—pointed me to valuable archival sources; I hotly await her book on the South Shore Bank.

Among the institutions to which I'm grateful for providing help and support are Boston College, the Chicago History Museum, the Chicago Public Library's Special Collections and Vivian G. Harsh Research Collection, the Special Collections section of the Richard J. Daley Library at the University of Illinois at Chicago, and South Shore International College Preparatory High School. I profited from thoughtful responses by colleagues and students, and by audiences at lectures hosted by, among others, the Friends of Fairsted, the Seminar on Modern American Society and Culture at the Massachusetts Historical Society, the Columbia University Society of Fellows, Yale University, and the Obermann Humanities Symposium at the University of Iowa.

I have drawn, mostly in the "Lost Cities" chapter, on material that appeared in different form in three preliminary studies of South Shore: "The Old Neighborhood," in *Story and Sustainability: Planning, Practice, and Possibility for American Cities*, edited by Barbara Eckstein and James Throgmorton (Cambridge, MA: MIT Press, 2003); "Into South Shore," first published in *City 2000*, edited by Teri Boyd (Chicago: 3 Book Publishing, 2006); and "The Dogs of South Shore," first published in my *Playing in Time: Essays, Profiles, and Other True Stories* (Chicago: University of Chicago Press, 2012).

This is both a very personal book and an experimental one, and I have been touched by the willingness of expert collaborators to get what it's up to and make it better on its own idiosyncratic terms. For the University of Chicago Press, Timothy Mennel shepherded the book through the publishing process with his usual firm hand and battle-tested good humor, and he and Erin DeWitt edited it with sensitivity and a satisfying attention to matters of craft; Isaac Tobin, Lauren Nassef, and Paul D'Amato, a trio of gifted artists, infused it with beauty and visual precision; Levi Stahl ushered it into the world; Rachel Kelly Unger took care of business; Eileen Quam prepared the index; and Bill Savage, Wendy Griswold, and an anonymous reader offered open-minded and useful readings of the manuscript.

Tina Klein told me to write this book and helped me in a thousand ways to write it. She and our daughters, Ling-li and Yuan, were remarkably good sports about my incessant travel, physical and mental, to Chicago. My brothers, Sebastian and Sal, contributed reminiscences, contacts, readings of drafts, and deep thoughts about the true meaning of "Can I get a ride on your bike?" My parents, Salvatore and Pilar Rotella, told me their South Shore stories, answered my many questions, sent me things to read, offered prompt and helpful responses to drafts, and lovingly inquired as to when I expected to be done.

This book is dedicated to my next-door neighbors in South Shore, the Passmans, Thigpens, Trainers, and Earps. The high standard of decency and respect for others set by their early example—close by and always ready to lend a hand, but recognizing the value of a cordial tolerant distance—shaped my strong feeling for the place where I grew up and my lifelong interest in neighborhood.

NOTES ON SOURCES

INTRODUCTION: 71ST AND OGLESBY TO 69TH AND EUCLID

1 **The compact brick house . . .** The Chicago Bungalow Association, formerly the Historic Chicago Bungalow Association, keeps authoritative track of houses in the city that qualify by its standards as historic Chicago bungalows. Some numbers, a history of the relevant architectural styles, and a checklist of defining characteristics can be found at https://www.chicagobungalow.org/chicago-bungalow (accessed August 3, 2018).

1 **It doesn't approach the Wild West highs . . .** For the spike in crime in South Shore in the 1970s, from below the city's average to more than double the rate, see, e.g., Richard P. Taub, E. Garth Taylor, and Jan D. Dunham, *Paths of Neighborhood Change: Race and Crime in Urban America* (Chicago: University of Chicago Press, 1984), 52; and Richard P. Taub, *Community Capitalism: The South Shore Bank's Strategy for Neighborhood Revitalization* (Cambridge, MA: Harvard Business School Press, 1994 [1988]), 35. See also Phyllis Betts Otti, "The Nature and Dynamics of Local Black Activism in an Urban Area: The Case of South Shore" (PhD diss., University of Chicago, 1978), 51, 56.

3 **It's apparently an aspect of being human . . .** I have learned a great deal from the archaeologist Michael E. Smith and his colleagues. See, e.g., Michael E. Smith et al., "Comparative Methods for Premodern Cities: Coding for Governance and Class Mobility," *Cross-Cultural Research* (2016): 1-37; Michael E. Smith, "Form and Meaning in the Earliest Cities: A New Approach to Ancient Urban Planning," *Journal of Planning History*, (February 2007): 3-47; Michael E. Smith, "The Archaeological Study of Neighborhoods and Districts in Ancient Cities," *Journal of Anthropological Archaeology* 29 (2010): 137-54; Michael E. Smith, "Empirical Urban Theory for Archaeologists," *Journal of Archaeological Method and Theory* 18 (2011): 167-92; Michael E. Smith, "The Role of Ancient Cities in Research on Contemporary Urbanization," *UGEC Viewpoints* 8 (2012): 14-19; Michael E. Smith et al., "Neighborhood Formation in Semi-Urban Settlements," *Journal of Urbanism* (2014): 1-26; Abigail M. York et al., "Ethnic and Class Clustering through the Ages: A Transdisciplinary Approach to Urban Neighbourhood Social Patterns," *Urban Studies* 48 (August 2011): 2399-415.

3   **Rather, as the sociologist Robert Sampson puts it** . . . Robert J. Sampson, *Great American City: Chicago and the Enduring Neighborhood Effect* (Chicago: University of Chicago Press, 2012), 22.

3   **Sampson, the leading scholar of neighborhood effects** . . . Sampson has graciously shared with me both published and unpublished South Shore data drawn primarily from his Project on Human Development in Chicago Neighborhoods, a massive undertaking that provided the foundational data for his masterwork, *Great American City*. Supported by additional original research studies, census data, and a wealth of archival records on health, crime, violence, housing, and organizations, the project included a longitudinal cohort study of 6,200 children and their families, followed wherever they moved in the United States for approximately seven years; a representative community survey of more than 8,000 residents of Chicago conducted in 1995 and another of 3,000 residents conducted in 2002; a Network Panel Study of more than 2,800 key leaders in 47 community areas, interviewed in 1995 and again in 2002; a study of more than 4,000 collective action events in the metro area from 1970 to 2000; and a "lost letter" experiment designed to measure altruism in public space, conducted in 2002 and 2010. For a description of the research design, see Sampson, *Great American City*, 24–25, 71–93.

4   **As Sampson says, "When people act as if neighborhood matters** . . ." Carlo Rotella, "Neighborhood Has Always Mattered," *Boston Globe*, May 26, 2014, https://www.bostonglobe.com/opinion/2014/05/25/neighborhood-has-always-mattered/WGsMwEivxomPfz6OaoCbDP/story.html (accessed October 23, 2017).

4   **The Sicilian crime writer Andrea Camilleri** . . . Sebastian Rotella, "Italian Mystery Writer Andrea Camilleri Keeps Montalbano on the Case," *Los Angeles Times*, February 3, 2009, http://www.latimes.com/world/europe/la-et-andrea-camilleri3-2009feb03-story.html (accessed October 23, 2017). Camilleri credited the line to Dostoevsky, though so far I haven't found it in Dostoevsky's work.

5   **With a vacancy rate above 50%** . . . Fran Spielman, "Grocery Store Finally Coming to South Shore Site of Shuttered Dominick's," *Chicago Sun-Times*, February 2, 2018, https://chicago.suntimes.com/news/grocery-store-finally-coming-to-south-shore-site-of-shuttered-dominicks/ (accessed April 10, 2018).

6   **Its population of about 50,000** . . . The Chicago Metropolitan Agency for Planning (CMAP) summarizes census information by community area: https://datahub.cmap.illinois.gov/dataset/2010-census-data-summarized-to-chicago-community-areas (accessed October 31, 2017). On mid-twentieth-century population, see Evelyn M. Kitagawa and Karl E. Taeuber, eds., *Local Community Fact Book: Chicago Metropolitan Area, 1960* (Chicago: University of Chicago and City of Chicago, 1963), 101.

6   . . . **187 homicides . . . disturbingly high.** The *Chicago Tribune* tracked homicides in Chicago by community area between January 10, 2006, and July 5, 2015: see http://homicides.redeyechicago.com/neighborhood/south-shore/ (accessed Octo-

ber 25, 2017). Data on rates of infant mortality, teen pregnancy, and low birth weight courtesy of Robert Sampson.

7   **It's composed** . . . The official South Shore community area still includes a vestigial section west of Stony Island Avenue that South Siders haven't thought of as part of the neighborhood for at least half a century, if they ever did.

7   **"If you're looking . . ."** Robert Sampson, interview with the author, January 29, 2015.

8   **Your mind is housed in a body** . . . In *From the Ground Up: Translating Geography into Community through Neighbor Networks* (Princeton, NJ: Princeton University Press, 2009), Rick Grannis offers a compelling account of the enduring importance of geography on the human scale in the dynamics of neighborhood.

9   **The voucher program** . . . Mike Dumke, Brett Chase, Tim Novak, and Chris Fusco, "The CHA's Great Upheaval—A Sun-Times/BGA Special Report," *Chicago Sun-Times*, June 29, 2016, https://chicago.suntimes.com/chicago-politics/the-chas -great-upheaval-a-sun-timesbga-special-report/ (accessed October 23, 2017).

9   **A recent study found that 47% of black men** . . . Teresa L. Cordova and Matthew D. Wilson, "Lost: The Crisis of Jobless and Out of School Teens and Young Adults in Chicago, Illinois and the U.S." (Great Cities Institute, University of Illinois at Chicago, January 2016), https://greatcities.uic.edu/wp-content/uploads/2016/02 /ASN-Report-v5.2.pdf (accessed June 26, 2018).

9   **"The world is always coming to an end in South Shore."** Allan Hamilton quoted in L. F. Palmer Jr., "South Shore Divisions Run Deep," *Chicago Daily News*, February 26, 1969, 3-4.

9   **. . . over 95% black by 1980.** Chicago Fact Book Consortium, *Local Community Fact Book: Chicago Metropolitan Area* (Chicago: Chicago Review Press, 1984), 117.

11   **When the Chicago Housing Authority** . . . In 1999 the *Chicago Tribune* reported that South Shore was receiving more relocated families from razed CHA projects than any other community area; see Flynn McRoberts and Abdon Pallasch, "Neighbors Wary of New Arrivals," *Chicago Tribune*, December 28, 1999, 1, 12-13. Relevant studies of the consequences of the Chicago Housing Authority's Plan for Transformation include a paper by Paul Fischer of Lake Forest College entitled "Where Are All the Public Housing Families Going: An Update" (2003) and several studies available from the Urban Institute (https://www.urban.org/research), including Susan J. Popkin et al., "The CHA's Plan for Transformation: How Have Residents Fared?" (Urban Institute, August 2010); "The Plan for Transformation: An Update on Relocation" (Chicago Housing Authority, April 2011); Susan J. Popkin et al., "CHA Residents and the Plan for Transformation" (Urban Institute, January 2013); and Larry Buron, Christopher Hayes, and Chantal Hailey, "An Improved Living Environment, but . . ." (Urban Institute, January 2013).

12   **But the experience of being a have-not . . .** Richard Wilkinson and Kate Pickett, *The Spirit Level: Why Greater Equality Makes Societies Stronger* (New York: Bloomsbury, 2009).

12   **The numbers tell the story . . . 20 times as much.** I am indebted to Jared Schachner of Harvard University for his expert assistance in analyzing the census data on class in South Shore summarized in this paragraph. We used the Pew Research Center's definitions of middle class (an annual income between 66% and 200% of the national average), lower class (income below 66% of the national average), and upper class (income above 200% of the national average). The income gap between richest and poorest is expressed as a 90:10 ratio and an 80:20 ratio— the income of those in the neighborhood's 90th income percentile expressed as a multiple of the income of those in the 10th percentile, and the income of the 80th percentile as a multiple of the 20th. Between 1980 and 2014, the 90:10 ratio rose from 11.8 to 20.1, the 80:20 from 5.1 to 7.3.

13   **I see the speed bumps . . .** Damien Cave made a similar point about the *topes* of Mexico in "The Deeper Meaning of Mexico's Giant Speed Bumps," *New York Times*, June 15, 2016, https://www.nytimes.com/2016/06/16/world/what-in-the-world/the -deeper-meaning-of-mexicos-giant-speed-bumps.html (accessed October 23, 2017).

13   **Other writers have abundantly demonstrated . . .** See, e.g., Mary Pattillo, *Black Picket Fences: Privilege and Peril among the Black Middle Class* (Chicago: University of Chicago Press, 1999) and *Black on the Block: The Politics of Race and Class in the City* (Chicago: University of Chicago Press, 2007); Margo Jefferson, *Negroland: A Memoir* (New York: Pantheon, 2015); Robert Stepto, *Blue as the Lake: A Personal Geography* (Boston: Beacon, 1998); Natalie Y. Moore, *The South Side: A Portrait of Chicago and American Segregation* (New York: St. Martin, 2016).

14   **By equipment for living I mean . . .** I got the idea of culture as equipment for living from one of my graduate school mentors, Michael Denning, who got it from Kenneth Burke, "Literature as Equipment for Living," in *Philosophy of the Literary Form: Studies in Symbolic Action*, 3rd ed. (Berkeley: University of California Press, 1973), 293–304.

17   **In 2015 Michelle Obama . . .** "Transcript of Michelle Obama's Commencement Address," *Chicago Tribune*, June 9, 2015, http://www.chicagotribune.com/news /ct-michelle-obama-commencement-address-transcript-20150609-story.html (accessed October 23, 2017).

20   **At times she has dwelt on . . .** See, e.g., "Michelle Obama Recalls Stressful Childhood in South Shore, at Whitney Young," *DNAInfo*, October 14, 2014, https:// www.dnainfo.com/chicago/20141014/south-shore-above-79th/michelle-obama -recalls-stressful-childhood-south-shore-at-whitney-young (accessed November 15, 2017); "Michelle Obama: Whitney Young Teachers Doubted Me, Said 'Sights Too High,'" *DNAInfo*, November 13, 2013, https://www.dnainfo.com/chicago/20131112 /near-west-side/michelle-obama-whitney-young-teachers-doubted-me-said -sights-too-high (accessed November 15, 2017); "Michelle Obama Recalls Child-

hood Eat-Fests of Ribs, Burgers, Shakes," *DNAInfo*, July 23, 2013, https://www
.dnainfo.com/chicago/20130723/south-shore-above-79th/michele-obama-recalls
-childhood-eat-fests-of-ribs-burgers-shakes (accessed November 15, 2017);
Michelle Obama, *American Grown: The Story of the White House Kitchen Garden and
Gardens across America* (New York: Crown, 2012), 12–17. See also Michelle Obama,
Becoming (New York: Crown, 2018), esp. 3–67.

20 **"Life is too complicated . . ."** Harvey Luskin Molotch, *Managed Integration:
Dilemmas of Doing Good in the City* (Berkeley: University of California Press, 1972), x.

22 **"Behold! . . ."** H. P. Lovecraft, *The Dream-Quest of Unknown Kadath* (New York:
Ballantine, 1970 [1943]), 132.

A STRANGE SENSE OF COMMUNITY

29 **In her remarks she drew freely . . . "economic development plan."** Carol
Adams, "South Shore—Working Together, for a Change," *South Shore Current*,
March 2016, 11.

29 **. . . institutional investors and other outsiders . . .** See, e.g., Sam Cholke,
"With $9.5 Million Sale, Real Estate Investors Betting Big on South Shore," *DNAInfo*,
December 3, 2015, https://www.dnainfo.com/chicago/20151203/jackson-highlands
/with-95-million-sale-real-estate-investors-betting-big-on-south-shore (accessed
November 8, 2017); Sam Cholke, "With Another $3.5 Million Sale, Investors Double
Down on South Shore Real Estate," *DNAInfo*, January 21, 2016, https://www.dnainfo
.com/chicago/20160121/jackson-highlands/with-another-35m-sale-investors
-double-down-on-south-shore-real-estate (accessed November 8, 2017). In September 2015, I spoke with Jeff Brown, CEO and chief investment officer of T2 Capital
Management, a private equity real estate firm that owned four large apartment
complexes in South Shore, at 69th and Paxton, 72nd and Yates, 73rd and Yates, and
75th and Coles. "We seek out subsidized tenants—CHA, Section Eight, HUD," he
explained. "Their options are limited and poor, and our play is to provide high quality: high ceilings, hardwood floors, granite countertops, security. It's easy to stand
out there, and doesn't cost that much more. They pay on the first of the month—
typically, the CHA will pay, say, $800 out of $1000, and the tenant is responsible for
paying the other $200." These reliable rents were the investment's principal attrac-
tion. "Whether the property appreciates or not would be gravy," Brown said. "Our
bread and butter is the rents." He said that his firm, based in the suburbs of Chicago,
had been active in "the South Shore" for three years, and that during this time he
had not visited the neighborhood or had any contact with local organizations. He
was looking to buy more property there, but he added, "Our appetite for additional
South Shore properties is confined to residential. It's not a good climate for commercial properties. The prospects for securing a good tenant who will be there for
a while aren't good."

31 **Between 2000 and 2010, the net gain . . .** Calvin Holmes of the Chicago Community Trust pointed out these numbers to me; they are handily summarized in

"South Shore Housing Fact Sheet," a document available from the Chicago Rehab Network, using an analysis of information from the 2000 and 2010 Census provided by the University of Illinois at Chicago's Nathalie P. Voorhees Center for Neighborhood and Community Improvement: http://www.chicagorehab.org/resources/docs/fact_books/2013_ca_fact_sheets/south_shore.pdf (accessed November 8, 2017).

32   **This is typical of public meetings . . .** In the last census, about one-third of South Shore's population had an income that fell above the poverty line but below the 66% of the national average that the Pew Research Center uses to define the bottom end of the middle class. The dominance of middle-class voices in public discourse in South Shore has a long history, a tradition copiously documented by Molotch's *Managed Integration*, based on his dissertation, and two other, unpublished dissertations in sociology at the University of Chicago: Otti, "The Nature and Dynamics of Local Black Activism in an Urban Area" (1978), and Theodoric Manley Jr., "By the Color of Their Skins: Socio-Political Transformations in a Chicago Neighborhood" (1986).

32   **. . . the study showing that in 2014, 47% of black men . . .** Teresa L. Cordova and Matthew D. Wilson, "Lost: The Crisis of Jobless and Out of School Teens and Young Adults in Chicago, Illinois and the U.S." (Great Cities Institute, University of Illinois at Chicago, January 2016), https://greatcities.uic.edu/wp-content/uploads/2016/02/ASN-Report-v5.2.pdf (accessed June 26, 2018).

34   **The flood of recognition and recall . . .** There's another 71st Street photograph of mid-1970s vintage that moves me even more strangely. It's a nighttime shot by Michael Abramson of a late IC train passing by a lounge called The Patio, and it calls up a false memory of the train's sudden rumble and clang momentarily interrupting the desolation of 71st Street at night, drowning out the Syl Johnson tune leaking out to the sidewalk from the jukebox and setting The Patio's Andeker beer sign a-creak on its rusted frame. I wasn't there but I feel as if I was, and that some essential secret truth of South Shore was almost revealed in that moment.

35   **That's a picture of leaders . . .** Sampson, *Great American City*, 17, 346.

36   **More broadly, Sampson found . . . to the opposite.** The findings in the book are further supported by unpublished data from the same set of studies, which Sampson generously shared with me. All data are expressed as a percentile rating for South Shore among the 77 community areas in Chicago. For these categories, a lower percentile indicates poorer performance in that category: participation in civic organizations (54.55), neighborhood leaders' level of trust in others (20), reciprocal exchange (2.60), adult-child connections (42.86), perception of shared values with neighbors (37.06), anonymous altruism (1.3), collective efficacy (29.87), perception among key informants of collective efficacy (26.67). For these categories, a higher percentile indicates poorer performance: sensitivity to disorder (74.03), perception of violence (76.32), fear of crime (59.74).

37   **There are significant exceptions . . .** Since my principal research ended in the summer of 2016, there have been fresh stirrings of organizational fervor in South

Shore, principally sparked by plans for the Obama Presidential Center and a Tiger Woods–designed upgrade of the golf course in Jackson Park. The most comprehensive of the responses to the opportunities opened up by these new developments was an effort coordinated by Val Free, who led the Planning Coalition and the Southeast Side Block Club Alliance and collaborated with Carol Adams in leading South Shore Works, to create more block clubs and revive the area councils that were active in the 1970s. There was even talk of reviving the South Shore Commission. But greater cohesion and effectiveness, if they came at all, would be slow in coming. After Free parted ways with the Planning Coalition in April 2018, she told me in an email that her contributions were not valued at South Shore Works and that "leadership in South Shore is no cake walk."

39 . . . **Pat Somers Cronin wrote . . .** Pat Somers Cronin, "The Agony of South Shore," *Chicago Daily News Panorama*, February 4, 1968, 5.

43 . . . **98% of students in the three schools . . .** Details about those three schools can be retrieved from the Chicago Public Schools website by putting in their names—Parkside, Bouchet, O'Keeffe—in the search box at http://schoolinfo .cps.edu/schoolprofile/FindaSchool.aspx (accessed August 3, 2018). The figure of 98% of students in those schools qualifying as economically disadvantaged comes from a check of the numbers shortly after I spoke with Henry English in 2014. When I checked again on November 8, 2017, "economically disadvantaged" had been replaced with "low-income," and the percentages of those students in the three schools had shifted slightly but not significantly (93.2 for Parkside, 98.5 for Bouchet, 95.1 for O'Keeffe).

56 **The middle class and those aspiring . . .** See Otti, "The Nature and Dynamics of Local Black Activism in an Urban Area," and Manley, "By the Color of Their Skins."

EQUIPMENT FOR LIVING: HISTORY

62 . . . **"the incandescent midafternoon air."** The line appears in *Mi Vida*, a privately printed volume of reminiscences written for her children and grandchildren that my mother completed in 2015, upon which I have drawn for my account of her wartime memories. Thanks, Mom.

SOMETHING FOR EVERYBODY

67 . . . **a recording made in 1972 . . .** Yuri Rasovsky, "The Chicago Language Tape," https://www.youtube.com/watch?v=-U4ctUHWFOk (accessed May 8, 2018).

68 **"We are having a book sale . . ."** Letter from Bernice C. Smith, librarian at the South Shore Branch of the Chicago Public Library, to Edward Sheehy, Commander, Fourth Police District, Chicago Police Department, April 26, 1976. Chicago Public Library Special Collections, South Shore Collection, box 7, folder 11.

68   **By the mid-1970s . . .** Taub, *Community Capitalism*, 35.

69   **"Call it black flight . . ."** Donda West with Karen Hunter, *Raising Kanye: Life Lessons from the Mother of a Hip-Hop Superstar* (New York: Pocket Books, 2007), 97.

71   **As Robert J. Bursik and Harold G. Grasmick . . . other qualities and problems.** Robert J. Bursik Jr. and Harold G. Grasmick, *Neighborhoods and Crime: The Dimensions of Effective Community Control* (Lanham, MD: Lexington Books, 1993), 91, 93. Before he became an eminent criminologist, the late Bob Bursik tended bar at the Cove in Hyde Park, where I did a fair amount of underage drinking back in the day.

71   **One of the most important factors . . .** Sampson, *Great American City*, 141–42.

74   **He joined the Black Panther Party's Chicago chapter . . .** Lemieux speaks at length about his political history in "David Lemieux video interview and biography," Grand Valley State University Library Digital Collections, https://digital collections.library.gvsu.edu/document/24570 (accessed October 27, 2017).

86   **. . . hiring a private security service . . .** David Mamet's memories of growing up in the Jackson Park Highlands in the late 1950s include an account of "a policeman, or guard, hired by some sort of block or neighborhood association." The guard, whose name was Tex, "patrolled the street, with two stag-handled revolvers on his belt; one worn butt forward, the other worn butt-to-the-rear." So at some point, apparently, the Highlands did have an armed private security service. See Mamet, "Seventy-First and Jeffrey [*sic*]," in *Great Chicago Stories: Portraits and Stories*, ed. Tom Maday and Sam Landers (Chicago: TwoPress, 1994), no page numbers.

89   **We fell to talking about Glenn Evans . . . if he was convicted.** Erin Mayer and Ted Cox, "Police Cmdr. Put Gun in Man's Mouth, Threatened to Kill Him: Prosecutors," *DNAInfo*, August 28, 2014, https://www.dnainfo.com/chicago/20140828/north -lawndale/police-cmdr-put-gun-mans-mouth-threatened-kill-him-prosecutors (accessed November 6, 2017); Steve Schmadeke, "Judge Acquits Chicago Police Commander of Abuse Charge Despite DNA Evidence," *Chicago Tribune*, December 14, 2015, http://www.chicagotribune.com/news/local/breaking/ct-chicago-police -glenn-evans-trial-verdict-20151214-story.html (accessed October 27, 2017).

95   **It put me in mind of the passage . . .** Theodore Dreiser, *Sister Carrie* (Oxford: Oxford University Press, 1991 [1900]), 14.

97   **. . . and a plenipotent father figure.** Hamilton published an account of his career as a foster father, "Daddy's House," as told to Ian Blair (and edited by Jamilah Lemieux, daughter of his former CPD partner David Lemieux), in *Ebony*, June 2016, 68–69. See also Ofelia Cassilas, "Foster Children Find Love—and a Dad," *Chicago Tribune*, February 14, 2007, http://articles.chicagotribune.com/2007-02-14/news /0702140125_1_caregiver-foster-male (accessed November 6, 2017).

102   **During a conference call . . . as a matter of course.** The conference call was held on August 11, 2014.

103   **Michael Javen Fortner's timely book . . .** Michael Javen Fortner, *Black Silent Majority: The Rockefeller Drug Laws and the Politics of Punishment* (Cambridge, MA: Harvard University Press, 2015).

EQUIPMENT FOR LIVING: PULP

108   **"Smokes in here . . ."** Raymond Chandler, *Farewell, My Lovely* (New York: Ballantine, 1973 [1940]), 2.

108   **In the opening scene . . .** Chandler, *Farewell, My Lovely*, 1.

109   **. . . "a dinge joint" and a "shine box."** Chandler, *Farewell, My Lovely*, 3, 5.

115   **"Let's you and me nibble one" . . .** Chandler, *Farewell, My Lovely*, 6.

THE DIVIDE

117   **. . . relocation crises of the 1950s . . .** See, e.g., Preston H. Smith II, *Racial Democracy and the Black Metropolis: Housing Policy in Postwar Chicago* (Minneapolis: University of Minnesota Press, 2012).

118   **The neighborhood's median income . . .** See, again, the Chicago Metropolitan Agency for Planning (CMAP) summary of census information by community area: https://datahub.cmap.illinois.gov/dataset/2010-census-data-summarized-to -chicago-community-areas (accessed October 31, 2017).

118   **Only about 250 families . . . led all community areas in evictions.** Brett Chase, Mick Dumke, Chris Fusco, and Mike Novak, "Razing High-Rises Reshaped City—A Sun-Times/BGA Special Report," *Chicago Sun-Times*, June 29, 2016, https:// chicago.suntimes.com/chicago-politics/razing-high-rises-reshaped-city/ (accessed October 25, 2017); Maya Dukmasova, "South Shore Is Chicago's Eviction Capital," *Chicago Reader*, April 17, 2017, www.chicagoreader.com/Bleader/archives/2017/04 /17/south-shore-is-chicagos-eviction-capital (accessed April 11, 2018).

118   **Consider these numbers . . .** Again, I am indebted to Jared Schachner of Harvard University for his expert assistance in analyzing the census data on class in South Shore.

126   **This holds true . . .** Sampson, *Great American City*, 44–46; Benjamin Looker, *A Nation of Neighborhoods: Imagining Cities, Communities, and Democracy in Postwar America* (Chicago: University of Chicago Press, 2015), 6–7; Kenneth A. Scherzer, *The Unbounded Community: Neighborhood Life and Social Structure in New York City, 1830–1875* (Durham, NC: Duke University Press, 1992), 1–5.

134   **HUD describes its Housing Choice Vouchers . . .** HUD, "Housing Choice Vouchers Fact Sheet," https://www.hud.gov/program_offices/public_indian_housing /programs/hcv/about/fact_sheet (accessed October 30, 2017).

137   ..."of a clean, saving disposition"... Dreiser, *Sister Carrie*, 10.

138   ...the physical realm is still an important component of neighborhood. In addition to Grannis's *From the Ground Up*, already cited, see Ryan D. Enos, *The Space Between Us: Social Geography and Politics* (Cambridge: Cambridge University Press, 2017).

EQUIPMENT FOR LIVING: BALL

148   ..."I am Chun the Unavoidable." Jack Vance, *The Dying Earth* (New York: Pocket Books, 1977 [1950]), 79.

THE LAY OF THE LAND

155   ...an early booster described... Everett Chamberlin, *Chicago and Its Suburbs* (Chicago: T. A. Hungerford and Co., 1874), 359.

156   ...by poverty and racism. See Woods Fund Chicago, http://www.woodsfund .org/about-foundation/core-principles (accessed October 25, 2017).

158   Lynch tried to determine... moving through the cityscape. Kevin Lynch, *The Image of the City* (Cambridge, MA: MIT Press, 1960).

162   "Great physical forces ... Elgin, Joliet & Eastern Railroad." Kenneth J. Schoon, *Calumet Beginnings: Ancient Shorelines and Settlements at the South End of Lake Michigan* (Bloomington: Indiana University Press, 2003), 2–4.

163   In the 1600s... the Miami. Schoon, *Calumet Beginnings*, 46–47.

163   A map drawn in 1900... Albert Scharf, "Indian Trails and Villages of Chicago and of Cook, Dupage and Will Counties, Ills. (1804), as shown by weapons and implements of the Stone Age" (1900 and 1901). It is reproduced in Milo Milton Quaife, *Chicago's Highways, Old and New, from Indian Trail to Motor Road* (Chicago: D. F. Keller and Co., 1923), between pages 136 and 137.

164   ...plowing over and hauling away mounds... Schoon, *Calumet Beginnings*, 47.

164   By the 1850s... seven miles away. I assembled the early history of South Shore from documents in the archives of the Chicago History Museum, especially its collections of papers from the South Shore Historical Society and the South Shore Commission, and the South Shore Community Collection and South Shore Newspapers Collection held in the Chicago Public Library's Special Collections. Among the most useful of these were a number of newsletters and papers published or collected by the South Shore Historical Society (see especially box 4 and more generally boxes 1–7 of the Chicago History Museum's South Shore Historical Society collection), including "Early South Shore History: Gustav Rohn" (no author, prob-

ably 1930s); David S. Bird Sr., "Pioneers of South Shore: The Rohn Family" (1936); Frank Mayo, "The South Shore Region" (1937); "South Shore's Early Growth" (no author or date, a note states it was reprinted with permission of the South Shore Presbyterian Church); "Early Settlers" (no author, probably 1930s); "Early South Shore History: Catherine Boylan" (no author, 1930s); and also "Preliminary Staff Summary of Information on the Jackson Park Highlands District" (Commission on Chicago Landmarks, October 1988); "It Did Happen Here" (South Shore Chamber of Commerce, 1930); and "Bryn Mawr History and Families" (no author, probably 1930s), Chicago Public Library Special Collections, South Shore Collection, box 6, folder 15.

164   **In a speech he made . . . "beautiful dream."** George F. Clingman, "Early Bryn Mawr," *Newsletter: South Shore Historical Society* 1, no. 1 (Spring 1978): 6–8, in Chicago Public Library Special Collections, South Shore Collection, box 6, folder 13.

165   **"I remember . . . had a bell."** Donald Culross Peattie, "Some Scenes at the Dunes Years Ago Recalled with Great Pleasure," *Chicago Daily News*, December 15, 1936, reprinted in *Of Prairie, Woods, and Water: Two Centuries of Chicago Nature Writing*, ed. Joel Greenberg (Chicago: University of Chicago Press, 2008), 354-55.

166   **Though he recalls . . . "the Jews and the Catholics . . ."** Donald Culross Peattie, *The Road of a Naturalist* (San Antonio, TX: Trinity University Press, 2013 [1941]), 111–12, 61–62.

167   **Peattie relates . . . "the driver ant."** Peattie, *The Road of a Naturalist*, 62–63.

169   **The Chicago Bungalow Association . . . and South Sides.** For the Chicago Bungalow Association's checklist, see https://www.chicagobungalow.org/chicago -bungalow (accessed August 23, 2018). On the Chicago bungalow, see also Joseph C. Bigott, *From Cottage to Bungalow: Houses and the Working Class in Metropolitan Chicago, 1869-1929* (Chicago: University of Chicago Press, 2001); and Dominic Pacyga and Charles Shanabruch, eds., *The Chicago Bungalow* (Chicago: Chicago Architecture Foundation, 2003).

169   **This house, built in 1910 . . .** I checked my old address on Oglesby with the very helpful people at the Chicago Bungalow Association, who informed me that, though it otherwise meets all criteria of period and style for a historic Chicago bungalow, its full second story puts it in the "other bungalow" category. Strictly orthodox historic Chicago bungalows have a floor-and-a-half design.

172   **The image of the intrepid migrant . . .** Isabel Wilkerson, *The Warmth of Other Suns: The Epic Story of America's Great Migration* (New York: Random House, 2010), 506-7, 523.

172   **Half of the neighborhood's residents . . .** Taub, *Community Capitalism*, 35.

172   **So, too, did the changing economic climate . . .** South Shore was always more of a bedroom community than a factory neighborhood, but, even so, it lost three thousand industrial jobs in the 1960s and 1970s, the decades in which it

became a black neighborhood, according to "The State of Commerce and Industry in South Shore," a study conducted by the Neighborhood Institute, an arm of the Illinois Neighborhood Development Corporation, the holding company that controlled the South Shore Bank. Cited in "Upbeat Study of South Shore," *Chicago Journal*, October 17, 1979, 3.

173   **Black workers disproportionately** . . . John P. Koval, "An Overview and Point of View," 4–6; David Moberg, "Economic Restructuring: Chicago's Precarious Balance," 39–41; both in *The New Chicago: A Social and Cultural Analysis*, ed. John Koval et al. (Philadelphia: Temple University Press, 2006). For more on Chicago's postindustrial transformation, especially its cultural consequences, see Carlo Rotella, *Good with Their Hands: Boxers, Bluesmen, and Other Characters from the Rust Belt* (Berkeley: University of California Press, 2002), 51–103, and *October Cities: The Redevelopment of Urban Literature* (Berkeley: University of California Press, 1998), 19–115.

173   **The combination of forces . . . greater atomization** . . . Kevin T. Leicht and Scott T. Fitzgerald cogently summarize the causes and consequences of the hollowing out of the middle class in *Middle Class Meltdown in America: Causes, Consequences, and Remedies*, 2nd ed. (New York: Routledge, 2014).

174   **. . . precise count of the Chicago Bungalow Association.** The 1,011 houses in South Shore that qualify as historic Chicago bungalows are identified in "Chicago Bungalow Mapping—South Shore Community Area," a spreadsheet listing maintained by the Chicago Bungalow Association.

EQUIPMENT FOR LIVING: PURPOSE

181   **And there was Kwai Chang Caine . . . when he said it.** Everybody agrees it was too bad that Bruce Lee didn't get the part of Caine, and it's true that David Carradine's kung fu was stiff and halting, like his affected fake-Chinaman diction, but that was part of his rightness for the role. Hollywood might have been foolishly unready for an Asian leading man, but Bruce Lee, whose characters were variations on the type of the superbly gifted jock brimming with galvanic fury, was all wrong for the part of Kwai Chang Caine. Carradine played him as a wandering philosophe who happened to be all out of weed at the moment and so was making do with meditation, medicinal herbs, and the occasional brisk sparring session with murderous racists.

LIMITED LIABILITY

185   **The story of the origin** . . . Harvey Molotch tells the most complete version of the story of the South Shore Commission in *Managed Integration*. I have also consulted Otti, "The Nature and Dynamics of Local Black Activism in an Urban Area," especially 29–38; I have interviewed Bob Keeley, Milton Davis, and others who worked for and with the commission; and I have drawn on the South Shore

Commission materials collected in the archives of the Chicago History Museum and the Chicago Public Library.

186   **By 1966 . . . one of the strongest community groups . . .** In *Managed Integration*, Molotch described the South Shore Commission as "perhaps the largest community organization in the United States" (9), and one academic reviewer described Molotch's book as "a case study of the largest and best-organized 'self-help' voluntary organization in the United States." W. Scott Ford, "Review of *Managed Integration*," *American Journal of Sociology* 79, no. 6 (May 1974): 1537.

187   **The turn was decisively marked . . . "and 50% white."** "SSC Board Approves Managed Integration," *South Shore Scene*, December 1966, 1-2.

188   **. . . a soul group who named themselves . . .** Warren Haygood, once upon a time the drummer of the South Shore Commission, told me the story of naming the band when I tracked him down by phone in California in 2014.

188   **Janowitz may have been . . .** Molotch's judiciously worded acknowledgment of Janowitz in *Managed Integration* offers no actual thanks but notes that he "provided enough threats to keep things moving as well as an informed critique" (x).

189   **He introduced the concept in 1952 . . .** Morris Janowitz, *The Community Press in an Urban Setting: The Social Elements of Urbanism* (Chicago: University of Chicago Press, 1967 [1952]), especially 210-13.

189   **Gerald Suttles . . .** Gerald Suttles, *The Social Construction of Communities* (Chicago: University of Chicago Press, 1972), especially 21-43.

190   **" . . . you could always tell . . ."** Mike Royko, *Boss: Richard J. Daley of Chicago* (New York: E. P. Dutton, 1971), 30-31.

190   **"The efforts of the South Shore Commission . . ."** Molotch, *Managed Integration*, 204-5.

191   **And the commission had formulated . . .** See, for example, the South Shore Commission, "The South Shore Community Plan: A Comprehensive Plan for Present and Future by the Residents of South Shore" (Chicago: South Shore Commission, 1967).

191   **The commission's focus had shifted . . .** Molotch, *Managed Integration*, 224.

196   **The bank, eventually renamed . . .** Taub's *Community Capitalism* is currently the most complete published account of the South Shore Bank, though with the qualification that it is written in forthright sympathy with the bank's mission and management. (Taub, a University of Chicago sociologist, was Ron Grzywinski's neighbor in Hyde Park.) My understanding of the bank's role in the neighborhood also draws on interviews with Grzywinski, Taub, Mary Houghton, Milton Davis, Steve Perkins, Carol Adams, and Bob Keeley; the holdings of the ShoreBank

Corporation Records in the Special Collections section of the Richard J. Daley Library of the University of Illinois at Chicago (especially box 2, folders 10–11; box 4, folder 24; box 84, folders 619, 622, 624; box 85, folders 624, 627; box 91); and Grazina Keeley's even more unabashedly partisan MA thesis, "The Neighborhood Bank in a Changing Neighborhood: The South Shore National Bank Experience" (University of Chicago, 1975). While I was working on this book, the historian Beryl Satter, whose family once lived next door to the house in which I later lived on the 6900 block of Euclid, was working on a book about the bank that will no doubt become the definitive one-volume account. She has been unfailingly collegial and generous whenever our respective South Shore projects crossed paths.

197   **Until it was done in** . . . Sheila Bair, former chairman of the Federal Deposit Insurance Corporation, examines the political dimensions of ShoreBank's demise in *Bull by the Horns: Fighting to Save Main Street from Wall Street and Wall Street from Itself* (New York: Simon & Schuster, 2013 [2012]): 283–90. See also James E. Post and Fiona S. Wilson, "Too Good to Fail," *Stanford Social Innovation Review*, Fall 2011, 66–71. The self-reported numbers on the bank's investments and housing units in South Shore come from Lynn Railsback, a veteran of ShoreBank to whom Ron Grzywinski referred me because she was "the very best keeper of data (among other things) at ShoreBank." According to Railsback, in an email sent on April 19, 2016, "Total bank investment in Chicago, 1974–2009: $2,912,590,121. Total bank investment in South Shore neighborhood only, 1974–2006*: $739,329,504. (*In 2007 we changed data collection systems and only the Chicago area totals were reported while the detail was retained in a database I don't have access to.) Total multifamily units in South Shore financed by bank: 18,195."

198   **A second major victory** . . . My account of the campaign to save the country club is based on conversations with Henry English, Milton Davis, Bob Keeley, Phyllis Betts (formerly Phyllis Betts Otti, whose dissertation, "The Nature and Dynamics of Local Black Activism in an Urban Area" [216–65], offers a thorough account of the early phases of the campaign, as of 1978), and others, as well the papers of the Coalition to Save South Shore Country Club Park, the organization that eventually took the lead in the long battle to prevent the Park District from demolishing the country club and instead compel it to turn the facility into the South Shore Cultural Center. These papers, fourteen linear feet of material held at the Chicago Public Library's Vivian G. Harsh Research Collection at 95th and Halsted and as yet uncataloged when I read them, include internal documents (strategy papers, lists of members, memos), press clippings, drawings and plans for the renovation of the country club, and so on. There's also memorabilia redolent of its moment, like a program for a concert at the contested country club site in July 1978, featuring a group led by the local soul saxophone veteran Gene Barge. The set list included "Gonna Fly Now," "Sara Smile," "Three Times a Lady," "Night Fever," and the themes from *Shaft*, *2001: A Space Odyssey*, and *Star Wars*.

199   **On November 5, 1974** . . . Otti, "The Nature and Dynamics of Local Black Activism in an Urban Area," 178.

200   . . . **"Superfly individuals, bums, and wineheads,"** . . . *Chicago Daily News*,

September 27, 1974, quoted in Otti, "The Nature and Dynamics of Local Black Activism in an Urban Area," 159.

200   **A letter to the editor . . . mail delivery was rendered "unsteady" . . .** *South Shore Scene*, November 3, 1974, quoted in Otti, "The Nature and Dynamics of Local Black Activism in an Urban Area," 171.

201   **The public debate . . . "don't drink" . . .** Otti, "The Nature and Dynamics of Local Black Activism in an Urban Area," 167-78.

201   **The photographer Michael Abramson . . .** Michael Abramson and various artists, *Light: On the South Side: The Photographs of Michael Abramson* (Chicago: The Numero Group, 2009); Patricia Smith and Michael Abramson, *Gotta Go Gotta Flow: Life, Love, and Lust on Chicago's South Side* (Chicago: CityFiles Press, 2015).

201   **Among these big wins . . .** I have pieced together the story of the Phoenix Partnership from conversations with Steve Perkins, Carol Adams, and Ron Grzywinski; Taub, *Community Capitalism*, 92-100; and solid reporting in the long-defunct *Chicago Journal*: Frank Gibney, "South Shore: Bringing It All Back Home," November 9, 1977, 6-7; Max Wiley, "Making Plans for a Better Future," September 27, 1978, 8-9; Eugene Forrester, "South Shore Has a Rough Street," August 12, 1981, 2.

202   **South Shore was over-endowed . . .** Taub, *Community Capitalism*, 94.

LOST CITIES

214   **. . . they did find guns . . .** Joe Ward, "Car, Streetlight, Axes, Knives among Junk Found in Jackson Park Lagoon," *DNAInfo*, September 5, 2015, https://www.dna info.com/chicago/20150905/woodlawn/car-streetlight-axes-knives-among-junk -found-jackson-park-lagoon (accessed October 30, 2017).

217   **. . . "the long thoughts."** Stuart Dybek, *Childhood and Other Neighborhoods* (New York: Ecco, 1986), 101.

221   **I sent it all to Philip Landrigan . . .** I quote from an email received on September 8, 2015, from Philip Landrigan, now director of Boston College's Global Public Health Initiative, who at the time was director of the Children's Environmental Health Center and Ethel Wise Professor and chair of the Department of Preventive Medicine at Mount Sinai Medical Center in New York City.

223   **The result might well turn . . .** Not that anyone asked me, but I still think that the perfect location for the OPC would have been just west of 71st and Stony Island, rather than in the park.

224   **Markovitz has caught . . . "regardless of race and religion."** Caryn Lazar Amster, *The Pied Piper of South Shore: Toys and Tragedy in Chicago* (Medinah, IL: CMA Publishing, 2005), 13-14. Amster refers to Darrell Cannon by a pseudonym,

Thomas Gunn, in the book; for his real name and details of the murder, see, e.g., "Gang Member Seized in Store Owner's Death," *Chicago Tribune*, February 12, 1970.

226   **"The day 'Mr. Wee Folks' was shot . . . regardless of race and religion."** Amster, *The Pied Piper of South Shore*, 13–14.

226   **". . . good people . . . appreciate in value."** Amster, *The Pied Piper of South Shore*, 131.

226   **"We were gullible . . . let people push us around?"** Amster, *The Pied Piper of South Shore*, 132.

228   **There are other self-published South Shore memoirs . . .** Gerald Lewis, *South Shore Days: 1940's and '50's* (2009); L. Curt Erler, *Southside Kid* (2006); Dorothy Sinclair, *You Can Take the Girl Out of Chicago . . . : Tales of My Wayward Youth* (Bloomington, IN: iUniverse, 2013); Gladys Keenan Henry, *The Innocent Days: Poems and Nostalgic Narratives* (Ontario, CA: Patrick Press, 1978); Gerry O'Brien and Bob O'Brien, eds., *The Heart of Chicago's South Shore: Memoirs 1920–2001* (Chicago: McCarthy Ventures, 2001). Add to these self-published memoirs some trade-published ones with a South Shore connection, among them Lee Kingsmill, *Safe Inside: A Memoir* (Chicago: Eckhartz Press, 2017); Jerald Walker, *Street Shadows: A Memoir of Race, Rebellion, and Redemption* (New York: Bantam, 2010); Craig Robinson, *A Game of Character: A Family Journey from Chicago's Southside to the Ivy League and Beyond* (New York: Gotham Books, 2010); and the previously mentioned West, *Raising Kanye*. The celebrated playwright David Mamet has also written essays about growing up in South Shore, including "Capture-the-Flag, Monotheism, and the Techniques of Arbitration," in *Writing in Restaurants* (New York: Viking Penguin, 1986), 3–7, and "Seventy-First and Jeffrey [*sic*]," in *Great Chicago Stories: Portraits and Stories*, ed. Tom Maday and Sam Landers (Chicago: TwoPress, 1994), no page numbers. And, of course, there is Michelle Obama's *Becoming*, esp. 3–67.

228   **One George Petros wrote . . .** George Petros in *South Shore News Spot Newsletter*, ed. Caryn Lazar Amster, May/June 2016. This is a monthly newsletter, distributed via email; subscription information at chicagosouthshore.wordpress.com/south -shore-news-spot-newsletter/ (accessed November 14, 2017).

228   **Extending beyond South Shore . . .** Louis Rosen, *The South Side: The Racial Transformation of an American Neighborhood* (Chicago: Ivan R. Dee, 1999); Ray Hanania, *Midnight Flight: The Story of White Flight in Chicago—1968* (self-published online, 1996), https://suburbanchicagoland.com/2017/06/01/midnight-flight -online-book-race-chicago/ (accessed November 15, 2017); Alan Ehrenhalt, *The Lost City: Recovering the Forgotten Virtues of Community in the Chicago of the 1950s* (New York: Basic, 1995).

230   **"What happened? . . . in the suburbs."** O'Brien and O'Brien, *The Heart of Chicago's South Shore*, 415–16.

230   **". . . the 'what might have been,' . . . cosmic collision" . . .** O'Brien and O'Brien, *The Heart of Chicago's South Shore*, 416.

233   **Still, whether the projections** . . . As of this writing in December 2018, Kanye West had announced that he would help fund the theater's renovation, but the Avalon still had not held its grand reopening, which had been announced and then postponed more than once in the previous months.

234   **. . . Gary was moved to quote Adam Smith** . . . Adam Smith, *An Inquiry into the Nature and Causes of the Wealth of Nations* (Edinburgh: Thomas Nelson and Peter Brown, 1827), 130–31.

236   **. . . read the novels' landscape right.** James T. Farrell, *Studs Lonigan: A Trilogy Comprising* Young Lonigan, The Young Manhood of Studs Lonigan, *and* Judgment Day (Champaign: University of Illinois Press, 1993 [1932, 1934, 1935]). For scenes at 71st and Jeffery, see 687, 797.

237   **In her essay . . . cries herself to sleep.** Gayle Pemberton, "Waiting for Godot on Jeffery Boulevard," in *The Hottest Water in Chicago: On Family, Race, Time, and American Culture* (Boston: Faber and Faber, 1992), 176–93.

238   **I'm not overly patient** . . . My antipathy to such readings proceeds from the conviction that they usually seem like an excuse to beat up the author for the sin of not being a like-minded critic.

239   **It's getting harder** . . . Bayo Ojikutu, *Free Burning* (New York: Three Rivers Press, 2006). See 303–5 for the scene at 71st and Jeffery. Ojikutu told me that he wrote the novel in 2002–2004 when I interviewed him in 2014.

240   **Here's a snippet . . . the *Tribune* story that quoted** . . . Flynn McRoberts and Abdon Pallasch, "Neighbors Wary of New Arrivals," *Chicago Tribune*, December 28, 1999, 1, 12–13.

240   **Looking back** . . . David Mamet, *The Old Neighborhood* (New York: Random House, 1999), 29. I saw the play on Broadway in 1997.

241   **A character named Deeny comes closest** . . . "Isn't it?" Mamet, *The Old Neighborhood*, 93–95.

242   **In Michael Bertiaux's *The Voudon Gnostic Workbook* . . . "invisible energy"** . . . Michael Bertiaux, *The Voudon Gnostic Workbook*, expanded ed. (San Francisco: Weiser Books, 2007 [1988]), 325–26.

242   **It's part of the bigger story** . . . Owen Davies, *Grimoires: A History of Magic Books* (Oxford: Oxford University Press, 2009), 210–24.

245   **"You know, when the Irish came . . . we are black now"** . . . Allan Hamilton quoted in L. F. Palmer Jr., "South Shore Divisions Run Deep," *Chicago Daily News*, February 26, 1969, 3–4.

CONCLUSION: 69TH AND EUCLID TO 71ST AND OGLESBY

249 **As the sociologist Matthew Desmond . . .** Matthew Desmond, *Evicted: Poverty and Profit in the American City* (New York: Crown, 2016), 323.

249 **. . . as Ian Frazier once observed . . .** Ian Frazier, *Hogs Wild: Selected Reporting Pieces* (New York: Farrar, Straus and Giroux, 2016), 274.

INDEX